AF844317

Studies in Energy, Resource and Environmental Economics

Series Editors

Georg Erdmann, Former Chair of Energy Systems, Technical University of Berlin, Oberrieden, Zürich, Switzerland

Anne Neumann, Norwegian University of Science and Tech, Trondheim, Norway

Andreas Loeschel, Ruhr-Universität Bochum, Bochum, Nordrhein-Westfalen, Germany

This book series offers an outlet for cutting-edge research on all areas of energy, environmental and resource economics. The series welcomes theoretically sound and empirically robust monographs and edited volumes, as well as textbooks and handbooks from various disciplines and approaches on topics such as energy and resource markets, the economics of climate change, environmental evaluation, policy issues, and related fields. All titles in the series are peer-reviewed.

Lina Dagilienė · Jurgita Bruneckienė ·
Viktorija Varaniūtė · Justina Banionienė

Circular Business Models in the Manufacturing Industry

Insights from Small Open Economies

Springer

Lina Dagilienė
Kaunas University of Technology
Kaunas, Lithuania

Jurgita Bruneckienė
Kaunas University of Technology
Kaunas, Lithuania

Viktorija Varaniūtė
Kaunas University of Technology
Kaunas, Lithuania

Justina Banionienė
Kaunas University of Technology
Kaunas, Lithuania

ISSN 2731-3409 ISSN 2731-3417 (electronic)
Studies in Energy, Resource and Environmental Economics
ISBN 978-3-031-28808-1 ISBN 978-3-031-28809-8 (eBook)
https://doi.org/10.1007/978-3-031-28809-8

© The Editor(s) (if applicable) and The Author(s), under exclusive license to Springer Nature Switzerland AG 2023
This work is subject to copyright. All rights are solely and exclusively licensed by the Publisher, whether the whole or part of the material is concerned, specifically the rights of translation, reprinting, reuse of illustrations, recitation, broadcasting, reproduction on microfilms or in any other physical way, and transmission or information storage and retrieval, electronic adaptation, computer software, or by similar or dissimilar methodology now known or hereafter developed.
The use of general descriptive names, registered names, trademarks, service marks, etc. in this publication does not imply, even in the absence of a specific statement, that such names are exempt from the relevant protective laws and regulations and therefore free for general use.
The publisher, the authors, and the editors are safe to assume that the advice and information in this book are believed to be true and accurate at the date of publication. Neither the publisher nor the authors or the editors give a warranty, expressed or implied, with respect to the material contained herein or for any errors or omissions that may have been made. The publisher remains neutral with regard to jurisdictional claims in published maps and institutional affiliations.

This Springer imprint is published by the registered company Springer Nature Switzerland AG
The registered company address is: Gewerbestrasse 11, 6330 Cham, Switzerland

Preface

This monograph takes a multi-level perspective, focusing on circular business models by manufacturing industries in European small open economies. The book conceptualizes circular business models and combines theoretical foundations with best practices when such models appeared in the textile, furniture, and plastics industries. It also explores barriers, drivers, challenges, and opportunities for leading manufacturing companies to implement circular activities across the value chain. This book offers a qualitative and transformative approach, spread across three different manufacturing industries, towards a circular transition. The findings will be of interest to practitioners and managers (generally in the fields of circular economy, sustainability, innovation, and corporate social responsibility, as well as those engaged in the industries explored herein), policymakers, and general readers who are interested in the circular economy and sustainability.

Kaunas, Lithuania

Lina Dagilienė
Jurgita Bruneckienė
Viktorija Varaniūtė
Justina Banionienė

Acknowledgements

This monograph is one of the outputs of a research project called "Circular economy modelling and empowerment perspectives in a small open economy" (Contract No. S-MIP-19-38), funded by the Research Council of Lithuania. Lithuania, itself an example of a small open economy, has started creating and implementing its national circular economy policy. During 2019–2022, the authors from Kaunas University of Technology gathered a lot of valuable information about ongoing circular economy related processes and assessed it through a multi-level perspective.

We are extremely grateful to our reviewers, Prof. Toomas Haldma, Prof. Joanna Kulczycka, and Prof. Kristina Rudžionienė, for their valuable comments designed to improve our book. We thank the experts and the Lithuanian manufacturing companies that agreed to participate in the survey. The support from the Digitalization Research Group and the Sustainable Economy Research Group, both at Kaunas University of Technology, helped enormously in the creation of this monograph.

Contents

Abbreviations

B2B	Business-to-business
B2C	Business-to-consumer
CE	Circular Economy
CO_2	Carbon dioxide
EC	European Commission
EU	European Union
GDP	Gross domestic product
NACE	The Nomenclature of Economic Activities
OECD	Organisation for Economic Co-operation and Development
PSSs	Product-Service System(-s)
R&D	Research and Development
RPA	Robotic process automation
SOEs	Small open economy(-ies)

Chapter 1
Introduction to a Circular Economy

Abstract This chapter introduces the concept of the circular economy, its connection with sustainable development, and the importance of taking a multi-level perspective. This chapter also presents the objectives and research questions, the logic of the book's overall structure, the applied research methodology, and the empirical focus. The chapter concludes with a discussion of the originality of the work, the theoretical contributions, and the practical implications.

Keywords Circular economy · Circular transition · Concept · Industrial strategy · Multi-level perspective

1.1 Concept of a Circular Economy

The prevailing linear economic model is predicated upon the intensive use of natural resources, and increases in the amount of waste produced, leading to increasingly negative impacts on the stability of the economy and nature. It pursues economies of scale through mass production and global supply chains that are highly polluting, resource-intensive, and lack the flexibility to deal with disruptions like the COVID-19 pandemic and the war between Russia and Ukraine. The adoption of neo-liberal economic policies led to significantly increased consumption (Murray et al. 2017) and only served to strengthen the industrial and societal reliance on the use of natural resources.

Governments respond by creating environmental policies, both nationally and globally, that are developed, at least in theory, to create a win–win between the environment and the economy. The first reference to this idea can be found in the well-known Brundtland Report:

> In most countries, environmental policies are directed at the symptoms of harmful growth … Experience in the industrialized nations has proved that anti-pollution technology has been cost-effective in terms of health, property and environmental damage avoided and that it has made many industries more profitable by making them more resource efficient. (World Commission on Environment and Development, 1988)

One possible route to sustainable economic growth is the circular economy (CE), often seen as a practical strategy for implementing sustainable development.

© The Author(s), under exclusive license to Springer Nature Switzerland AG 2023
L. Dagilienė et al., *Circular Business Models in the Manufacturing Industry*, Studies in Energy, Resource and Environmental Economics,
https://doi.org/10.1007/978-3-031-28809-8_1

However, the CE tends to focus on the role of businesses as drivers of economic performance, while sustainable development has a broader focus that includes addressing environmental and social issues for the benefit of the world's future (Kirchherr & Piscicelli, 2019).

The European Union (EU) aims to become a leader in sustainable growth, and, as a result, a whole series of strategic, integrally related policies and directives have been adopted. The European Commission (EC) has recognized the need to move towards a CE and has approved the Circular Economy Action Plan in 2015, last amended in 2020. The Circular Economy Action Plan (2020)[1] sets out a proactive agenda to achieve a cleaner, more competitive Europe, involving business organizations, consumers, citizens, and the broader civil society. It is one of the main elements of the European Green Deal,[2] the new European strategy for sustainable economic growth. In addition, the European Industrial Strategy[3] emphasizes the integration of both CE and digitalization and encourages Member States and industrial companies to apply the latest technologies to enable the creation and adaptation of circular innovations, as well as the creation of sustainable products, services, and business models. The Industrial Strategy includes actions to support both the green and digital transition of EU industry. Although such strategic goals seem ambitious, only a fraction of them is precise and quantifiable. Therefore, in February 2021, members of the European Parliament voted to strengthen the EU's Green Deal, naming specific goals and measures focused on areas such as product-specific and/or sector-specific binding targets for recycled content, and encouraging the development of circular business models.[4]

The CE has been implemented for economic purposes for hundreds of years (Velenturf & Purnell, 2021) and historic examples of industrial symbiosis, where the by-products of one industry become the raw materials of another industry, illustrate this. The roots of the CE may have grown out of a vast number of concepts from the systems ecology literature. The most well-known ones include cradle-to-cradle, which stresses the transformation of waste into a valuable resource (Braungart & McDonough, 2002); the so-called performance economy (Stahel, 2010), which predicts that the ownership of a product will become less important, replaced by a servitization model, whereby the customer pays for a service, rather than buying the hardware required to provide that service; and industrial ecology (Graedel & Allenby, 1995). The current environmental and industrial configurations aim to optimize resource flows and waste management, and sometimes the CE is considered only as a more appropriate approach towards waste (Ghisellini et al., 2016). This

[1] European Commission (2020). Circular Economy Action Plan. https://environment.ec.europa.eu/strategy/circular-economy-action-plan_en.

[2] European Green Deal. https://ec.europa.eu/info/strategy/priorities-2019-2024/european-green-deal_en.

[3] European Industrial Strategy. https://ec.europa.eu/info/strategy/priorities-2019-2024/europe-fit-digital-age/european-industrial-strategy_en.

[4] Circular economy: MEPs call for tighter EU consumption and recycling rules. https://www.europarl.europa.eu/news/en/press-room/20210204IPR97114/circular-economy-meps-call-for-tighter-eu-consumption-and-recycling-rules.

is not surprising because proper waste collecting and recycling have long been the subject of political and economic focus (Murray et al., 2017). However, the CE should be much more than an answer to waste management and resource efficiency goals that are too often focused on low-quality recycling (Blomsma & Brennan, 2017), i.e., processing waste into lower-quality products and materials.

The CE concept is still developing and the CE literature is full of different interpretations of this concept. Umbrella constructs tend to emerge in academic fields where there is no theoretical consensus (Hirsch & Levin, 1999). Therefore, our study follows an umbrella approach to the CE (Blomsma & Brennan, 2017), which is described "*as a broad concept or idea used loosely to encompass and account for a set of diverse phenomena*" (Hirsch & Levin, 1999, p. 200). The CE, as an umbrella construct, covers many different but related elements and topics, such as eco-design, responsible resource management, circular business model, circularity-oriented innovation, cleaner production, waste management, and sustainable consumption. The concept of the CE is still in a state of excitement (Hirsch & Levin, 1999), but there is rarely consensus on how to operationalize the CE. Nevertheless, here are the most commonly used definitions of the CE. The CE can be defined as an "*economic model wherein planning, resourcing, procurement, production and reprocessing are designed and managed, as both process and output, to maximize ecosystem functioning and human well-being*" (Murray et al., 2017, p. 369). The CE is an industrial economy in which resource use, waste costs, emissions levels, and energy losses are reduced through proper management and integration into a closed chain of energy and materials (Geissdoerfer et al., 2017). Homrich et al. (2018) consider the CE to be in opposition to linear open systems, and it can be deployed to overcome the challenges of resource scarcity and waste through a win–win approach from both economic and environmental perspectives. Finally, to emphasize the multi-level perspective, Kirchherr et al. (2017) define the CE as:

> an economic system that is based on business models which replace the 'end-of-life' concept with reducing, alternatively reusing, recycling and recovering materials in production/distribution and consumption processes, thus operating at the micro level (products, companies, consumers), meso level (eco-industrial parks) and macro level (city, region, nation and beyond), to accomplish sustainable development, which implies creating environmental quality, economic prosperity and social equity, to the benefit of current and future generations.

The CE is also widely discussed by many who are neither academic researchers nor policymakers, including professional, non-governmental organizations (NGOs) such as the Ellen MacArthur Foundation, which emphasizes three principles for the CE that keep the focus on design; these are "*eliminate waste and pollution, circulate products and materials (at their highest value), and regenerate nature*".[5]

The CE is currently seen as a necessary concept that requires fundamental changes in today's dominant business models (Stahel, 2010). However, to arrive at such

[5] What is a Circular Economy? https://ellenmacarthurfoundation.org/topics/circular-economy-introduction/overview.

a regenerative and sustainable economy, manufacturing industries and companies need to change how they operate (Bocken et al., 2016).

1.2 Multi-level Perspective, Structural Logic and Aim

No single actor can radically drive institutional change and innovate business models in isolation. The systemic alignment processes that shape business models can only be understood when viewed from various system levels (e.g., micro, meso, and macro levels of aggregation) (Kirchherr et al., 2017). The CE is inherently complex, systemic, and multidimensional. The prevailing research does not focus on one or more specific sectors, spatial settings, or types of actors, but rather highlights the meta-principles that may shape the transition to the CE across industries since many characteristics are common to various sectors (Bauwens et al., 2020). However, a significant transition to the CE depends heavily on companies and other key actors across the value chain, their dynamic interactions, industrial readiness, and integration of the CE into the whole ecosystem. Although the CE principles have been gradually integrated into some industrial practices, and some individual companies managed to boost the impact of their sustainability programmes, there has yet to be a breakthrough that fundamentally reshapes the structures and dynamics of entire industries. Progress has been very slow so far, and the manufacturing sector, which is underdeveloped in the CE context, is perfectly suited to this research.

Over the years, the manufacturing sector has followed traditional processes, without paying much attention to the resulting negative impacts (Lacy et al., 2020). The current linear economic system still largely fails to hold businesses accountable for the negative consequences of their activities, such as social inequality and ecological degradation. Therefore, it is essential to understand manufacturing companies in the broader context and provide empirical data about institutional changes by adopting a multi-level perspective.

Manufacturing companies play an important role in the transition towards CE through sustainable product design, product-service systems, and waste management. This monograph brings a qualitative and transformative approach, spread across different manufacturing industries, towards a circular transition. Moreover, the CE concept covers both technical and biological cycles.[6] In the technical cycle, products and materials are kept in circulation through reuse, repair, remanufacture, and recycling, while in the biological cycle, biodegradable materials are returned to the Earth to regenerate nature. The research presented in this monograph focuses on the technical cycle within manufacturing industries.

Despite the strong commitment that the EU is making through various communications and recommendations to promote the decisive implementation of a CE

[6] The butterfly diagram: visualising the Circular Economy. https://ellenmacarthurfoundation.org/circular-economy-diagram.

model in the common European space, it does not ensure homogeneous results for the EU member countries that have already integrated the CE principles, and there are strong divergences among the results obtained by different countries (Rodríguez-Antón et al., 2022). Moreover, small open EU countries have different strategies and conditions in terms of their transition to the CE (Dagilienė et al., 2023), which ultimately lead to different rates of progress. More than half of the EU countries are small open economies (SOEs), and the homogeneous transformation towards the CE of the entire EU significantly depends on these countries. SOEs in the CE are relatively blessed with viability, flexibility, a greater openness to change, agility, and efficient decision-making processes. The adaptive capacities of these small economies, and their higher homogeneity, can help overcome the narrowness of their domestic markets (Robinson, 1960). The ever-changing global situation and adaptive capacities of the small economies lead us to conclude that SOEs have untapped potential and can, indeed, be drivers of growth, but only if the context is favourable. Economic smallness does not necessarily hurt micro-state performance, and smallness does not appear to be a disadvantage in this regard (Armstrong et al., 1998).

The CE principles are gradually being integrated into the practices of manufacturing industries and revealed through best case studies (Bocken et al., 2016; Lacy et al., 2020). However, there are so far few studies that holistically cover the capabilities of companies and manufacturing industries, the drivers and barriers of CE implementation and link them to macro indicators.

This monograph aims to identify drivers, barriers, challenges, and opportunities around the development of circular business models, with a particular focus on manufacturing industries in SOEs.

To achieve this aim, the structure of the monograph is organized around four research questions:

1. What changes need to be made to business models in a transition to the CE?
2. How can European SOEs be characterized in the context of the CE?
3. What are the key drivers, barriers, challenges, and opportunities for the Lithuanian manufacturing sector in a transition to the CE?
4. What is the industry-specific nature of circular business models in relation to the product value chain?

1.3 Applied Research Methodology and Empirical Focus

Although manufacturing companies play a relatively small part in a product life cycle, they have a significant impact on both the user of the product and on the product's end-of-life destination, through product design and development (Bjørnbet et al., 2021).

Manufacturing companies typically apply two main strategies when assessing opportunities around the transition to the CE:

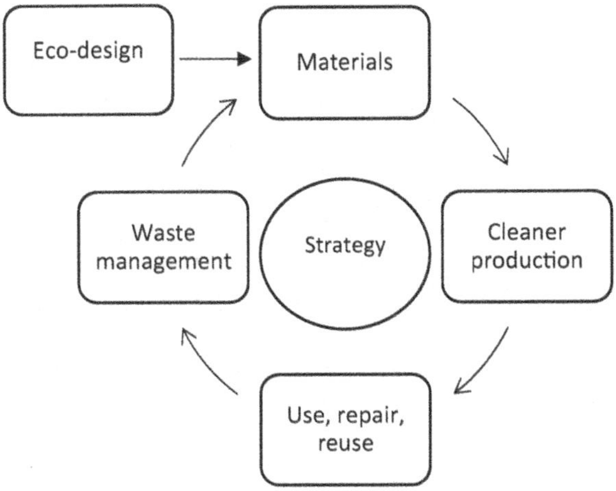

Fig. 1.1 Product value chain approach in the CE

- **Focus on product design innovation** (Blomsma & Brennan, 2017; Bocken et al., 2016). For example, manufacturing companies produce technologically long-lasting goods that use fewer raw materials and less energy, are easy to repair, or are easy to recycle at the end of the product's life cycle.
- **Focus on cleaner production innovation processes, reduced emissions, and waste management** (Lacy et al., 2020).

By exploring the transition to the CE in manufacturing industries and companies, we emphasize system theory and a product's value chain approach (see Fig. 1.1).

The CE is characterized by a sectoral approach. The empirical focus of our study is on manufacturing companies (the C sector, according to the Nomenclature of Economic Activities (NACE) classification) in the SOEs in the EU, specifically Belgium, Czech Republic, Denmark, Estonia, Ireland, Cyprus, Latvia, Lithuania, Luxembourg, Malta, The Netherlands, Austria, Slovenia, Slovakia, Finland, and Sweden.

The selection of the manufacturing industries was based on these criteria: they are priority industries, according to the EU strategic documents for the CE,[7,8] contribution of added value created,[9] and have a significant number of employees.[10]

The survey presented in this monograph examines manufacturing companies, specifically textile, plastic and furniture, in Lithuania, one of the SOEs in the EU, as a set of case studies.

[7] European Cluster Observatory Report. Priority Sector Report: Circular Economy: https://ec.europa.eu/docsroom/documents/24681/attachments/3/translations/en/renditions/native.

[8] Circular economy Update. Overview of Circular Economy in Europe: https://ecopreneur.eu/wp-content/uploads/2019/05/Ecopreneur-Circular-Economy-Update-report-2019.pdf.

[9] Value-add created: https://ec.europa.eu/eurostat/web/main/data/database.

[10] Number of employees: https://ec.europa.eu/eurostat/web/main/data/database.

The Lithuanian manufacturing ecosystem is highly fragmented because of the wide range of demands pressing upon companies. The explored industries are characterized by a high use of energy and raw materials, and increasing levels of post-consumer waste. The Lithuanian textile industry is mainly engaged in subcontracted production, which means relatively large volumes of imported, sorted, and exported second-hand textiles and clothes. The industry suffers from the same technological recycling shortfalls as the rest of Europe. Both the plastic and furniture industries are highly technologically developed, with the former focusing on innovations in alignment with the CE, and the latter seeing an increasing focus on digitalization.

The research methodology deployed in this monograph consists of:

- **Literature review**—academic and grey literature, including strategic documents and market reviews.
- **Analysis of established data sets**—including Eurostat and Statistics Lithuania, to baseline the current CE performance of the European SOEs.
- **Quantitative survey**—of 139 manufacturing companies, each with more than 20 employees.
- **Multiple case studies**—identifying the best cases and practices in moving towards the CE within the selected manufacturing industries.

1.4 Theoretical and Practical Contributions

1.4.1 Theoretical Contributions

This monograph takes a multi-level perspective by focusing on three specific manufacturing industries within the European SOEs. We conceptualize circular business models and combine theoretical foundations with best practices found in the selected industries. The novelty of this monograph lies in our exclusive focus on SOEs and the provision of practical solutions for local manufacturing companies to become more circular.

There are many books and articles already published on the CE. Some publications are academic and analyse the conceptual background of the CE and CE frameworks, while others are orientated more towards engineering and environmental specifics. This monograph makes contributions to the academic literature around sustainable economics and business practices, as it explores the causes of circular transformation from the perspective of individual companies and the industrial value chains that surround them. We find that the academic literature focuses mainly on technological innovations that are driving the transition to a CE, while the grey literature (especially EU reports) increasingly emphasizes the importance of systemic innovations (de Jesus & Mendonça, 2018). The role of the social sciences is undoubtedly important in implementing circular business models in the market.

We contribute to the sustainable economic and business literature by:

- exploring circular business models as catalysts for a transition to the CE through specific frameworks, strategies, and transformational factors;
- examining different circular business models which are more relevant to different industries;
- combining theoretical foundations with rational, practical suggestions for integrating circularity at the strategic management level;
- identifying the role and features of SOEs in the CE;
- identifying external uncertainties and threats, as well as possible scenarios for a future circular economy.

We also provide a relevant understanding of systemically important transition issues and of the changes in business model required to facilitate a move to the CE.

1.4.2 Practical Contributions

This monograph provides original empirical evidence and identifies the relevant drivers, barriers, challenges, and opportunities for Lithuanian manufacturing companies. We draw upon previous research papers and combine these with our original survey data regarding a transition to the CE, and then provide a number of sector-specific insights. We identify and assess the circular business models that are both dominant and successful across different industries, with consideration of the local context, to help practitioners and managers to design and implement such models more efficiently in their own companies, as well as accelerate the systemic transition of the whole industry to the CE.

For policymakers, systemic and multi-perspective knowledge of the CE is vital to effectively achieve the goals of the EU, and we provide an overview of the circularity and economic performance within these European SOEs. Understanding the patterns seen in the three selected industries as they transition towards the CE will supplement and deepen existing knowledge in a local context.

The remaining chapters of the monograph are organized as follows.

- Chapter 2 conceptualizes circular business models, presents key frameworks and strategies, and identifies drivers and barriers in circular transformation.
- Chapter 3 discusses the CE potential of SOEs, presents the dynamics of CE performance, and the economic performance of SOEs.
- The original results of the survey on the relevant CE patterns of Lithuanian manufacturing companies for CE are discussed in Chapter 4.
- Chapters 5 analyses drivers, barriers, challenges and future opportunities, and prevailing business models in the textile industry.
- Chapters 6 analyses drivers, barriers, challenges and future opportunities, and prevailing business models in the furniture industry.

- Chapters 7 analyses drivers, barriers, challenges and future opportunities, and prevailing business models in the plastic industry.
- Finally, Chapter 8 provides concluding remarks and a global future perspective for the CE.

References

Armstrong, H., De Kervenoael, R. J., Li, X., & Read, R. (1998). A comparison of the economic performance of different micro-states, and between micro-states and larger countries. *World Development, 26*(4), 639–656. https://doi.org/10.1016/S0305-750X(98)00006-0

Bauwens, T., Hekkert, M., & Kirchherr, J. (2020). Circular futures: What will they look like? *Ecological Economics, 175*, 106703. https://doi.org/10.1016/j.ecolecon.2020.106703

Bjørnbet, M. M., Skaar, C., Fet, A. M., & Schulte, K. Ø. (2021). Circular economy in manufacturing companies: A review of case study literature. *Journal of Cleaner Production, 294*, 126268. https://doi.org/10.1016/j.jclepro.2021.126268

Blomsma, F., & Brennan, G. (2017). The emergence of circular economy: A new framing around prolonging resource productivity. *Journal of Industrial Ecology, 21*, 603–614. https://doi.org/10.1111/jiec.12603

Bocken, N. M. P., Pauw, I., Bakker, C. A., & van der Grinten, B. (2016). Product design and business model strategies for a circular economy. *Journal of Industrial and Production Engineering, 3*(5), 308–320. https://doi.org/10.1080/21681015.2016.1172124

Braungart, M., & McDonough, W. (2002). *Cradle to cradle: Remaking the way we make things* (1st ed.). North Point.

Circular Economy Action Plan. (2020). https://eur-lex.europa.eu/legal-content/EN/TXT/?qid=1583933814386&uri=COM:2020:98:FIN

Dagilienė, L., Bruneckienė, J., Varaniūtė, V., & Lukauskas, M. (2023). The circular economy for sustainable development: Implementation strategies in advanced small open economies. *International Journal of Environment and Sustainable Development, 22*, 51–76. https://doi.org/10.1504/IJESD.2021.10040657

De Jesus, A., & Mendonça, S. (2018). Lost in transition? Drivers and barriers in the eco-innovation road to the circular economy. *Ecological Economics, 145*, 75–89. https://doi.org/10.1016/j.ecolecon.2017.08.001

Geissdoerfer, M., Savaget, P., Bocken, N. M. P., & Hultink, E. J. (2017). The circular economy—A new sustainability paradigm? *Journal of Cleaner Production, 143*, 757–768. https://doi.org/10.1016/j.jclepro.2016.12.048

Ghisellini, P., Cialani, C., & Ulgiati, S. (2016). A review on circular economy: The expected transition to a balanced interplay of environmental and economic systems. *Journal of Cleaner Production, 114*, 11–32. https://doi.org/10.1016/j.jclepro.2015.09.007

Graedel, T., & Allenby, B. (1995). *Industrial ecology*. Prentice Hall.

Hirsch, P., & Levin, D. (1999). Umbrella advocates versus validity police: A life-cycle model. *Organization Science, 10*(2), 199–212. https://doi.org/10.1287/orsc.10.2.199

Homrich, A. S., Galvão, G., Abadia, L. G., & Carvalho, M. M. (2018). The circular economy umbrella: Trends and gaps on integrating pathways. *Journal of Cleaner Production, 175*, 525–543. https://doi.org/10.1016/j.jclepro.2017.11.064

Kirchherr, J., & Piscicelli, L. (2019). Towards an education for the circular economy (ECE): Five teaching principles and a case study. *Resources, Conservation and Recycling, 150*, 104406. https://doi.org/10.1016/j.resconrec.2019.104406

Kirchherr, J., Reike, D., & Hekkert, M. (2017). Conceptualizing the circular economy: An analysis of 114 definitions. *Resources, Conservation and Recycling, 127*, 221–232. https://doi.org/10.1016/j.resconrec.2017.09.005

Lacy, P., Long. J., & Spindler, W. (2020). *The circular economy handbook: Realizing the circular advantage* (p. 363). Springer, ISBN 978-1-349-95967-9. https://doi.org/10.1057/978-1-349-95968-6

Murray, A., Skene, K., & Haynes, K. (2017). The circular economy: An interdisciplinary exploration of the concept and application in a global context. *Journal of Business Ethics, 140*, 369–380. https://doi.org/10.1007/s10551-015-2693-2

Robinson, E. A. G. (1960). *Economic consequences of the size of nations*. Palgrave Macmillan. https://doi.org/10.1007/978-1-349-15210-0

Rodríguez-Antón, J. M., Rubio-Andrada, L., & Celemín-Pedroche, M. S. (2022). From the circular economy to the sustainable development goals in the European Union: An empirical comparison. *International Environmental Agreements: Politics, Law and Economics, 22*, 67–95. https://doi.org/10.1007/s10784-021-09553-4

Stahel, W. R. (2010). *The performance economy*. Palgrave Macmillan.

Velenturf, A. P. M., & Purnell, P. (2021). Principles for a sustainable circular economy. *Sustainable Production and Consumption, 27*, 1437–1457. https://doi.org/10.1016/J.SPC.2021.02.018

World Commission on Environment and Development. (1988). The Brundtland Report: "Our Common Future." *4*(1), 17–25. https://doi.org/10.1080/07488008808408783

Chapter 2
Transition to Circular Business Models

Abstract This chapter discusses the role of business models as a catalyst for circular transformation. It starts with the conceptualization of circular business models before moving on to presenting several circular business model frameworks, as well as unifying strategies and circular economy principles. This chapter also outlines the enablers (or drivers) of and barriers to move towards circular business models.

Keywords Circular business model · Circular transformation · Drivers and barriers · Product-Service Systems · Resource cycles · Strategies

2.1 Business Models in the Circular Economy

The world's first biomimetic carpet tile (the so-called Entropy product) was created in 2000 by Interface and was highly successful. "*When we set our moonshot, we knew it wasn't just about making greener products. To achieve Mission Zero®, we had to radically transform our entire business, starting with our thinking*" (Interface Report, 2020).[1] While some individual companies have succeeded in increasing the impact of their sustainability programmes, they have not created breakthrough multi-company business models that fundamentally change the structures and dynamics of entire industries. Therefore, an appropriate business model is one of the catalysts that might upscale circular initiatives and activities.

Business models and business model innovation occupy a very distinct position in the circular economy (CE) as tools for fundamentally changing the way business is done and driving it towards social and environmental innovation (Bocken et al., 2016; De Angelis, 2022; Fehrer & Wieland, 2021). A key challenge for companies implementing the CE principles is to rethink their value chains and how they create and deliver value through their business models (Lüdeke-Freund et al., 2019).

The academic literature around sustainable business models and, more specifically, circular business models, has only emerged quite recently. Sustainable business

[1] Interface. Lessons for the future. http://interfaceinc.scene7.com/is/content/InterfaceInc/Interface/Americas/WebsiteContentAssets/Documents/Sustainability%2025yr%20Report/25yr%20Report%20Booklet%20Interface_MissionZeroCel.pdf.

© The Author(s), under exclusive license to Springer Nature Switzerland AG 2023
L. Dagilienė et al., *Circular Business Models in the Manufacturing Industry*, Studies in Energy, Resource and Environmental Economics,
https://doi.org/10.1007/978-3-031-28809-8_2

models encompass a broader understanding of value creation for various stakeholders since they are designed to "*capture economic value while maintaining or regenerating natural, social and economic capital beyond its organisational boundaries*" (Schaltegger et al., 2016, p. 6). A circular business model is usually understood to be a type of sustainable business model (Bocken et al., 2014).

One of the most comprehensive definitions of the circular business model is given by Frishammar and Parida (2019, p. 8): "*a circular business model is one in which a focal company, together with partners, uses innovation to create, capture, and deliver value to improve resource efficiency by extending the lifespan of products and parts, thereby realising environmental, social, and economic benefits*". This definition emphasizes a systemic approach, which together with other actors in the value chain, create products and services based on the CE principles.

Circular business models are key levers for the transition to the CE (Geissdoerfer et al., 2020) and circular supply chains (Farooque et al., 2019; Masi et al., 2017; Yang et al., 2018). Inherently circular business models operate at different levels of the economic system—micro (products, companies, consumers), meso (industries, eco-industrial parks, cities, regions) and macro (Kirchherr et al., 2018), with the involvement of a broad range of stakeholders, including suppliers and customers (Urbinati et al., 2017) through value networks and collaboration (Bocken et al., 2014). Circular business models show how companies create value by using the principles of the CE, namely reduce, reuse, repair, remanufacture, recycle, recover, and repurpose (Reike et al., 2018; Winans et al., 2017) in production, distribution, and consumption processes (Lüdeke-Freund et al., 2019), which are compatible both with sustainability (Geissdoerfer et al., 2018; Ünal et al., 2019) and profitability (Zucchella & Previtali, 2019). Companies that are willing to design and implement a circular business model need to rethink the value propositions by consuming fewer resources, and/or consuming recycled materials, to create circular value chains (Farooque et al., 2019; Masi et al., 2017) while at the same time improving environmental quality, economic prosperity, and social equity (Kirchherr et al., 2018).

Even though the CE is gaining momentum, there is still a considerable lack of clarity about the conceptual and dimensional ambiguities of circular business models (De Angelis, 2022; Geissdoerfer et al., 2020), as well as their contribution to the circular transformation in different industries. The conceptualization of sector-specific circular business models may clarify and elucidate specific knowledge for value proposition, value capture, value delivery (i.e., customer involvement), and value creation (Rosa et al., 2019), and help managers implement circular business models in their companies more efficiently, as well as accelerate the systemic industrial transition to the CE.

The broader upscaling of circular business models across different industries, as well as consumer awareness and acceptance of novel value propositions (Kirchherr et al., 2018), is still in the initial stages. Integrating the CE principles in ways that are supportive of business performance is a challenge. This new kind of business model seeks to keep the created economic value embedded into products to the end of their life cycle and beyond and deploy it in new types of market offerings (Rosa et al., 2019). Importantly, there is a lack of guidance and orienting management practices (De Angelis, 2022) in terms of consolidated circular practices guiding companies in improving the circularity of either their products or services (Rosa et al., 2019). As Fehrer and Wieland (2021) note, quite often, circular business models are conceptualized as holistic descriptions of how organizations create value for their stakeholders, optimize resource loops, and thereby capture value (Bocken et al., 2014, 2016).

2.2 Circular Business Model Frameworks

The dynamics and complexity of closed-loop value chains, and the needs of multiple actors, lead to a fairly large variety of circular business models. Table 2.1 presents a non-exhaustive range of conceptual frameworks of circular business models in the academic and grey literature. Scholars have observed that circular business models usually combine various principles of the CE concept—3R, 4R, 6R, and 10R[2] (Reike et al., 2018; Salvador et al., 2021; Winans et al., 2017). For example, the Ellen MacArthur Foundation (2015), Bocken et al. (2016), and Geissdoerfer et al. (2020), all propose circular business model frameworks that are characterized by different intensifications of circular (so-called R loops) flows, starting from resource optimization, prolonging the product's life cycle, and ending with the recovery of useful materials at the end of product life. Meanwhile, Urbinati et al. (2017) and Lüdeke-Freund et al. (2019) apply a Business Model Canvas—value creation, value delivery, and value capture—as a basis for circular business model frameworks. However, a systemic and institutional view highlights that the widely adopted Business Model Canvas logic does not adequately explain circular value flows (Fehrer & Wieland, 2021), because simplified, step-by-step process steps do not reflect the complexity associated with circular innovation.

Another prevalent classification, this time identifying five types of circular business models, was proposed by OECD (2019), Lacy et al. (2020).

- **Circular supplies** (also known as "*circular inputs*" or "*circular supply chains*") is one of the most prevalent circular business models. The idea is to replace a linear type of resource in its supply chain with renewable resources, renewable bio-based materials, or renewable man-made materials.
- **Resource recovery** is a business model in which the product, at the end of its useful life, is fully recycled, refurbished, and integrated into the life cycle of a new product. Here the focus is set on closed-loop recycling, industrial symbiosis, and cradle-to-cradle designs (McDonough & Braungart, 2002) that recycle waste into new resources.

[2] 3R—reduce, reuse, recycle; 4R—reduce, reuse, recycle, recover; 5R—reduce, reuse repair, recycle, and regulate; 6R—includes 3R and redesign, recover, remanufacture; 10R—includes 3R and refuse, rethink, repair, refurbish, recover, remanufacture, repurpose. The higher number of R shows the higher level of detail. There are also existing combinations of 7R, 8R, 9R.

Table 2.1 The range of circular business model conceptual frameworks

Author	Name	Description
Ellen MacArthur Foundation (2015)	Regenerate	Shift to renewable energy and materials; reclaim, retain, and regenerate the health of the ecosystem and return recovered biological resources to the biosphere
	Share	Keep product loop speed low and maximize utilization of products by sharing them among users (peer-to-peer sharing of privately owned products or public sharing of a pool of products), reusing them throughout their technical lifetime (second-hand), and prolonging their life through maintenance, repair, and design for durability
	Optimize	Increase performance/efficiency of a product; remove waste from the production process and the supply chain (from sourcing and logistics to production, use, and end-of-use collection); leverage big data, automation, remote sensing, and steering. None of these actions requires a change in the product or technology
	Loop	Keep components and materials in closed loops and prioritize inner loops. For finite materials, this means remanufacturing products or components and, as a last resort, recycling material. For renewable materials, this means anaerobic digestion and extracting biochemical from organic waste
	Virtualize	Dematerialize and deliver utility virtually—books or music, online shopping, fleets of autonomous vehicles, and virtual offices

(continued)

Table 2.1 (continued)

Author	Name	Description
	Exchange	Replace old materials with advanced, non-renewable materials; apply new technologies (e.g. 3D printing); choose new products and services (e.g. electric motors). Essentially, these are processes of changing, upgrading, or replacing older ways of doing things
Geissdoerfer et al. (2020)	Cycling	Entails the implementation of a number of end-of-use strategies, such as reuse, repair, and remanufacturing
	Extending	Aims at keeping the product in use to the highest extent possible, being mainly enabled by design and operation practices
	Intensifying	Leads to the implementation of new value propositions around sharing models, enabled by capacity management, digital capabilities, and customer relationship management
	Dematerializing	Decreases the use of physical resources by enhancing the value created by intangible solutions, such as services and software
Lacy et al. (2020), OECD (2019)	Circular supplies	Phasing out scarce resources by using fully renewable, recyclable, or biodegradable resources, removing inefficiencies, and cutting waste. This model is a good fit for companies that deal with scarce commodities or have a significant environmental footprint

(continued)

Table 2.1 (continued)

Author	Name	Description
	Resource recovery	Capturing embedded value at the end of one product life cycle to feed into another via innovative recycling and upcycling services. This model is based on next generation recycling using new technologies and capabilities. Cradle-to-cradle certified products created through industrial symbiosis and closed-loop recycling are examples of this business model
	Product life extension	This business model is concerned with extending the life cycle of products and assets by repairing, upgrading, remanufacturing, or remarketing products. This type of business model is appropriate for capital-intensive, business-to-business companies, such as industrial equipment manufacturers, and for business-to-consumer companies in markets where new products bring only marginal extra performance over the previous version
	Sharing platforms	This encourages collaboration among product users, whether individuals or organizations. The platform facilitates the sharing of overcapacity or underutilization, thereby increasing productivity
	Product as a service	Provides products through lease or pay-for-use arrangements. In this business model, the company has to ensure durability and upgradability

(continued)

Table 2.1 (continued)

Author	Name	Description
Urbinati et al. (2017)	Downstream circular	Companies adopt a pricing scheme or a marketing campaign that is based on the “use” and “reuse” of products, but where internal practices and design procedures for products do not seem to reflect the characteristics of a circular adopter. In this way, the firm is focusing on the market acceptance of the pay-per-use model, whereas non-relevant changes are made at the level of product design, internal activities or suppliers
	Upstream circular	Companies adopt circularity principles in their product design activities and eventually establish effective relationships with new suppliers. However, they do not make visible to their final customers their adoption of CE practices, either in the price or in the marketing campaigns. In this case, the focus of upstream circular companies is on the cost structure and the advantage is tied to cost efficiency
	Fully circular	Companies who are circular both internally and externally not only manage the production system according to the CE principles, but the involvement of suppliers in its circular production system is also relevant and effective. Moreover, these companies communicate clearly to customers the implementation of circular practices in their internal activities because this is considered of value
Tukker (2015)	Product-oriented	Selling products and providing additional services such as technical services or product-related consultancy
	Use-oriented	Leasing or renting products and providing additional services

(continued)

Table 2.1 (continued)

Author	Name	Description
	Result-oriented	Selling a result by offering a pure service, for example, selling industrial gas rather than gas generators
Bocken et al. (2016)	Access and performance model	Companies provide the capability or services to satisfy users' needs without the ownership of any physical products. The access and performance model is similar to Product-Service Systems (PSSs) and is focused on narrowing resource flows or slowing resource loops
	Extending product value	Companies exploit the residual value of products after their market life through remanufacturing, repair, or other product life extension designs. The business model is focused on slowing resource loops
	Classic long-life model	Companies focus on delivering long-life products, supported by design for durability and repair. This business model is focused on slowing resource loops
	Encourage sufficiency	Companies encourage sufficiency (i.e., reducing end user consumption) through principles, such as durability, upgradability, service, warranties and reparability, and a non-consumerist approach to marketing and sales. This business model is orientated towards slowing resource loops
	Extending resource value	Companies exploit the residual value of resources (products at the end of their life) through collection and sourcing of waste or resources to turn into new forms of value. This business model is focused on closing resource loops

(continued)

Table 2.1 (continued)

Author	Name	Description
	Industrial symbiosis	The use of the residual output of one company's process as a raw material for another process is often characterized by the geographical proximity of the business. The business model is focused on closing resource loops
Lüdeke-Freund et al. (2019)	Repair and maintenance	Repair and maintenance prolong the life of a product by carrying out checks and servicing that preserve or restore its function. This model focuses on repair, product life extension, and creating long-life products
	Reuse and redistribution	Reuse and redistribution refer to the reuse of a product with minor improvements or changes. In a commercial environment, ownership is usually transferred from the original user to the second-hand user
	Refurbishment and remanufacturing	Refurbishment and remanufacturing refer to the major overhaul of products, replacing parts that are failing or likely to fail soon. Refurbished products generally do not reach the quality level of remanufactured products. Remanufacturing ensures that products meet the performance specifications of the original equipment manufacturer
	Recycling	Recycling should already follow the above ways of extending the product life cycle. To enable closed-loop production product materials can be separated, collected, recycled, and put into the process of making new products

(continued)

Table 2.1 (continued)

Author	Name	Description
	Cascading and repurposing	Closing the cycles of biological materials through the use of biodegradable materials and their eventual return to the environment can include cascading and repurposing, as well as the extraction of biochemical feedstock
	Organic feedstock	Once all technically and economically feasible cascades are implemented, organic residuals can be processed via biomass conversion, composting, or anaerobic digestion
Fehrer and Wieland (2021)	Efficient material-technical loops	Efficient material-technical loops support the use of fully renewable, recyclable, or biodegradable resources
	Effective product-service loops	Effective product-service loops are mainly related to product-service systems
	Social-collaborative loops	Following the logic of social-collaborative loops, customers engage in alternative consumption systems based on sharing, which utilize idling capacity of already produced but rarely used goods, or individuals' spare time and skills
	Symbiotic ecosystems	Symbiotic ecosystems create value by closing resource loops built on collective action and collaboration of various actors

- **Product life extension** focuses on extending the use of a product in its intended application and lifespan through design considerations, repairs, refurbishing, component reconditioning, upgrades, and resale on secondary markets.
- **Sharing platforms** can facilitate collaboration between product users, manufacturers, and services providers based on product sharing and leasing.
- Finally, **product as a service** is a business model in which the products are used on a rental/lease or pay-per-use basis.

The development of **Product-Service Systems** (PSSs) (the official term for "product as a service"), oriented to circularity, provides new opportunities for a transformation towards circular business models. PSSs emphasize the idea of product integrity (Stahel, 2010), durability, and renewal, promoting a shift from product ownership to usage on a service basis. PSSs include design, planning and additional capabilities such as a customer service desk or reverse logistics systems, and are considered business model innovations in the CE (Rosa et al., 2019). PSSs imply a return flow to the producer from users, though there can be intermediaries between the two parties (Linder & Williander, 2017). Companies have an incentive to prolong product life cycles, to ensure they are used as intensively as possible, to make them as cost- and material-efficiently as possible, and to reuse parts as much as possible after the end of the product's life (Guldmann & Huulgaard, 2020; Tukker, 2015; Yang et al., 2018). In addition, manufacturing industries have different product life spans and consumption patterns, leading to a variety of circular practices. Focusing on slowing the loops by presenting products as a service to users may increase resource efficiency through reuse, as well as increase jobs related to the economies that support this service model (Patwa et al., 2021).

Generally, there are three types of PSSs (Tukker, 2015; Yang et al., 2018), namely product-oriented, use-oriented, and result-oriented. In product-oriented PSSs, products are sold to the user, and optional services can be added on, such as maintenance or product-related consultancy. Use-oriented PSSs propose selling the product function through leasing or renting, while the product remains the property of the PSSs provider. Result-oriented PSSs are closest to pure service delivery, as they aim to displace more resource-intensive systems and reduce the need for resources at the time of use. A transfer of product ownership can also be advanced through sharing platforms and digital solutions (Hansen et al., 2021). In this case, PSSs fit the specific business model of a sharing platform (Lacy et al., 2020), as it enables product swapping, renting by using digital platforms.

The most common business models described in the CE literature are various recycling practices and use-oriented PSSs (Kjaer et al., 2019; Rosa et al., 2019). Tukker (2015) shows that use-oriented PSSs potentially enhance and improve the use of materials and products by reducing their consumption. However, a less careful use could lead to more rapid product substitution (Rosa et al., 2019). Therefore, rebound effects may also occur (Zink & Geyer, 2017). Circularity may lead to rebound either by failing to compete effectively with virgin materials, or by lowering prices and thus increasing consumption (Zink & Geyer, 2017). Adapted user behaviour is a common cause of rebound effects, for example, when a more fuel-efficient car encourages users to drive more (Kjaer et al., 2019).

Finally, an emerging stream of research emphasizes the systemic and symbiotic perspective of circular business models as a response to the CE complexity and multidimensionality (Fehrer & Wieland, 2021). Companies need to establish new processes and infrastructures for the circular design of products and services through circular value creation (Hansen et al., 2021).

2.3 Circular Business Model Strategies

In academic and grey literature, the approach for the classification of circular business model strategies, which has become the basis of other researchers' studies (Geissdoerfer et al., 2018, 2020; Guldmann & Huulgaard, 2020), is resource cycles (Bocken et al., 2016; McDonough & Braungart, 2002; Stahel, 2010):

- Narrowing resource flows.
- Slowing resource loops.
- Closing resource loops.

Resource conservation is related to the reduction of resource use associated with the product and the production process. Although **narrowing resource flows** is often not considered a sufficient strategy transitioning to the CE (Bocken et al., 2016), we will present it as well. Narrowing resource flows seeks to achieve resource efficiency and optimization. This means less consumption of products, components, materials, and energy in design and manufacture (Geissdoerfer et al., 2018) as well as in supply, use, and refurbishment (Bocken et al., 2016). It is a strategy where products and services are of at least the same quality to the consumer, but where the product itself, or the processes used to produce and deliver it, have a lower negative environmental impact.

At the product level, the narrowing resource flows involves design focused on low-impact inputs (Tukker, 2015), product lightness, or multifunctionality (Konietzko et al., 2020), as well as eliminating waste in the production process, and/or optimizing the supply chain (Konietzko et al., 2020). At the ecosystem level, this strategy is concerned with maximizing the potential use of products and materials (Konietzko et al., 2020). This often includes sharing activities where several user groups (e.g., industrial manufacturers) have access to the same resources in the ecosystem and share excess resources. Notably, narrowing resource flows is the least suitable in the CE, as it is focused mostly on reducing material and energy resources (Bocken et al., 2016; McDonough & Braungart, 2002), but does not emphasize the fundamental transformation of product design or consumer habits and preferences.

The **slowing resource loops** strategy involves longer and reusable use of products, components, and materials (Bocken et al., 2016), and transformation of single-use products into reusable ones. This strategy is usually related to "physical durability design" and product maintenance and repair options (e.g., reassembly, refurbishment, and standardization). According to Bocken et al. (2016), slowing resource loops strategies are related to designing long-life products (designed for attachment and trust, as well as for reliability and durability) and/or designed for product-life extension (ease of maintenance and repair, upgradeability and adaptability, standardization and compatibility, as well as designed for disassembly and reassembly). Mass consumption due to planned, technological, and foreseeable obsolescence is emerging as a resource-related issue for many product groups (Kjaer et al., 2019). Thus, slowing resource loops quite strategy often relates to the PSSs design for the CE (Lacy et al., 2020; Tukker, 2015; Yang et al., 2018). PSSs can help users to extend the use phase and thus potentially reduce resource consumption throughout the life cycle. The development of repair, remanufacture, or refurbishment services, or consultancy services that allow consumers to take care of their product themselves illustrates the implementation of this strategy. Bocken et al. (2016) identify these circular business models based on slowing resource loops: the access and performance model, extending product value, the classic long-life model, and encouraging self-sufficiency.

Closing resource loops strategies relate to companies' efforts to reintegrate waste (e.g., paper, plastic, glass, metal) into supply chains and to reuse and recycle it (Kjaer et al., 2019). At the product level, this strategy usually involves design using materials suitable for primary processing of the product (Bocken et al., 2016) to enable the return of the product and its components back to the value chain. Products can be made from either recycled materials derived from other products and components, or derived from the same product. According to Bocken et al. (2016), closing resource loops strategies could be related to designing for technological and biological cycles, and designing for recycling that only fits into a linear economy (covering secondary recycling or downcycling, tertiary recycling or feedstock recycling, as well as quaternary recycling or thermal recycling). Business models tend to focus on extending the value of resources and/or industrial symbiosis that is enabled by an appropriate ecosystem for turning waste into raw materials.

An important role is played by industrial symbiosis, where products, materials, waste, and energy are shared between businesses that are close to one another. Industrial symbiosis is a form of brokering to bring companies together in innovative collaborations, finding ways to use the waste from one as raw material for another. Local or wider cooperation in industrial symbiosis can reduce the need for virgin raw material and waste disposal, thereby closing the material loop—a fundamental feature of the circular economy and a driver for green growth and eco-innovative solutions. It can also reduce emissions and energy use and create new revenue streams.[3]

Circular business models differ in the degree of change they contribute to sustainable development. Those business models that systematically change the behaviour of society and companies have a stronger impact (Fehrer & Wieland, 2021) than

[3] What is industrial symbiosis? https://fissacproject.eu/en/what-is-industrial-symbiosis/.

those that focus mainly on reducing the environmental footprint (Hussain & Malik, 2020). Narrowing resource flows is treated as a business model strategy that makes a relatively gradual and weak improvement in sustainability (Bocken et al., 2016). Closing resource loops is similar in this regard, but if this business model is applied in the context of the whole ecosystem (e.g. industrial symbiosis), then it is treated as a business model that makes a radical and strong change. Slowing resource loops strategies may be considered as more radical and strong strategies that have an impact on consumer behaviour and value creation (Hussain & Malik, 2020).

Finally, business models are embedded in industrial value chains. Depending on the dominant circular business strategy, so-called circular value chains can be respectively orientated towards closing loops, slowing loops, narrowing resource flows, as well as intensifying loops and dematerializing loops (Geissdoerfer et al., 2018). Companies that are oriented towards higher-quality circularity strategies might create or maintain their competitive advantage by seeking greater vertical integration, which enables higher levels of loop closing and better feedback into the product design (Hansen et al., 2021).

In business practice, there are often hybrid circular strategies and business models. Taken individually, or in combination, these strategies help to transform linear approaches to production and consumption into circular ones.

2.4 Drivers and Barriers for Circular Business Models

As the CE is inherently multidimensional and complex, organizations face many factors that can encourage or hinder their transition to more circular business models. Summarized drivers (enablers) and barriers with selected references are presented in Table 2.2.

Recent circular economy policies promote eco-design, extended producer responsibilities and innovative ways of reducing, reusing, and recycling for manufacturing companies (Dagilienė et al., 2021). Organizations are institutions that have to adapt to **norms and regulations**. This includes both legal norms and industry standards. Therefore, managers are forced to adopt novel and sustainable environmental practices driven by coercive, normative, and cognitive pressures from their main stakeholders (Gusmerotti et al., 2019). A combination of formal and informal institutions either restricts or enables the extent to which companies can implement a circular business model (Ranta et al., 2018). Compliance with environmental regulations is also one of the means of risk minimization, and revenue and image protection (Dangelico & Pujari, 2010). Williamson et al. (2006) indicate that regulation plays a vital role in improving the environmental practices of small and medium sized manufacturing companies. Finally, the anticipation of future legal requirements (Bansal et al., 2018) may enhance more sustainable environmental practices. A series of directives and national legislation, particularly related to waste management issues, recycling, packaging, and product safety encourage companies to proactively change their business models and processes. The role of governments is also important because

Table 2.2 Drivers and barriers to transformation to circular business models

		WHAT	
	Factors	Drivers (enablers)	Barriers
HOW	Regulative	Environmental regulations (Ranta et al., 2018; Seuring & Müller, 2008), e.g., laws concerning product take-back (Govindan & Hasanagic, 2018) and compliance with legal regulations for risk management (Dangelico & Pujari, 2010) Anticipate future legal requirements (Bansal et al., 2018) Green public procurement (Guldmann & Huulgaard, 2020) Tax policies and subsidies (Tura et al., 2019) Educational programs and facilitate infrastructure development (Patwa et al., 2021)	Lack of regulation (Guldmann & Huulgaard, 2020) Taxation of labour rather material (Stahel, 2010) Confusion over legal definitions regarding recaptured goods (Guldmann & Huulgaard, 2020)
	Market (consumer)	Consumer environmental awareness and preferences (de Jesus & Mendonça, 2018) Consumer responsibility and self-sufficiency (Bocken et al., 2014; Govindan & Hasanagic, 2018)	Lack of consumer interest and unclear market demand (Kirchherr et al., 2018) Consumer irrationality (prefer ownership of a product even if temporary usage is more economical) (Sousa-Zommer et al., 2018) The possibility of buying cheaper products made from cheaper raw materials (Kirchherr et al., 2018)

(continued)

Table 2.2 (continued)

		WHAT	
	Factors	Drivers (enablers)	Barriers
	Economic	Economic benefits such as profitability, competitive advantage, and market share (Dangelico & Pujari, 2010; Gusmerotti et al., 2019; Lieder & Rashid, 2016) Resource scarcity and efficiency (Lieder & Rashid, 2016; Linder & Williander, 2017; Tura et al., 2019)	Cost increase and lack of evidence of economic benefits (Lieder & Rashid, 2016; Guldmann & Huulgaard, 2020; Gusmerotti et al., 2019) Low price of raw (virgin) materials (Kirchherr et al., 2018; Mah, 2021; Ranta et al., 2018)
	Financial	Favourable financial conditions (Tura et al., 2019)	Funding difficulties, high upfront costs (Guldmann & Huulgaard, 2020; Kirchherr et al., 2018; Masi et al., 2018)
	Technological	Technologies for redesign, remanufacturing, and reuse (Govindan & Hasanagic, 2018) Advanced technologies for turning waste into secondary raw materials (Suchek et al., 2021)	High technological uncertainty (Tura et al., 2019) Linear technologies, challenges in separating the bio- from the techno-cycle (Masi et al., 2018) Technological dependence and high adoption costs (Suchek et al., 2021)
	Supply chain	Inter-firm collaboration; industry leader; information sharing (Moktadir et al., 2018; Sousa-Zommer et al., 2018; Suchek et al., 2021); supply chain coordination (Fischer & Pascucci, 2017) Product as service arrangements (Fischer & Pascucci, 2017)	Complexity and lack of supply chain integration (Geissdoerfer et al., 2018; Guldmann & Huulgaard, 2020); lack of industry standards (Kirchherr et al., 2018) Difficulties for business collaboration and mutual trust, lack of knowledge (Fischer & Pascucci, 2017), insufficient or missing communication (Seuring & Müller, 2008)
	Social	Maturity of society and social awareness (de Jesus & Mendonça, 2018); environmental and social pressure groups (Mah, 2021)	Lack of awareness and sense of urgency (Masi et al., 2018)

(continued)

Table 2.2 (continued)

		WHAT	
	Factors	Drivers (enablers)	Barriers
	Organizational (strategy)	Integrating environmental and social goals (Geissdoerfer et al., 2018); change of mindset (Bocken et al., 2014; Sousa-Zommer et al., 2018) Knowledge of the CE (Moktadir et al., 2018)	Resistance to change, unawareness (Kirchherr et al., 2018; Masi et al., 2018) Narrow focus of existing sustainability strategies (Guldmann & Huulgaard, 2020)
	Organizational (implemention)	Fit and change of organizational structure and strategy; leadership and multifunctional teams (Sousa-Zommer et al., 2018; Tura et al., 2019)	Lack of expertise, technical skills (Tura et al., 2019); lack of capabilities, resources and adaptability (Guldmann & Huulgaard, 2020; Suchek et al., 2021)
	Product design and innovation	Product innovation (radical versus incremental) (Bakker et al., 2014; Dangelico & Pujari, 2010) Certification (Hansen et al., 2021); warranties; circular product design strategies, and business models (Bocken et al., 2016) Product testing and experimentation (Sousa-Zommer et al., 2018) Systemic innovation (de Jesus & Mendonça, 2018)	Concerns about quality control of returned products, complexity in product design (Guldmann & Huulgaard, 2020) Product design limitations and fashion vulnerability (Linder & Williander, 2017)

they **initiate educational programs** and **facilitate infrastructure development** (Patwa et al., 2021) for circular transformation.

The megatrends of increasing international political tensions and sustainability push more towards the shortening of global value chains and favouring regionalization (Mariotti, 2022). The importance of regional value chains in the CE manifests through focusing on the domestic market and shortening the value chains. The agendas of governments are boosting regional value chains, especially in the food industry.

Importantly, the same **factor** can be **both motivating and hindering**, depending on the contextual conditions and circumstances. Therefore, regulative factors (e.g., limited circular procurement, obstructing laws and regulations) are also seen as insufficiently coercive mechanisms in the CE context. Regulative institutions tend not to create a sufficiently robust environment for a successful transition to the CE (Levänen et al., 2018; Moreau et al., 2017; Ranta et al., 2018), yet they do not appear among the main CE barriers in EU countries (Kirchherr et al., 2018). Indeed, informal normative and cultural-cognitive preferences may negate regulative efforts aimed towards the CE; for example, customers often prefer new products over refurbished ones (Ranta et al., 2018). **A lack of consumer interest and awareness**, and hesitant company approach and culture (Guldmann & Huulgaard, 2020) appear to be the most important barriers to the CE (Kirchherr et al., 2018). **Consumer acceptance of circular business models** (e.g., Product-Service Systems, performance-based contracting, sharing platforms) is increasing only gradually because of inertia (de Jesus & Mendonça, 2018). The expectations, habits, and behaviours of end users and business customers are changing slowly. Therefore, dissemination of information and the sharing of knowledge and good practices are treated as stimulating factors in the CE. Among other stakeholders, the **consumer's responsibility** should be the key driver, forcing companies to keep up with CE principles (Govindan & Hasanagic, 2018). When making a decision to buy a circular product, consumers often pay attention to its price and they are usually very **cost-conscious**. The fact that primary raw materials are often cheaper than secondary ones (Kirchherr et al., 2018) leads to a higher price of the circular product and the difficulty of competing, especially in the lower income consumer segment. Thus, the possibility to produce from cheaper primary raw materials is still a barrier in the CE transformation. This has been the case in the plastics industry, where periods of low oil prices have threatened the viability of plastics recycling and the development of recycling projects (Mah, 2021).

Proponents of the CE announce opportunities for companies to create market-based solutions that can be profitable while also addressing environmental concerns (Gusmerotti et al., 2019). Paradoxically, quite often, the **most important factors appear to be only the economic and financial** ones (Gusmerotti et al., 2019; Lieder & Rashid, 2016; Tura et al., 2019). In particular, small and medium-sized enterprises with innovative business models and high expertise often require financial support in order to make their novel ideas a reality (Reike et al., 2018). Based on the survey results of more than 800 Italian manufacturing companies, Gusmerotti et al. (2019) identify that companies seek to improve their own efficiency by optimizing logistics and waste management through the reduction of waste and recovering material in their own production processes. Lieder and Rashid (2016) emphasize the triple motivation for manufacturing organizations for successful CE transition, namely **resource scarcity, environmental impacts, and economic benefits**. Industrial activity fundamentally depends on the resources necessary to manufacture products and their components. Resource scarcity, lack of critical materials, volatile prices of resources, and supply risks strongly influence corporate decisions to rethink their linear business models and to develop circular solutions (Tura et al., 2019). Finally, perceiving end-of-life products as resources rather than waste (Lieder & Rashid, 2016) and proactive environmental management contribute to minimizing negative environmental impacts. Usually, economic motivation, followed by cost reduction and an increase in competitiveness, are related to the strategy of narrowing or closing the loops that lead to resource value management (Gusmerotti et al., 2019; Lieder & Rashid, 2016).

Technologies and technological innovations such as 3D printing, the Internet of Things (IoT), automation, and digitization can improve waste management by turning waste into new raw materials (Suchek et al., 2021). Advanced technology may also assist designers and producers to redesign, remanufacture, and reuse the used product effectively (Govindan & Hasanagic, 2018) in environmentally friendly ways. Technological challenges are considered to be among the key barriers to a transition towards the CE, because technologies very often come with high costs (Suchek et al., 2021) that many companies are unable to meet. Interestingly, despite available technical solutions, even more technological innovation seems to be required to enable the CE (de Jesus & Mendonça, 2018; Govindan & Hasanagic, 2018). However, the CE not only requires technical implementation, but also has fundamental organizational implications as essential components of success (Reike et al., 2018).

Inter-firm collaboration across the value chain is thought to be another very important driver for circular industrial systems (Sousa-Zommer et al., 2018; Suchek et al., 2021). New forms of collaboration and supply chain coordination, such as digital platforms or technology developers, are necessary to facilitate the process in the CE context. However, companies struggle to cope with the dynamics of closed-loop systems (Lieder & Rashid, 2016) and to arrange proper business collaborations (Fischer & Pascucci, 2017), since the prevailing business models, products, and supply chains have been developed for operating in linear systems. Chain coordination, financial mechanisms, and the contracting out of products as services are key drivers for a transition into circular material flows (Fischer & Pascucci, 2017). Green supply chain management involves optimizing the flow of raw materials, components, and waste, and sharing information throughout the supply chain to eliminate or reduce any negative environmental impacts without impacting product quality, productivity, and cost (Masi et al., 2017).

Despite the long-term environmental and economic benefits, the adoption of a circular business model might have **higher associated business risks** than the adoption of a conventional (linear) business model (Linder & Williander, 2017). One reason is that the life of a product is becoming longer as a result of post-consumption return and reuse. Through the integration of circular services, a company makes such services available to the customers (Guldmann & Huulgaard, 2020), e.g., implementing take-back systems to collect products from consumers at the end of the product's life. Thus, the adoption of a circular business model requires more spatial and temporal organizational adaptability, knowledge, and resources and, from an **internal organizational point of view**, the barriers are often related to a lack of management support and knowledge about the CE (Moktadir et al., 2018), resources, incentive structures, organizational adaptability, unclear business cases, and complexity of product design (Guldmann & Huulgaard, 2020). Companies need to know and care about the necessary resources, competencies, and capacities that may, in turn, act either as barriers or as drivers when transitioning to circular business models (Suchek et al., 2021). Moreover, the role of leadership and multifunctional teams, as well as the integration of key stakeholders into circular business development processes (Sousa-Zommer et al., 2018), is particularly important enablers. Additionally, based on Lacy et al. (2020), it is very important to include all actors in the circular value chain in business strategy and planning. Testing and experimenting with products (as value propositions) and developing testing procedures are also necessary for the implementation of a circular business model (Sousa-Zommer et al., 2018). Circular business models require extraordinary intra-organizational governance of complex physical flows of material and energy, as well as coordinated efforts from actors in the value chain.

Nevertheless, **circular product design** is crucial to sustainable production and consumption (Bakker et al., 2014; Bocken et al., 2014), especially in connection with critical materials (Lieder & Rashid, 2016) and the emotional and technical durability of products (Bakker et al., 2014). The cradle-to-cradle design philosophy, developed by McDonough and Braungart (2002), has inspired many companies and designers to adopt a circular approach to product design. Bocken et al. (2016) also note that business model innovation closely aligns with product innovation for circularity. For example, solutions to reduce end user consumption through principles, such as durability, adaptability, modularity, warranties, and repairability involve changes in both product design and the underlying business model. Standardization activities and possible **certifications** related to circular product design might also be a benefit for organizations (Hansen et al., 2021).

Linder and Williander (2017) highlight issues such as **fashion vulnerability** and **changing customer preferences,** and their impact on product design. Product design should reflect durability and adaptability to uncertainty (Bocken et al., 2016), changes in technology, functionality, and cost-effectiveness (Linder & Williander, 2017).

A growing stream of research emphasizes the importance of **innovations in CE** implementation (Bocken et al., 2016; Suchek et al., 2021). Relevant innovation policy and support of R&D, aligned with education and training policies, may fill the gap in CE knowledge and create the required skills and toolkits. In the field of innovation, de Jesus and Mendonça (2018) divide the drivers and constraints of eco-innovation into "harder" (technological and economic) and "softer" (institutional, social, cultural) factors. To facilitate a successful circular transition, eco-innovation should be treated as more than just green technology (i.e., devices that provide environmentally beneficial effects), extending into a strategic and systematic enabler of the transformation of the entire value chain (de Jesus & Mendonça, 2018).

Circular innovation can open up new opportunities for small and medium-sized enterprises, as they are more flexible, more responsive, and more adaptable to external changes. Research by Shevchenko et al. (2016) has proven that small, innovative companies guide their decision-making based on their internal readiness to change and, therefore, might reach true sustainability faster than some of the larger companies. Suchek et al. (2021) also found that incumbent companies might influence a circular transformation of entire value chains, but they may be less flexible than start-ups in capturing opportunities and developing radical innovations.

A critical assessment of drivers (enablers) and barriers to CE transformation is provided herein. A holistic understanding of these motivating and non-motivating factors and their interaction helps us better understand how linear business models can be transformed into circular ones.

Key Highlights

- Circular business models belong to the broader literature of sustainable business models.
- The upscaling of circular business models across different industries is still in the initial stages, because integrating CE principles while maintaining business performance is a challenge.
- In business practice, there are often impure, hybrid circular business models. Taken individually, or in combination, these help to transform linear approaches to production and consumption into circular ones.
- The development of PSSs, focused on circularity, might open up new opportunities for a move towards circular business models.
- Companies should orientate towards higher-quality circularity strategies, starting with circular product and service design.
- Manufacturing organizations face many factors that can encourage or hinder their transition to more circular business models. Importantly, the same factor can be both motivating and hindering, depending on the contextual characteristics (industry, product type), the institutional environment, as well as ecological values.
- Motivating and non-motivating factors can arise from regulations, the market, the economy, the supply chain, product design and innovation, or can be financial, technological, social, or organizational.
- Barriers to circular transformation (non-motivating factors) are uncertainty around regulations, a lack of consumer interest and awareness, changing consumer preferences, a lack of financial resources, a lack of technologies or difficulties in accessing them, a lack of management support, a lack of knowledge, and a shortage of tools.

- Key drivers for circular transformation (motivating factors) are clear legislation and external financial support, consumer acceptance of circular products and services, the need for certification, resource scarcity, technological and social innovation, and collaboration.

References

Bakker, C., Hollander, den M., Hinte, van E., & Zijlstra, Y. (2014). *Product that last*. Product Design for Circular Business Models, TU Delft Library, Delft.

Bansal, P., Anna, K. I. M., & Wood, M. O. (2018). Hidden in plain sight: The importance of scale in organizations' attention to issues. *Academy of Management Review, 43*(2), 217–241. https://doi.org/10.5465/amr.2014.0238

Bocken, N. M. P., Pauw, I., Bakker, C. A., & van der Grinten, B. (2016). Product design and business model strategies for a circular economy. *Journal of Industrial and Production Engineering, 3*(5), 308–320. https://doi.org/10.1080/21681015.2016.1172124

Bocken, N. M. P., Short, S. W., Rana, P., & Evans, S. (2014). A literature and practice review to develop sustainable business model archetypes. *Journal of Cleaner Production, 65*, 42–56. https://doi.org/10.1016/j.jclepro.2013.11.039

Dagilienė, L., Varaniūtė, V., & Bruneckienė, J. (2021). Local government's perspective on implementing the circular economy: A framework for future solutions. *Journal of Cleaner Production, 310*, 127340. https://doi.org/10.1016/j.jclepro.2021.127340

Dangelico, R. M., & Pujari, D. (2010). Mainstreaming green product innovation: Why and how companies integrate environmental sustainability. *Journal of Business Ethics, 95*(3), 471–486. https://doi.org/10.1007/s10551-010-0434-0

De Angelis, R. (2022). Circular economy business models as resilient complex adaptive systems. *Business Strategy and the Environment, 31*(September 2021), 2245–2255. https://doi.org/10.1002/bse.3019

De Jesus, A., & Mendonça, S. (2018). Lost in transition? Drivers and barriers in the eco-innovation road to the circular economy. *Ecological Economics, 145*, 75–89. https://doi.org/10.1016/j.ecolecon.2017.08.001

Ellen MacArthur Foundation. (2015). *Towards the circular economy, economic and business rationale for an accelerated transition*. https://www.ellenmacarthurfoundation.org/assets/downloads/publications/TCE_Ellen-MacArthur-Foundation_26-Nov-2015.pdf

Farooque, M., Zang, A., Thurer, M., Qu, T., & Huisingh, D. (2019). Circular supply chain management: A definition and structured literature review. *Journal of Cleaner Production, 228*. https://doi.org/10.1016/j.jclepro.2019.04.303

Fehrer, J. A., & Wieland, H. (2021). A systemic logic for circular business models. *Journal of Business Research, 125*, 609–620. https://doi.org/10.1016/j.jbusres.2020.02.010

Fischer, A., & Pascucci, S. (2017). Institutional incentives in circular economy transition: The case of material use in the Dutch textile industry. *Journal of Cleaner Production, 155*, 17–32. https://doi.org/10.1016/j.jclepro.2016.12.038

Frishammar, J., & Parida, V. (2019). Circular business model transformation: A roadmap for incumbent firms. *California Management Review, 61*(2). https://doi.org/10.1177/0008125618811926

Geissdoerfer, M., Morioka, S. N., de Carvalho, M. M., & Evans, S. (2018). Business models and supply chains for the circular economy. *Journal of Cleaner Production, 190*, 712–721. https://doi.org/10.1016/j.jclepro.2018.04.159

Geissdoerfer, M., Pieroni, P. P. M., Pigosso, C. A., & Soufani, K. (2020). Circular business models: A review. *Journal of Cleaner Production, 277*, 123741. https://doi.org/10.1016/j.jclepro.2020.123741

Govindan, K., & Hasanagic, M. (2018). A systematic review on drivers, barriers, and practices towards circular economy: A supply chain perspective. *International Journal of Production Research, 56*(1/2), 278–311. https://doi.org/10.1080/00207543.2017.1402141

Guldmann, E., & Huulgaard, R. D. (2020). Barriers to circular business model innovation: A multiple-case study. *Journal of Cleaner Production, 243*. https://doi.org/10.1016/j.jclepro.2019.118160

Gusmerotti, N. M., Testa, F., Corsini, F., Pretner, G., & Iraldo, F. (2019). Drivers and approaches to the circular economy in manufacturing firms. *Journal of Cleaner Production, 230*, 314–327. https://doi.org/10.1016/j.jclepro.2019.05.044

Hansen, E. G., Revellio, F., Schmitt, J., Schrack, D., Alcayaga, A., & Dick, A., (2021). *Successfully implementing a circular economy: The role of innovation, quality standards & digitalization* (White paper). Quality Austria—Trainings, Zertifizierungs und Begutachtungs GmbH, Vienna, Austria.

Hussain, M., & Malik, M. (2020). Organizational enablers for circular economy in the context of sustainable supply chain management. *Journal of Cleaner Production, 256*. https://doi.org/10.1016/j.jclepro.2020.120375

Kirchherr, J., Piscicelli, L., Bour, R., Kostense-Smit, E., Muller, J., Huibrechtse-Truijens, A., & Hekkert, M. (2018). Barriers to the circular economy: Evidence from the European Union (EU). *Ecological Economics, 150*, 264–272. https://doi.org/10.1016/j.ecolecon.2018.04.028

Kjaer, L. L., Pigosso, D. C. A., Niero, M., Bech, N. M., & McAloone, T. C. (2019). Product/service-systems for a circular economy: The Route to decoupling economic growth from resource consumption? *Journal of Industrial Ecology, 23*(1), 22–35. https://doi.org/10.1111/jiec.12747

Konietzko, J., Bocken, N., & Hultink, E. (2020). A tool to analyze, ideate and develop circular innovation ecosystems. *Sustainability, 12*(1). https://doi.org/10.3390/su12010417

Lacy, P., Long. J., & Spindler, W. (2020). *The circular economy handbook: Realizing the circular advantage* (p. 363). Springer, ISBN 978-1-349-95967-9. https://doi.org/10.1057/978-1-349-95968-6

Levänen, J., Lyytinen, T., & Gatica, S. (2018). Modelling the interplay between institutions and circular economy business models: A case study of battery recycling in Finland and Chile. *Ecological Economics, 154*, 373–382. https://doi.org/10.1016/j.ecolecon.2018.08.018

Lieder, M., & Rashid, A. (2016). Towards circular economy implementation: A comprehensive review in context of manufacturing industry. *Journal of Cleaner Production, 115*, 36–51 https://doi.org/10.1016/j.jclepro.2015.12.042

Linder, M., & Williander, M. (2017). Circular business model innovation: Inherent uncertainties. *Business Strategy and the Environment, 26*, 182–196. https://doi.org/10.1002/bse.1906

Lüdeke-Freund, F., Gold, S., & Bocken, N. (2019). A review and typology of circular economy business model patterns. *Journal of Industrial Ecology, 23*. https://doi.org/10.1111/jiec.12763

Mah, A. (2021). Future-proofing capitalism: The paradox of the circular economy for plastics. *Global Environmental Politics, 21*(2), 121–142. https://doi.org/10.1162/glep_a_00594

Mariotti, S. (2022). A warning from the Russian-Ukrainian war: Avoiding a future that rhymes with the past. *Journal of Industrial and Business Economics*. https://doi.org/10.1007/s40812-022-00219-z

Masi D., Day S., & Godsell J. (2017). Supply chain configurations in the circular economy: A systematic literature review. *Sustainability, 9*. https://doi.org/10.3390/su9091602

Masi, D., Kumar, V., Garza-Reyes, J. A., & Godsell, J. (2018). Towards a more circular economy: Exploring the awareness, practices, and barriers from a focal firm perspective. *Production Planning and Control, 29*(6), 539–550. https://doi.org/10.1080/09537287.2018.1449246

McDonough, W., & Braungart, M. (2002). *Cradle to cradle: Remaking the way we make things* (1st ed.). North Point Press.

Moktadir, M. A., Rahman, T., Rahman, M. H., Syed, M. A., & Sanjoy, K. P. (2018). Drivers to sustainable manufacturing practices and circular economy: A perspective of leather industries in Bangladesh. *Journal of Cleaner Production, 174*, 1366–1380. https://doi.org/10.1016/j.jclepro.2017.11.063

Moreau, V., Sahakian, M., Van Griethuysen, P., & Vuille, F. (2017). Coming full circle: Why social and institutional dimensions matter for the circular economy. *Journal of Industrial Ecology, 21*(3), 497–506. https://doi.org/10.1111/jiec.12598

OECD. (2019). *Business models for the circular economy: Opportunities and challenges for policy*. OECD Publishing, Paris. https://doi.org/10.1787/g2g9dd62-en

Patwa, N., Sivarajah, U., Seetharaman, A., Sarkar, S., Maiti, K. P., & Hingorani, K. (2021). Towards a circular economy: An emerging economies context. *Journal of Business Research, 122*, 725–735. https://doi.org/10.1016/j.jbusres.2020.05.015

Ranta, V., Aarikka-Stenroos, L., & Mäkinen, S. J. (2018). Creating value in the circular economy: A structured multiple-case analysis of business models. *Journal of Cleaner Production, 201*, 988–1000. https://doi.org/10.1016/j.jclepro.2018.08.072

Reike, D., Vermeulen, W. J. V., & Witjes, S. (2018). The circular economy: New or refurbished as CE 3.0?—Exploring controversies in the conceptualization of the circular economy through a focus on history and resource value retention options. *Resources, Conservation & Recycling, 135*(1), 246–264. https://doi.org/10.1016/j.resconrec.2017.08.027

Rosa, P., Sasanelli, C., & Terzi, S. (2019). Towards circular business models: A systematic literature review on classification frameworks and archetypes. *Journal of Cleaner Production, 236*, 117696. https://doi.org/10.1016/j.jclepro.2019.117696

Salvador, R., Barros, M., Freire, F., Halog, A., Piekarski, C., & De Francisco, A. (2021). Circular economy strategies on business modelling: Identifying the greatest influences. *Journal of Cleaner Production, 299*. https://doi.org/10.1016/j.jclepro.2021.126918

Seuring, S., & Müller, M. (2008). From a literature review to a conceptual framework for sustainable supply chain management. *Journal of Cleaner Production, 16*, 1699–1710. https://doi.org/10.1016/j.jclepro.2008.04.020

Schaltegger, S., Lüdeke-Freund, F., & Hansen, E. G. (2016). Business models for sustainability: A co-evolutionary analysis of sustainable entrepreneurship, innovation, and transformation. *Organization & Environment, 29*(3), 264–289. https://doi.org/10.1177/1086026616633272

Shevchenko, A., Lévesque, M., & Pagell, M. (2016). Why firms delay reaching true sustainability. *Journal of Management Studies, 53*(5), 911–935. https://doi.org/10.1111/joms.12199

Sousa-Zommer, T. T., Magalhães, S., Zancul, E., & Cauchick-Miguel, P. A. (2018). Exploring the challenges for circular business implementation in manufacturing companies: An empirical investigation of a pay-per-use service provider. *Resources, Conservation & Recycling, 135*, 3–13. https://doi.org/10.1016/j.resconrec.2017.10.033

Stahel, W. R. (2010). *The performance economy*. Palgrave Macmillan.

Suchek, N., Fernandes, C. I., Kraus, S., Filser, M., & Sjögrén, H. (2021). Innovation and the circular economy: A systemic literature review. *Business Strategy and the Environment, 30*, 3686–3702. https://doi.org/10.1002/bse.2834

Tukker, A. (2015). Product services for a resource-efficient and circular economy—A review. *Journal of Cleaner Production, 97*, 76–91. https://doi.org/10.1016/j.jclepro.2013.11.049

Tura, N., Hanski, J., Ahola, T., Ståhle, M., Piiparinen, S., & Valkokari, P. (2019). Unlocking circular business: A framework of barriers and drivers. *Journal of Cleaner Production, 212*, 90–98. https://doi.org/10.1016/j.jclepro.2018.11.202

Ünal, E., Urbinati, A., Chiaroni, D., & Manzini, R. (2019). Value creation in circular business models: The case of a US small medium enterprise in the building sector. *Resources, Conservation and Recycling, 146*, 291–307. https://doi.org/10.1016/j.resconrec.2018.12.034

Urbinati, A., Chiaroni, D., & Chiesa, V. (2017). Towards a new taxonomy of circular economy business models. *Journal of Cleaner Production, 168*, 487–498. https://doi.org/10.1016/j.jclepro.2017.09.047

Williamson, D., Lynch-Wood, G., & Ramsay, J. (2006). Drivers of environmental behaviour in manufacturing SMEs and the implications for CSR. *Journal of Business Ethics, 67*, 317–330. https://doi.org/10.1007/s10551-006-9187-1

Winans, K., Kendall, A., & Deng, H. (2017). The history and current applications of the circular economy concept. *Renewable and Sustainable Energy Reviews, 68*(1), 825–833. https://doi.org/10.1016/j.rser.2016.09.123

Yang, M., Smart, P., Kumar, M., Jolly, M., & Evans, S. (2018). Product-service systems business models for circular supply chains. *Production Planning & Control, 29*(6), 498–508. https://doi.org/10.1080/09537287.2018.1449247

Zink, T., & Geyer, R. (2017). Circular economy rebound. *Journal of Industrial Ecology, 21*, 593–602. https://doi.org/10.1111/jiec.12545

Zucchella, A., & Previtali, P. (2019). Circular business models for sustainable development: A "waste is food" restorative ecosystem. *Business Strategy and the Environment, 28*, 274–285. https://doi.org/10.1002/bse.2216

Chapter 3
Circular Performance of Small Open Economies

Abstract This chapter analyses the characteristics and adaptive features of small open economies; reviews and compares previous studies on circularity performance; and identifies drivers and barriers among small open economies and large economies in the European Union. Finally, it concludes with an assessment of circularity and economic performance of selected manufacturing industries in selected small open economies.

Keywords Small open economies · Circular performance · Economic performance

3.1 Adaptive Features of Small Open Economies

Only a limited number of studies address the potential of the circular economy (CE) at the macro level (Geerken et al., 2019), none of which are peer-reviewed, and most of the CE research is noticeably focused on large economies, such as the USA, China, Japan, Germany, and the UK. There is an argument that a large economy is one that has a substantial impact on global GDP, prices (as price makers), global interest rates, and various economic, social, technological, and other conditions. In contrast to these countries, small open economies (SOEs) intensively participate in international trade (open economies), but in smaller volumes, and their policies do not impact world prices, interest rates, or incomes. According to Carlin and Soskice (2003), SOEs are assumed to be too small to influence the level of world output and prices, meaning that they are price takers, and are affected by the actions of some of the larger players in the world markets.

SOEs leverage the advantages of smallness to make the most of their potential via viability, flexibility, greater openness to change, agility, decision-making efficiency, greater social homogeneity, and cohesion. The adaptive capacities of small economies and their higher homogeneity can help mitigate the narrowness of their domestic markets (Robinson, 1960). Smaller cities, in fact, tend to enjoy the advantages of being a city without the diseconomies that arise in rapidly growing cities (Frick & Rodríguez-Pose, 2018).

© The Author(s), under exclusive license to Springer Nature Switzerland AG 2023

L. Dagilienė et al., *Circular Business Models in the Manufacturing Industry*, Studies in Energy, Resource and Environmental Economics,
https://doi.org/10.1007/978-3-031-28809-8_3

Despite their limited influence on global output and conditions, a large body of research has shown the specific role of SOEs in the global economy, which is derived from the core characteristics of these countries (see Table 3.1).

Economic development is highly context dependent. Over the past decade, the world has changed significantly, and multiple situations have become uncertain, temporary, rapidly changing, or requiring transformation (such situations are named as "New Normal"), which has blurred the links between the size of the economy and its productivity/growth. According to Frick and Rodríguez-Pose (2018), the largest cities in the world today are not necessarily the most productive. Many micro-states have, however, demonstrated that they are much more adept at surviving economically and politically than some earlier studies presupposed (Armstrong et al., 1998). The "New Normal" highlighted the importance of agility, flexibility, intelligence, that are often independent of economic size. According to Camagni et al. (2013) and Frick, Rodríguez-Pose (2018), factors such as well-developed infrastructure, industry composition, matching of skills, institutional capacity, an adequate level of governance effectiveness, networking, and efficient interactions between economic actors are now becoming more important for economic development.

The changed situation in the world and the characteristics of SOEs allow us to conclude that SOEs have potential and can indeed be drivers of growth, but only if the context is favourable. Economic smallness does not necessarily have an adverse impact on micro-state performance and appears to be no particular handicap in this regard (Armstrong et al., 1998).

3.2 Overview of Studies of Countries' Circular Performance

The literature review of circularity performance of SOEs was carried out in three ways: (a) an overview of countries' CE research in the European Union (EU); (b) an overview of CE performance with a focus on SOEs; and (c) an overview of drivers and barriers of SOEs and large economies.

The aim of this literature review is to examine empirical papers that explore certain aspects of circularity performance at the country level. A summary of previous research papers is presented in Tables 3.2 and 3.3. We note that SOE circularity performance is usually analysed across several countries.

Now that CE has become the EU strategy for green growth, recent research seeks to evaluate circularity performance from different angles, and quite often compares it to economic development (usually measured by GDP). Mayer et al. (2019) explore progress towards CE on an economy-wide scale, specifically whether absolute reductions in resource use and waste flows were achieved. The authors propose a comprehensive biophysical assessment of CE, supported by official statistics on resource extraction, use, and waste flows using a mass-balanced approach. Considering the fact that the EU has strict waste regulations, smart waste collection and recovery

Table 3.1 Main features of SOEs

Characteristics	Description	Authors
The trade openness is higher than large economies	Small economies benefit more from openness to trade than larger ones, in relative terms. Export-led growth increases the productivity of the tradable sector, fuelling the growth of the GDP of smaller economies Small economies may be more viable in a globalized world economy The trade balance-to-GDP ratio is weakly countercyclical There is likely to be a substantial asymmetry between the domestic patterns of production and consumption of a SOEs that is alleviated by imports. As a result, the proportion of imports in domestic consumption can be expected to be extremely high	Kuznets (1960), Chen et al. (2018), Alouini and Hubert (2019)
Small-scale economies	Small domestic market A large land area may provide significant natural resources. A large population provides a labour force and a wide domestic market with scale economies A high share of industries that benefit from agglomeration economies, a well-developed urban infrastructure, and an adequate level of governance effectiveness allow countries to take advantage of the benefits of agglomeration from larger cities	Briguglio (1995), Milner and Weyman-Jones (2003), Frick and Rodríguez-Pose (2018), Alouini and Hubert (2019)
Small and/or poor domestic resource base	Since the geographic area of a micro-state is small, it is likely that natural resources are both limited and relatively undiversified	Armstrong et al. (1998)

(continued)

Table 3.1 (continued)

Characteristics	Description	Authors
More sensitive to global changes	Small and very open economies should be more sensitive to changes in terms of trade and capital flows, for instance Inflation in SOEs may be very sensitive to exchange rate fluctuations	Alouini and Hubert (2019), Corbo and Di Casola (2022)
More volatile output than in large economies	Small and very open economies are sensitive to output fluctuations Consumption is less volatile than output	Chen et al. (2018); Alouini and Hubert (2019)
More volatile investments than in large economies	Investment is more volatile than outputs A high GDP results from a capital or technology-intensive industrial base capable of generating endogenous growth	Chen et al. (2018), Alouini and Hubert (2019)
More volatile consumption than in large economies	SOEs have a lower degree of marketization, stronger family ties, and a higher degree of labour intensity where more hours are spent working in the home sector A positive technology shock reduces leisure and significantly increases consumption	Parente et al. (2000), Chen et al. (2018)

(continued)

Table 3.1 (continued)

Characteristics	Description	Authors
Less resilient to economic shocks than large economies	Micro-states have long been particularly vulnerable to forces beyond their control An excessive dependence upon a small number of dominant activities exposes a micro-state economy to the risk of exogenous shocks to its principal activities A high GDP hints at the fact that a country may be close to its steady state and will thus witness a slower pace of growth A high GDP may be associated with slower growth rates as income and development levels are already high, but also with better infrastructure, greater human capital, and so a higher growth potential Both economic policy uncertainty and risk aversion shocks have negative spill overs for SOEs	Holmes (1976), Armstrong et al. (1998), Alouini and Hubert (2019), Kim et al. (2020)
SOEs have more homogeneous and specialized economies than large economies	Larger economies have a higher proportion of slower-growing regions than smaller economies because of diseconomies of scale in managing larger territories with more administrative entities Larger countries are characterized by a larger number of sectors, whereas smaller economies tend to be more specialized Large cities lead to greater productivity and economic growth through the generation of agglomeration economies which allow for a more productive use of available resources The narrowness of the domestic production structure in a micro-state is also a key determinant of its narrow range of exports and export markets	Armstrong et al. (1998), Imbs (2007), Melo et al. (2009), Alouini and Hubert (2019)

(continued)

Table 3.1 (continued)

Characteristics	Description	Authors
In some cases, more efficient governance	A large land area may prove difficult and costly to manage with regard to public services and transportation. A large population may incur larger administrative costs if it is heterogeneous	Alouini and Hubert (2019)
Close relationships with nearby countries	Micro-states tend to be inextricably linked-in with their regional country partners	Armstrong et al. (1998)

Table 3.2 Overview of CE performance research in the EU

Author	Focus	Method	Indicators deployed	Time period(s) and countries
Mayer et al. (2019)	Comprehensive and economy-wide biophysical assessment of a CE	Economy-wide material flow accounting	Mass-based CE indicators: scale indicators; circularity rates (socioeconomic cycling, ecological cycling potential, non-circularity)	2014 EU28
Giannakitsidou et al. (2020)	Municipal solid waste (MSW) management	Data envelopment analysis (DEA)	MSW generated; recycling waste of MSW; circular material use ratio; social progress index	2014 and 2017 26 EU countries
Škrinjarić (2020)	Waste management (mainly recycling), innovation and competitiveness	Grey Relational Analysis	Energy recovery per capita; recycling material per capita; gross investment in tangible goods; number employed as contributors to the CE; circular material use rate; number of patents related to recycling and secondary raw materials	2010–2016 22 EU countries

(continued)

Table 3.2 (continued)

Author	Focus	Method	Indicators deployed	Time period(s) and countries
Mavi and Mavi (2019)	Energy and environmental efficiency	Malmquist productivity index, DEA	Labour force; energy use; gross domestic product; renewable energy; greenhouse gas emissions; municipal waste	2012–2015 34 OECD countries
Mitrovic and Milan (2018)	Sustainable resource management, societal behaviour, business operations, innovation, and competitiveness	Composite index, DEA	Resource productivity; recycling rate of municipal waste; recycling rate of e-waste; circular material use rate; generation of municipal waste per capita; citizens who have chosen alternatives to buying new products; repair of computers and personal and household goods; share of enterprises that facilitated recycling of products after use; enterprises that extended product life through more durable products, by innovating; enterprises that recycled waste; water or materials for their own use or sale within the enterprises by innovating	22 EU countries

(continued)

Table 3.2 (continued)

Author	Focus	Method	Indicators deployed	Time period(s) and countries
Agovino et al. (2020)	Relationship between achieved recycling rates of different waste streams and company competitiveness	Stochastic Frontier Analysis	Recycling rate of packaging waste; recycling rate of e-waste; recycling rate of bio-waste; company competitiveness	2010–2016 17 EU countries
Momete (2020)	Economic, social and environmental performance	Composite index, DEA	Value-added at factor cost for required rate of return (Recovery, Return & Reintegration sector (RRR)); generation of waste, excluding major mineral wastes, per GDP; persons employed in RRR; patents related to recycling and secondary raw materials; circular material use rate; waste disposal landfill	2016 24 EU countries
Marino and Pariso (2020)	Economic performance; waste management; CE investment	Statistical analysis	GDP; produced municipal waste; produced food waste; municipal waste recycling rate; domestic material consumption; material reuse rate; market rate of recyclable raw materials	2006–2016 28 EU countries

(continued)

Table 3.2 (continued)

Author	Focus	Method	Indicators deployed	Time period(s) and countries
Stanković et al. (2021)	Comparison of CE development	Composite index, multi-criteria decision-making (MCDM) methods	Generation of municipal waste per capita; recycling rate of all waste excluding major mineral waste; recycling rate of municipal waste; recycling rate of packaging waste by type of packaging; recycling of bio-waste; recovery rate of construction and demolition waste; recycling rate of e-waste; trade in recyclable raw materials; circular material use rate; private investments, jobs, and gross value-added related to CE sectors; patents related to recycling and secondary raw materials	EU countries
Dagilienė et al. (2023)	CE indicators over time; clustering of countries' CE implementation	Principal components analysis (PCA)	17 country-level indicators from the EU monitoring framework	2010 and 2017 13 SOEs of EU
García-Sánchez et al. (2021)	Moving from the physical properties of the productive activities to the CE and finally to their wider effects on the environment, the economy, and society	Multivariant index based on business actions	17 company-level environmental indicators	26,783 companies from 49 countries (some EU countries included); 2014–2019

(continued)

Table 3.2 (continued)

Author	Focus	Method	Indicators deployed	Time period(s) and countries
POLITICO's CE index	Statistical comparison	Ranking	Municipal waste per capita; food waste per capita; municipal waste recycling; proportion of goods traded that are recyclable raw materials; patents related to CE; material reuse rate; investment in CE sectors	28 EU countries

Table 3.3 Overview of "best" and "worst" CE performing countries

Author	"Best" CE performing countries	"Worst" CE performing countries
Giannakitsidou et al. (2020)	Belgium, Austria, Germany, Slovenia, the Netherlands	Cyprus, Greece, Romania, Croatia, Latvia
Škrinjarić (2020)	Germany, the Netherlands, Denmark, France, Italy	Bulgaria, Slovakia, Cyprus, Greece, Romania
Mitrovic and Milan (2018)	Luxembourg, Finland, Sweden, Germany, Slovakia	Cyprus, Romania, Malta, Bulgaria, Latvia
Agovino et al. (2020)	Northern Europe cluster (Sweden, Denmark—high efficiency; Lithuania, Latvia—low efficiency); Central Europe (Belgium, Austria, the UK—highest efficiency); Southern Europe (Spain—highest; Slovenia—the lowest)	
Momete (2020)	Ready for the CE (10 countries): Slovenia, Italy, France, Latvia, Poland, UK, Germany, Netherlands, Austria, Belgium	On-track to the CE (11 countries): Croatia, Lithuania, Denmark, Spain, Estonia, Hungary, Finland, Cyprus, Portugal, Slovakia, Sweden Not ready to the CE: Bulgaria, Greece, Romania
Marino and Pariso (2020)	Austria, Belgium, Germany, Luxembourg, the Netherlands	Bulgaria, Croatia, Czech Republic, Estonia, Hungary, Latvia, Lithuania, Poland, Romania, Slovakia, Slovenia
Mavi and Mavi (2019)	Switzerland, Ireland, Denmark	
Stanković et al. (2021)	Germany, the Netherlands, France, Austria	
Dagilienė et al. (2023)	The Netherlands, Belgium	Slovakia, Cyprus, Malta
García-Sánchez et al. (2021)	France, Finland, Spain, Germany	Qatar, Argentina, Peru, United Arab Emirates
POLITICO's CE index	Germany, UK, France, Czech Republic, Italy	Cyprus, Greece, Malta, Ireland, Bulgaria

systems, and high category-specific material recovery rates was surprisingly low (25% for biomass and 70% for metals).

With its comprehensive, all-encompassing content, the CE differs from earlier, partial attempts concerning only selective collection of waste or individual attempts to recycle or to increase energy efficiency (Bonciu, 2014). Though the European CE monitoring framework (European Commission, 2018) does not directly include any energy-related measures, some researchers use these indicators in evaluating the progress of the CE. Mavi and Mavi (2019) analyse the CE performance of OECD countries from an energy and environmental efficiency point of view and note that energy production is a critical issue in the CE. The CE aims at sustainable development by focusing more on renewable sources of energy and the precise management of waste. Reducing the generation of waste and limiting the extraction of natural resources are expected to benefit the environment (Velenturf & Purnell, 2021), but Millar et al. (2019) raise the discussion about the possibility of CE to promote economic growth while simultaneously protecting the natural environment and improving social equity for this generation and those to come.

Mavi and Mavi (2019) find a strong and direct relationship between energy use and greenhouse gas (GHG) emissions and that a higher priority is applied to input variables, such as energy use, compared to undesirable output variables like GHG emissions, especially for less efficient energy-intensive industries. Environmental research and development (R&D) investment is a crucial factor to develop eco-innovative technologies to improve energy and environmental efficiency.

Giannakitsidou et al. (2020) measure the environmental and CE performance of 26 EU countries by implementing Data Envelopment Analysis (DEA). They tackle this problem by focusing on effective municipal solid waste (MSW) strategies and using the generated quantity of MSW per capita. The performance gaps between the efficient and less efficient countries are significant, suggesting that the latter countries have the potential for large improvements in waste management and sustainable material policies.

Škrinjarić (2020) also seeks to assess the performance of the CE in 22 EU countries, but with a broader measurement focus than just effective waste management, using recycling ratios, CE innovation (patents), and CE employment data from the European CE monitoring framework (European Commission, 2018). The results indicate regional discrepancies between European countries. The best performing countries were shown to be those which have larger Per capita GDP and better infrastructure, better education, and greater R&D expenditure. It should be noted that Căutişanu et al. (2018) find that Per capita GDP and years of schooling have a direct positive effect on R&D expenditures regarding the CE. In economies based on overconsumption, the higher the per capita GDP, the higher consumption per capita which, in turn, generates a large amount of waste.

One more comparative study of the CE performance in the EU by Stanković et al. (2021) indicates a positive correlation between the development of CE at the national level and the socioeconomic development of the country, while progress in the CE has no immediate impact on environmental sustainability. Meanwhile, Agovino et al. (2020) explore the relationship between realized recycling rates and the competitiveness of firms working in CE sectors. Their results show that the recycling rates of packaging, waste from electrical and electronic equipment (widely known as WEEE or e-waste) and bio-waste affect corporate competitiveness in Europe. In the CE, environmental issues drive innovation and so they can be a source of competitiveness (Agovino et al., 2020).

Other studies attempt to improve countries' CE measurement approaches and techniques. Mitrovic and Milan (2018) propose a composite indicator of progress towards circularity in order to uniformly drive the creation of a zero-carbon, zero-waste, innovative, and prosperous CE. Again, the authors show that the share of the adoption of CE principles is larger in economically developed EU countries while other countries, especially those less developed, continue to operate on the linear economy principles. To assess the readiness of the economies belonging to the EU to shift towards the CE, Momete (2020) also proposes a composite index based on the triple bottom line approach and finds that 42% of the EU Member States are currently ready for the CE, showing a commitment to pursue the transition. Another study of country-level CE performance progress and "Reduction, Reuse, Recycling" actions was conducted by Marino and Pariso (2020). The findings suggest that there is a direct correlation between the volume of generated municipal waste and per capita GDP, and that different strategies are adopted by the 28 EU countries. In contrast to Momete (2020), only a few countries are considered effective in meeting the challenges of the CE, and these leading countries distinguish themselves with a higher per capita GDP in terms of the average values of purchasing power standards (PPS) and the GDP/CE investments (CEI) ratio, confirming a correlation between these economic elements and the degree of transition towards the CE.

García-Sánchez et al. (2021) propose the two-step composite Circular Economy Business Index, based on 17 environmental practices that companies have implemented to reduce the generation of waste and emissions and to increase the reuse and efficiency of materials and energy, among other actions. This global empirical study includes countries beyond the EU borders, i.e., a total of 49 countries. However, the EU countries are leading in circular business activities.

Importantly, the majority of the afore-mentioned articles utilize different combinations of indicators (quite often from the same databases), dedicated to show countries' performance and progress of the CE. Empirically, the findings based on these combinations of indicators sometimes lead to quite different CE measurements and ranking results (see Table 3.3). This emphasizes the shortcomings of the current measurement system and the lack of consistent macro-economic data that would enable researchers to describe CE progress accurately. One of the problems is that most of these studies are based on data from the European CE Monitoring Framework (European Commission, 2018). However, the focus of this framework is mainly on measuring material and waste production. It, therefore, misses out on relevant indicators in eco-design and CE business models (Moraga et al., 2019). Truly holistic assessments of the CE development are data intensive and major coordinated efforts are required to establish data systems to monitor the stocks and flows of materials and products within economies (Velenturf & Purnell, 2021).

3.2.1 Overview of CE Performance with the Focus on SOEs

By consulting official CE indicators from Eurostat and based on previous research (Garcia-Bernabeu et al., 2020; Marino & Pariso, 2020; Mazur-Wierzbicka, 2021; Politico, 2018; Škrinjarić, 2020), we can state that being a SOE appears to be no particular handicap with regard to creating a CE. The larger economies have the highest CE scores, namely Germany, the UK, and France; however, depending on the circularity calculation methodology used, top rankings also include SOEs like the Netherlands, Czech Republic, Denmark, Belgium, Lithuania, Slovenia, and Austria (see Table 3.4).

Table 3.4 Top 10 EU countries by circularity index

Authors	Circularity index Ranks										
	Year	1	2	3	4	5	6	7	8	9	10
Politico (2018)	2018	Germany	United Kingdom	France	Czech Republic	Italy	Poland	Slovenia	Belgium	Austria	Spain
Mazur-Wierzbicka (2021)	2018	Germany	Netherlands	Spain	Austria	Belgium	Italy	Lithuania	Sweden	France	Slovenia
Garcia-Bernabeu et al. (2020)	2016	Germany	United Kingdom	France	Netherlands	Italy	Belgium	Spain	Austria	Denmark	Lithuania
Škrinjarić (2020)	2016	Germany	Denmark	Netherlands	France	Lithuania	Finland	Italy	Belgium	Latvia	Austria

A deeper analysis of circularity indices shows a heterogeneous transition towards CE in the EU countries. Dagilienė et al. (2023) explore CE implementation strategies in advanced SOEs in the EU and revealed three, correlated with CE development stages: integrated in the value chain; focused on institutional compliance; and fragmented. Countries with higher GDP in terms of PPS and GDP/CEI ratio average values tend to have significant recycling and reuse capacity, private investment, and CE-related patents (Marino & Pariso, 2020). SOEs which have not yet reached significant transition outcomes still show a high degree of investment propensity due to the strong commitment of the EU.

However, countries that top the chart are not necessarily the greenest. According to Politico (2018), this is partly because practices that reduce impacts on health and the environment do not necessarily contribute to circularity. For example, burning waste for energy, a common practice in Nordic countries, minimizes the waste going to landfill, but does not help boost recycling and reuse rates, so it is not very circular and does not contribute to a country's ranking. Another factor that reduces the circularity is their tendency to produce a lot of garbage. Although the Netherlands, Denmark, and Sweden rank highly in innovation and recycling, their scores are dragged down by high levels of general waste and food waste.

Larger countries can manage their own economic policies relatively easily, but SOEs are, inversely, those that are forced to adjust to the policies proposed by their large neighbours; they do not have the autonomy to adopt only the favourable measures from abroad and to avoid the harmful ones (Damijan, 2001). In addition, large economies have done a great deal to support CE-related industries (Dagilienė et al., 2021). Geerken et al. (2019) emphasize that more competitive CE sectors in an open economy can benefit from new CE activities, both domestically and abroad.

More than half of EU countries belong to SOEs. The insufficiently researched topic related to country size and circularity within the 28 EU Member States makes SOEs an interesting case to investigate for finding the best possible ways to reduce the circularity gap. Even though Marino and Pariso (2020) find that the leading nations in terms of transition to CE all have a higher GDP and GDP/CEI ratio average values, confirming a correlation between these economic elements with the degree of transition towards the CE and the level of circularity is still highly context dependent. The same authors find a strong influence of the economic structures on national CE initiatives that result in best practices.

It is important to note that data-related limitations usually hamper CE macro-statistical analyses, therefore usage of multiple data sources and methods might add a deeper contribution to the research object (i.e., SOEs). According to the critical analysis of CE indicators discussed by Mayer et al. (2019), it is crucial to increase statistical reporting. Waste-related indicators (both waste generation and recycling) comprise 47.4% of all indicators. Given the context of competitiveness, less waste may be related more to low productivity than to CE. The monitoring of CE implementation by countries is crucial for long-term EU policy objectives, and therefore, data gathering and monitoring systems are essential for updating CE implementation and timely decision-making.

3.2.2 *Overview of CE Drivers, Barriers, Challenges and Opportunities Among SOEs and Large Economies*

During the analysis of the scientific literature, we notice that, when examining barriers, drivers, challenges, and opportunities that help or hinder companies to move to the CE, general studies, approaching the subject from a theoretical point of view, prevail (see Sect. 2.4). However, individual countries are now being increasingly analysed. It is clear that research on the topic of the CE in terms of drivers and barriers is relevant in large economies, such as China, Brazil, Australia, and India (see Table 3.5). We can state that the aspects of the CE are also widely analysed in the context of the EU (Cainelli et al., 2020; Robaina et al., 2020) or large economies in Europe, such as Germany, the UK, and Italy. As SOEs intensively participate in international trade, more and more research is being conducted in these countries, which tend to be more advanced along the CE path as it is easier for them to take actions towards a more CE. Recent CE research in SOEs is focused on individual national case studies in the Netherlands, Finland, Sweden, Denmark, etc. (see Table 3.5) that analyse resource productivity (Cainelli et al., 2020), best industrial practices (Paquin et al., 2015; Ranta et al., 2018), drivers (Fischer & Pascucci, 2017; Ranta et al., 2018; Seth et al., 2018), barriers (Golev et al., 2015; Vermunt et al., 2019; Whalen et al., 2018), and opportunities and benefits (Geerken et al., 2019). However, the main challenge for SOEs is competitiveness, which needs to be maintained when moving from a linear to a circular system due to their scarce resources. SOEs must focus on open trade through partnerships due to the resource issue and global environmental boundaries and challenges. Since environmental boundaries and challenges are global, solutions to environmental threats require very close cooperation among industries and companies.

Clearly, much of the research focuses on the manufacturing and textiles (or fashion) industries, as these are among the most polluting ones.

3.3 Circularity and Economic Performance of Manufacturing Industries in Small Open Economies

Researchers use various indicators to characterize an SOE, for example, GDP, population, and arable land (Alouini & Hubert, 2019), the ratio of the sum of imports and exports and GDP (Geerken et al., 2019). According to Keogh et al. (2018), the following sampling filters are used for the identification of advanced SOEs in the EU:

- Small population. Traditionally, population size has been used as a metric to identify a small economy. This research defines a small population as up to 20 million, according to OECD (2018) population statistics.
- Advanced. The International Monetary Fund (IMF, 2018) compiles an advanced economy list based on per capita income, export diversification, and degree of integration into the global financial system.
- Trade openness.[1] Countries were selected if their trade openness was more than 100% (The Global Economy, 2018).

Based on the above criteria, 16 of the EU countries are identified as advanced SOEs: Belgium, the Czech Republic, Denmark, Estonia, Ireland, Cyprus, Latvia, Lithuania, Luxembourg, Malta, the Netherlands, Austria, Slovenia, Slovakia, Finland, and Sweden.

3.3.1 Research Approach

This subsection describes the main principles for the analysis of circularity and economic performance. The statistical data were obtained from the Eurostat and Lithuanian Statistics databases. The period for the analysis runs from 2014 to 2018 because the availability of data for 2019–2020 is limited for all selected countries. The structure of industry input and output data is prepared using OECD database information. The latest information about input–output tables is available for the year 2015.

---

[1] Trade openness is measured as the sum of a country's exports and imports as a share of that country's GDP (in%) (The Global Economy, 2018).

Table 3.5 Research on drivers, barriers, challenges, and opportunities designed to lead companies and industries to implement circular activities

Author	Economy		Sector
	Large economy	Small economy	
Khan et al. (2022)	Pakistan		Manufacturing industry
Piila et al. (2022)		Finland	
Gavazzi et al. (2022)	Germany		Packaging industry
Upadhyay et al. (2021)	UK, South Africa, Australia		Mining industry
Hartley et al. (2022)		The Netherlands	Technical & interior textiles industries
Abdul-Hamid et al. (2021)	Malaysia		Palm oil industry
Ostermann et al. (2021)	Brazil		Fashion industry
Zhang et al. (2021)	China		Waste management
Smol et al. (2021)	Poland		Raw materials recovery sector
Hussain and Malik (2020)	United Arab Emirates		
Ünal et al. (2019)	Italy		Office supply industry
Agyemang et al. (2019)	Pakistan		Automobile manufacturing industry
Caldera et al. (2019)	Australia		
Buzuku and Kässi (2019)		Finland	Pulp and paper industry
Vermunt et al. (2019)		The Netherlands	
Ormazabal et al. (2019)	Spain		
Mishra et al. (2019)			Manufacturing
Gusmerotti et al. (2019)	Italy		Manufacturing
Päivi et al. (2019)		Finland	
Qin et al. (2019)	China		
Sehnem et al. (2019)	Brazil, Scotland		Agribusiness
Seth et al. (2018)	India		Manufacturing
Ranta et al. (2018)	China, USA, and Europe		Manufacturing
Moktadir et al. (2018)	Bangladesh		Leather industry

(continued)

Table 3.5 (continued)

Author	Economy		Sector
	Large economy	Small economy	
Aid et al. (2017)		Sweden	
Todeschini et al. (2017)	Brazil, Italy		Fashion industry
Castellacci and Lie (2017)	South Korea		
Mativenga et al. (2017)	UK, South Africa		
Fischer and Pascucci (2017)		The Netherlands	Textile industry
Ilić and Nikolić (2016)		Serbia	
Pitkänen et al. (2016)	France, Germany	Finland, the Netherlands, Denmark	
Zhang and Wang (2014)	China		Energy intensive industry
Zhu and Geng (2013)	China		Manufacturing industry
Bastein et al. (2013)		The Netherlands	

The indicators for the analysis (Table 3.6) were selected for the following reasons:

Table 3.6 Selection of indicators

Type	Industry	Indicator
Macro-economic	Whole economy	GDP, per capita GDP, population, employment, unemployment, wages and salaries, green patents, resource productivity
Industrial	C13–C14, C22, C31	Enterprises, persons employed, apparent labour productivity, average personnel costs, growth rate of employment, the share of value-added at factor cost in production value (the share of the gross income from operating activities after adjusting for operating subsidies and indirect taxes), investment rate, high-growth enterprises, enterprises with innovation activities
CE	C13–C15, C22/C20–C22, C31–C32/C31–C33	Environmental protection expenditures, investment in plant and equipment for pollution control, production input and output, energy use, carbon dioxide (CO_2) emissions, waste generation

- Macro-economic indicators—to build an overview of the economic performance of a country and define its main economic tendencies.
- Industrial indicators—to build an overview of the performance of selected industries for deeper evaluation of economic conditions.
- CE indicators—to build an overview of the progress towards a CE in particular industries (see Chapters 5, 6 and 7).

To reflect the dynamics of plastic, textile, and furniture industries, we selected the closest industries based on the available statistical information. The industries presented in Table 3.6 are identified according to the Nomenclature of Economic Activities (NACE) classifications:

- C13—manufacture of textiles.
- C14—manufacture of wearing apparel.
- C15—manufacture of leather and related products.
- C13–14—manufacture of textiles and wearing apparel.
- C13–15—manufacture of textiles, wearing apparel, leather, and related products.
- C22—manufacture of rubber and plastic products.
- C20–22—manufacture of chemical, pharmaceutical, rubber, and plastic products.
- C31—manufacture of furniture.
- C31–32—manufacture of furniture; other manufacturing.
- C31–33—manufacture of furniture; jewellery, musical instruments, toys; repair and installation of machinery and equipment.

The analysis of the CE indicators of selected industries, the results of which are presented in Chapters 5, 6 and 7, is done by comparing macro-economic indicators that could help to evaluate circularity. Similarly, five areas are distinguished in the analysis of the results of the survey presented in Chapter 4:

- vision and strategy, for which the indicators selected for evaluation relate to the motivation of companies. Circular activities are being implemented gradually, through innovation in production processes and changes in product design. To assess the motivation of companies and the possibilities to implement innovations to promote circularity, we chose to review the trends in the indicator of environmental protection expenditures;
- raw materials, secondary raw materials, and eco-design, for which sectorial indicators of production input are selected for analysis;
- cleaner production, for which an analysis is made of energy consumption and emissions levels;
- consumption, reuse, repair are measured through the production output indicator. To the best of our knowledge, there is no available aggregated statistical data at the industry level to evaluate reuse and repair activities;
- waste management.

These areas can be defined as components of the internal and external environment of the production process (see Fig. 3.1).

The average rate of change was calculated for each indicator for the period 2014–2018, and the values were distributed into intervals (see Fig. 3.2). Green shows an increase in an indicator, and decreases are shown in variations of red.

The statistical analysis is implemented by comparing indicators' values for the various SOEs and average or relative values of SOEs (16) as well as the average or relative values across the EU (28). The special interest here relates to the Lithuanian data.

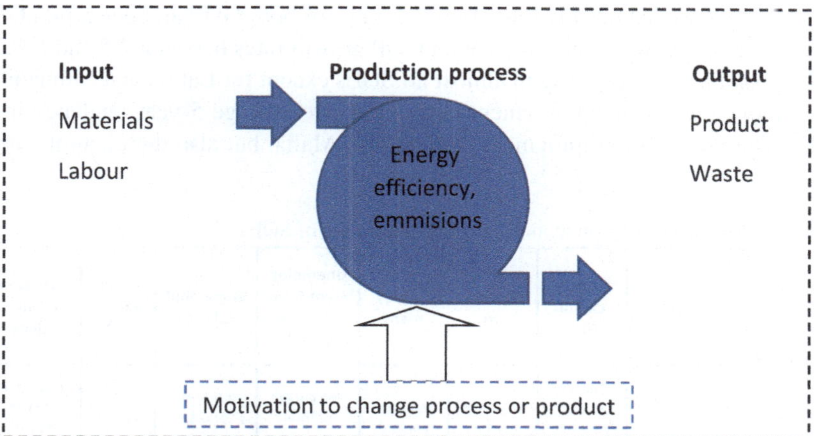

Fig. 3.1 Components of the internal and external environment of the production process

Fig. 3.2 Intervals of indicator changes

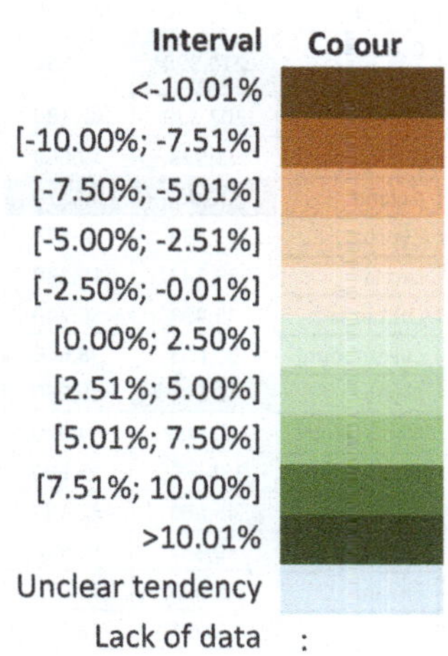

3.3.2 *The State of the Art of SOEs in the CE*

The results of our analysis of the macro-economic indicators and their tendencies are presented in Table 3.7. SOEs generate around 21.9% of the EU GDP and their average per capita GDP is higher than that of the EU (28). Moreover, the SOEs (16) have 17.5% of the total EU (28) population.

During the period 2014–2018, Ireland had the highest growth rate of GDP and per capita GDP, and is one of the most developed countries. Moreover, the relatively high per capita GDP growth rate is seen in almost all countries (Czech Republic, Estonia, Latvia, Lithuania, Malta) comparing with lower rates of per capita GDP in the EU (28). Sweden has the lowest growth rates of both GDP and per capita GDP. All the remaining SOEs have per capita GDP growth rates between 2.5 and 5%.

The population is growing in almost all SOEs except for Latvia and Lithuania.

Employment and unemployment have a positive average 5-year tendency in all SOEs. The growth of employment is highest in Malta, but also the unemployment

Table 3.7 Key macro-economic indicators and tendencies of SOEs

Economies	GDP	Per capita GDP	Populati on	Employ ment	Unemploy ment from 15 to 74 years*	Wages and salaries	Green patent s**	Resource produc-tivity
	Current prices, € million	Current prices, euro per capita	Thousand persons	Thousand persons	Percentage of total population	Current prices, € million	Number	€/kg, chain linked volumes (2015)
EU (28)	15,939,289	31,070	513,009	:	4.4	6,043,851	:	:
SOEs (16)	3,494,202	38,825	89,998	44 251	:	1,305,330	69.7	:
Belgium	460,370	40,290	11,427	4,901	3.6	168,451	14.7	2.88
Czech Republic	210,928	19,850	10,626	5,385	1.5	71,832	8.7	1.12
Denmark	302,329	52,180	5,794	2,925	3.5	142,992	5.5	2.13
Estonia	25,938	19,660	1,319	667	3.9	9,254	2.0	0.55
Ireland	326,986	67,270	4,861	2,216	3.9	78,548	1.1	2.69
Cyprus	21,433	24,630	870	429	5.7	7,780	0.0	1.34
Latvia	29,143	15,130	1,926	916	5.2	11,454	1.0	0.96
Lithuania	45,491	16,240	2,802	1,377	4.3	15,937	0.0	0.84
Luxembourg	60,053	98,640	609	265	3.6	25,704	1.5	4.12
Malta	12,595	25,960	485	236	2.4	4,956	0.0	1.88
Netherlands	773,987	44,920	17,232	9,238	2.7	290,635	15.7	4.60
Austria	385,362	43,600	8,838	4,382	3.3	152,388	3.9	2.19
Slovenia	45,863	22,130	2,072	1,029	3.4	19,607	0.0	1.47
Slovakia	89,357	16,410	5,446	2,567	4.2	28,450	0.1	1.18
Finland	233,696	42,370	5,516	2,622	4.9	90,067	10.5	1.19
Sweden	470,673	46,260	10,175	5,097	4.6	187,276	5.0	1.94

*Unemployment is decreasing, but the tendency is positive and green is used instead of red

**Data of the year 2016, the range was calculated as an average value of granted patents related to recycling and secondary raw materials of 2014–2016

level is one of the lowest of the SOEs. Cyprus has the highest unemployment level, but the employment indicator is growing more than the EU (28) average. Lithuania has an average unemployment rate compared with the EU (28), and slightly growing employment, but the population is decreasing.

Furthermore, wages and salaries are growing in all SOEs, though growth is faster in economies where GDP and per capita GDP growth are stronger (Czech Republic, Estonia, Latvia, Lithuania, Malta).

The number of new green patents is the highest in the Netherlands (15.7 on average per year) and Belgium (14.7). Besides, countries with lower per capita GDP than the EU (28) are more likely to submit only 1–2 green patents per year. Only Czech Republic has 8.7 green patents from this group of countries, but there is a decreasing number of patents over the five-year period.

The resource productivity indicator is the highest in the Netherlands (4.60) and Luxembourg (4.12), while in the Baltic states it remains low and is even decreasing in Latvia and Lithuania.

A more detailed investigation of the analysis of different industries is presented below.

3.3.3 Circularity and Economic Indicators of the Textile Industry

The overview of the textile industry's main economic indicators and their tendencies in SOEs are introduced in this subsection.

The textile and clothing industry is an important part of the European manufacturing sector. Based on the Eurostat Database (2021), this industry consists of 44,546 companies from the SOEs (23% of EU (28) textile and wearing apparel companies), employing 200,000 people (13% of the EU (28) total) and generating a turnover of €20 billion (13% of that for the EU (28) textile and wearing apparel sector). According to Euratex (2020), the industry in the EU (28) is dominated by small businesses, specifically micro (0–9 employees, 88.8% of the total) and small (10–249 employees, 11.0%). In the SOEs (16), 69% are clothing companies and 31% are textiles. Comparing employment statistics, textile companies employ about 53% of total SOEs (16) employees, while wearing apparel companies employ about 47%.

Of the SOEs (16), the largest concentration of textile and wearing apparel (C13–14) companies are in the Czech Republic, the Netherlands, Slovakia, and Lithuania, and the numbers are growing. Conversely, Luxembourg, Malta and Cyprus have the smallest number of enterprises and of employees in analysed SOEs. When we compare the number of employees in the industry, we see that the Czech Republic has 25% of the employees from SOEs (16) and the number is growing. However, the trend is decreasing in average value of SOEs (16) and in Belgium, Estonia, Latvia, Lithuania, Austria, Slovenia, Finland, and Sweden. Employment in the C13–C14 sector is growing the strongest in Denmark.

The analysis of apparent labour productivity shows that it is higher in the textile sector (C13) than in the wearing apparel sector (C14) in the EU (28) and in all SOEs (16). This indicator is trending upwards in all SOEs except in Ireland (both C13 and C14) and Austria (only C14). In Lithuania, apparent labour productivity is 35% higher in C13 than in C14, but the values remain less than half than in the EU (28). Latvia, Estonia, Cyprus, Czech Republic, and Slovakia have a lower apparent labour productivity than the EU (28) in both C13 and C14.

Average personnel costs are growing fastest in the Baltic states (Estonia (13.4), Lithuania (10.2), and Latvia (7.8)), but the values are still some of the smallest among the SOEs (16). The highest personnel costs are in the Netherlands (51.6) and Sweden (49.1).

Value-added in production value is higher in SOEs (16) than in the EU (28). The highest value-added is in Latvia (41.7) and Slovakia (41.5), with Lithuania (38.0) not far behind at 38% and growing.

C13–C14 has an investment rate of between 1% in Ireland and 16% in the Czech Republic, with an average value of 11.2% across the SOEs. Belgium, Czech Republic, Denmark, Estonia, Slovenia, and Slovakia have higher investment rates than the average in both the SOEs (16) and the EU (28), but the highest growth in investment is in Slovenia and Denmark.

The highest and growing sales profitability is found in Ireland and Slovenia, while Estonia has the lowest profitability rate of 6.7% and falling, but this could be explained by growing investment and personnel cost values. Compared with Lithuania, Estonia's investment rate is 9.5% but it is decreasing. Growing personnel costs could have influenced the investment and profitability of the sector because it employs a relatively large number of people (Table 3.8).

High-growth enterprise statistics show that Lithuania and the Czech Republic had the highest growth enterprises measured by turnover, but these numbers are decreasing. The Czech Republic also has the largest number of high-growth enterprises measured by employment, followed by Slovakia and the Netherlands. The results of this indicator in the EU (28) show that high growth is identified in enterprises with, on average, 62 persons employed in C13, while in C14 about 50 persons are employed. Compared with SOEs, this tendency is the opposite in Denmark, Estonia, Ireland, and Sweden.

The results show that the Czech Republic and Belgium had the largest number of enterprises with innovation activities among the SOEs in 2018.

The geographical position of a country is important for the development of the textile and wearing apparel industry. According to Euratex (2020), the southern and western EU, where most developed EU countries are located, such as Germany, France, and Italy, accounted for nearly 73.7% of EU's textile manufacturing in 2018. Southern countries such as Italy, Greece and Portugal, as well as Romania, Bulgaria, Poland, Lithuania, and, to a lesser extent, Spain and France, concentrate their manufacturing activities to clothing production. On the other hand, northern countries such as Germany, Belgium, the Netherlands, Austria, and Sweden concentrate their manufacturing activities to textile production, notably technical textiles. The medium-priced clothes products for consumption in the mass market are produced primarily

Table 3.8 Textile and wearing apparel sector (C13–C14) indicators and tendencies of SOEs

Economies in 2018	Enterprises	Persons employed	Apparent labour productivity		Average personnel costs	Value-added in production value	Investment rate	Sales profitability	High-growth enterprises				Enterprises with innovation activities during 2016 and 2018
									Measured in turnover	Measured in employment	Average size measured in employment		
	Number	Number	C13, (€'000)	C14, (€'000)	(€'000)	Percentage	Percentage	Percentage	Number	Number	Number, C13	Number, C14	Number
EU (28)	192,246	1,542,398	39	23	22.1	31.5	11.23	9.7	:	1,991	62.4	49.6	:
SOEs (16)	44,546	201,742	:	:	23.9	32.7	11.25	9.8	267	202	:	:	:
Belgium	1,652	17,892	60.7	52.0	44.2	28.8	13.88	9.0	:	6	71.2	:	204
Czech Republic	15,973	51,456	22.9	11.5	13.9	32.5	16.08	10.8	97	48	82.4	68.0	221
Denmark	665	5,372	82.9	76.5	55.4	30.7	14.04	10.6	:	10	38.0	48.5	57
Estonia	803	9,759	22.0	12.5	13.4	32.5	12.57	6.7	:	11	52.6	90.7	:
Ireland	827*	3,178*	49.4*	44.1*	35.4*	38.4*	1.36*	13.6*	:	9	28.4	30.0	33
Cyprus	269	900	22.4	13.5	14.4	40.7	3.52	11.7	:	2	:	0.0	6
Latvia	1,892	12,209	12.6	8.4	7.8	41.7	6.18	10.6	41	20	64.6	56.8	67
Lithuania	4,252	28,035	16.0	10.5	10.2	38.0	9.53	9.5	84	13	52.2*	:	:
Luxembourg	26	:	:	:	:	:	:	:	:	0	:	0.0	:
Malta	47**	213**	:	25.0	18.0**	25.9**	7.10**	10.9**	:	0	:	0.0	:
Netherlands	4,955	16,067	76.3	28.6	51.6	30.1	8.82	9.9	:	27	68.1	21.8	:
Austria	1,271	13,308	65.6	35.6	44.2	34.0	9.75	7.8	:	2	:	0.0	:
Slovenia	1,053	6,478	39.2	19.7	20.6	38.3	15.21	13.6	:	10	142.0	68.6	:
Slovakia	5,465	24,225	19.5	10.0	11.1	41.5	11.39	10.4	45	35	114.2	35.3	55
Finland	1,520	6,122*	48.9	44.9*	38.8*	33.4*	6.58*	9.1*	:	5	129.5	31.7	70
Sweden	3,876	6,528	62.7	53.9	49.1	37.1	7.71	11.0	:	4	56.3	211.0	68

*Data from 2017 were used for the analysis and calculations

**Data only from C14

by developing countries in Eastern and Southern Europe, such as Poland, Hungary and Romania, where labour is relatively cheap. The high-end luxury apparel is usually produced by developed Western EU countries, such as Italy, the UK, France, and Germany.

The data prove that manufacturing companies in SOEs in Eastern and Southern Europe have undergone radical change recently to maintain their competitiveness, moving towards high-value added products and have emerged as competitors to manufacturing companies in the larger economies.

European manufacturing companies in the SOEs (16) are becoming capital- and technology-intensive, actively investing in and adopting automation and digitalization technology, while labour productivity is also increasing.

3.3.4 Circularity and Economic Indicators of the Rubber and Plastics Industry

This subsection introduces the overview of the main economic indicators for the plastic industry, and their trends, in SOEs.

SOEs employ about 18% of the workforce and have about 21% of enterprises of all the EU (28) rubber and plastics sector. The number of enterprises is decreasing both in SOEs (16) and the EU (28), while the number of persons employed is increasing.

The largest number of enterprises is in the Czech Republic, Slovakia, the Netherlands, and Sweden, the latter of which has suffered, on average, a fall of 7.5% in the value of enterprises in the selected period, while the number of persons employed is growing by 1.7%. This tendency shows that, in Sweden, enterprises are growing. In Lithuania, the total number of enterprises is growing by 2% on average (Table 3.9).

The statistical analysis of the rubber and plastics industry shows that, in Lithuania, this sector employs only 9,415 people (0.5% of the EU (28) rubber and plastics sector employees) and this has grown by 2.6%, on average, in recent years. The Czech Republic has the most employees (30%) among SOEs, while Cyprus, Malta, and Latvia have the smallest number of persons employed in the industry. The highest employment growth is in Slovenia (5.7%), while this indicator is decreasing by 4.5% in Denmark.

The results show that the largest growth rate in employment in 2018 was in Latvia and Sweden, while Ireland, Belgium, Denmark, Lithuania, the Netherlands, and Slovakia saw employment decreasing.

Apparent labour productivity is growing in all countries except for Slovakia. The highest growth is in Latvia (8.9%), but the total value (€20,500) is the smallest among SOEs (16). In Latvia, Lithuania, Estonia, Cyprus, Malta, Slovakia, Czech Republic, and Slovenia, apparent labour productivity is lower than the EU (28) average. Furthermore, average personnel costs are the lowest in Latvia, Lithuania, and the Czech Republic, but are growing the most intensively by 11.4%, 9.6%, and 7.8%, respectively. The highest average personnel costs are in Belgium and Denmark.

Table 3.9 Rubber and plastics industry (C22) indicators and tendencies of SOEs

Economies in 2018	Enterprises	Persons employed	Growth rate of employment	Apparent labour productivity	Average personnel costs	Value-added in production value	Investment rate	Sales profitability	High-growth enterprises			Enterprises with innovation activities during 2016 and 2018
									Measured in turnover	Measured in employment	Average size measured in employment	
	Number	Number	Percentage	(€'000)	(€'000)	Percentage	Percentage	Percentage	Number	Number	Number	Number
EU (28)	61,214	1,784,167*	:	55*	36.0*	32.4	17.1	10.8*	:	2,673	100.00	:
SOEs (16)	12,641	316,445	:	:	:	:	:	:	:	492	:	:
Belgium	737	23,438	-3.3	95.0	60.8	29.4	19.1	10.4	:	19	98.42	:
Czech Republic	3,595	95,202	1.9	34.0	19.8	28.3	31.0	11.4	198	133	112.33	26
Denmark	478	12,740	-2.7	88.2	60.2	38.4	11.1	11.8	:	21	62.24	:
Estonia	199	4,130	3.2	31.0	20.6	29.1	20.3	9.4	:	8	85.00	:
Ireland	484*	9,481*	-4.7*	69.5*	45.1*	37.5*	2.3*	13.1*	:	27	61.56	:
Cyprus	78	995	7.8	31.6	21.1	32.9	29.2	10.0	:	1	:	:
Latvia	219	3,295	10.3	20.5	12.8	27.9	18.4	10.0	19	15	50.53	2
Lithuania	405	9,415	-1.4	28.0	15.3	23.8	30.1	10.8	50	20	:	:
Luxembourg	23	:	:	:	:	:	:	:	:	1	42.00	0
Malta	41	1,983	:	33.6	21.5	48.4	30.4	:	:	6	94.33	0
Netherlands	1,449	32,799	-1.4	89.0	55.0	31.3	13.9	11.3	:	66	65.71	:
Austria	574	32,288	7.0	77.3	57.1	35.3	14.6	8.7	:	22	79.23	:
Slovenia	966	16,646	5.5	40.5	26.1	34.3	23.0	11.2	:	38	80.63	:
Slovakia	1,765	36,373	-0.8	34.8	19.0	28.0	24.6	12.1	85	60	138.28	29
Finland	514	12,760	1.1	78.4	51.7	32.6	13.1	10.2	:	10	41.30	6
Sweden	1,114	24,900	9.7	72.7	55.3	35.1	12.1	10.6	:	45	43.07	9

*Data from 2017 were used for the analysis and calculations

Analysis of the value-added indicator shows that this varies between 23.8% of value-added in Lithuania, to 48.8% in Malta, while the Czech Republic, Denmark, the Netherlands, Austria, and Slovakia show a decreasing trend. The growth of value-added is the highest in Latvia.

The average investment rate of 17.1% across the EU (28) is almost twice as much in the Czech Republic, Lithuania, and Cyprus. The lowest investment is in Ireland, Denmark, Sweden, Finland, and Austria. Sales profitability varies from 8.7% in Austria to 13.1% in Ireland, but the highest growth of this indicator is in Sweden, at 10.5%. Lithuania has an average sales profitability of 10.8%, equal to that for the EU (28).

The analysis shows that four countries have the most high-growth enterprises as measured by turnover. The Czech Republic has four times as many as Lithuania and the indicator is decreasing. However, Slovakia have an increasing number of high-growth enterprises. Comparing the results with high-growth enterprises measured by employment, Czech Republic (133), Slovakia (60), and the Netherlands (66) have the leading positions. Lithuania has only 20 such enterprises and the number is decreasing. These collectively account for about 4% of the total number of high-growth enterprises measured by employment in SOEs (16).

The average size of high-growth enterprises is 100 persons in the EU (28), whereas it is below 100 employees in almost all SOEs except for the Czech Republic and Slovakia. Similarly, from the data of enterprises with innovation activities during 2016 and 2018, we see that the Czech Republic and Slovakia have the highest number of innovative enterprises.

3.3.5 Circularity and Economic Indicators of the Furniture Industry

The statistical analysis of the furniture industry shows that the Lithuanian furniture sector employs the most people (2.8% of EU (28) furniture sector employees) among SOEs and this indicator has grown, on average, by 2.6% in recent years. Only the Czech Republic, the Netherlands, and Austria have a higher number of furniture enterprises than Lithuania (Table 3.10).

The highest growth rate of employment is in Malta (9.0%), followed by Cyprus (8.5%), while this indicator is lower and decreasing in Lithuania (2.2%).

Apparent labour productivity in the furniture industry is increasing in all SOEs and the EU (28). The growth rate of this indicator is higher in the Czech Republic, Estonia, Latvia, and Lithuania, all economies with an apparent labour productivity level that is lower than the EU average. These countries also have a lower level of value-added than the EU (28) average, but due to growing productivity, this is also growing. Sweden has the highest apparent labour productivity in the furniture sector but also has the highest (and increasing) personnel costs.

Table 3.10 Furniture industry (C31) indicators and tendencies of SOEs

Economies in 2018	Enterprises	Persons employed	Growth rate of employment	Apparent labour productivity	Average personnel costs	Value-added at factor cost in production value	Investment rate	Sales profitability	High-growth enterprises			Enterprises with innovation activities during 2016 and 2018
									Measured in turnover	Measured in employment	Average size measured in employment	
	Number	Number	Percentage	(€'000)	(€'000)	Percentage	Percentage	Percentage	Number	Number	Number	Number
EU (28)	128,702	1,043,806	:	34	25.8	33.7	10.9	10	:	1,614	74.75	:
SOEs (16)	30,420	192,006	:	:	:	:	:	10	:	267	:	:
Belgium	1,736	12,366	2.4	52.2	44.1	33.9	26.3	9	:	3	24.00	173
Czech Republic	5,698	24,931	-3.2	19.7	15.5	30.8	17.3	11	87	31	66.19	199
Denmark	625	10,030	7.6	74.3	52.0	37.1	6.7	11	:	18	64.22	77
Estonia	736	7,915	1.3	22.1	17.1	30.0	13.8	7	:	8	64.25	:
Ireland	:	:	:	:	:	:	:	:	:	25	37.28	23
Cyprus	311	1,033	8.5	22.9	16.6	40.8	11.7	15	:	1	0.00*	13
Latvia	817	6,860	-1.4	13.4	10.2	32.0	10.6	9	16	9	22.78	42
Lithuania	2,236	30,018	2.2	18.0	12.6	32.7	27.4	10	110	36	112.67	:
Luxembourg	26	178	4.1	48.8	40.1	49.6	2.9	8	:	0	0.00	0
Malta	497	1,303	9.0	18.9	16.4	42.9	10.3	21	:	1	18.00	7
Netherlands	9,313	25,763	2.2	53.5	45.8	34.7	8.4	13	:	55	34.76	:
Austria	3,132	27,547	1.2	50.2	41.9	43.6	8.2	10	:	16	71.69	:
Slovenia	1,158	6,257	3.8	26.4	21.2	36.9	18.5	10	:	13	86.08	:
Slovakia	1,187	14,516	3.0	14.6	15.6	22.1	26.1	0	29	16	126.13	40
Finland	806	7,006	:	52.2	42.2	31.9	7.9	7	:	11	66.55	76
Sweden	2,142	16,283	6.6	60.7	52.6	37.7	8.7	8	:	24	43.67	138

Average personnel costs correlate with per capita GDP so are highly dependent on the overall level of development. Denmark and Sweden have the highest average personnel costs, while Latvia and Lithuania have the lowest, though here they are increasing.

The investment rate varies widely among SOEs in the furniture sector. Denmark, the Netherlands, Austria, Finland, and Sweden are investing less than the EU (28) average and about three times less than Lithuania, Belgium, and Slovakia. The average investment growth rate is the highest in Cyprus, Luxembourg, Malta, and Belgium. While the Czech Republic, Denmark, and Estonia have a decreasing investment rate, in the Czech Republic and Estonia it is still higher than the EU (28) average.

Sales profitability is highest in Malta at 21%, but this is decreasing, while countries such as the Czech Republic, Denmark, Cyprus, and the Netherlands have a higher-than-average value for this indicator (in both EU (28) and SOEs (16)).

Our results show that Lithuania had the highest number of high-growth enterprises (110) measured by turnover, or 36 high-growth enterprises measured by employment in 2018. On average, these enterprises employed around 112 people. The growth of the furniture industry has become less intensive in recent years. Compared with other SOEs, the Netherlands had around 21% of all high-growth enterprises measured by employment in SOEs (16) where, for the most part, the number of small enterprises with around 34 employees was growing.

Enterprises with innovation activities are concentrated in Belgium, Czech Republic, and Sweden.

Key Highlights

- The characteristics of SOEs show their potential for growth, but only if the context is favourable.
- Economic smallness does not necessarily have an adverse impact on CE performance.
- It is important to increase statistical reporting, as currently, CE macro-statistical analyses are limited due to the lack of data. Therefore, the use of multiple data sources and methods might add a deeper contribution to the research object.
- Waste-related indicators (both waste generation and recycling) comprise 47.4% of all indicators used for analysis in the CE field. Given the context of competitiveness, less waste generation may be related more to productivity than to CE progress.
- The national monitoring of CE implementation is crucial for long-term EU policy objectives. Therefore, data gathering and monitoring systems in each country are essential for updating the CE implementation picture and to enable timely decision-making.
- The scientific research tends to focus on the manufacturing and textile (or fashion) industries, as these industries generate the most pollution.
- 16 European SOEs were selected for analysis on the basis of three factors: small population; advanced economy (by per capita income); and trade openness. The

results show a very different economic potential to implement changes in the EU (28) countries with higher-than-average GDP, such as the Netherlands, Belgium, Luxembourg, and Denmark, compared to the EU (28) countries with a lower-than-average GDP, such as Slovenia, Slovakia, Latvia, Lithuania, and Cyprus.

- More green innovation and higher resource productivity are common for economically stronger SOEs, while those that are weaker use their economic growth to improve the social conditions of employees by increasing wages and salaries.
- Sectorial analysis showed that SOEs with leadership positions in the industry tend to implement more circular activities.

References

Abdul-Hamid, A. Q., Helmi Ali, M., Osman, L. H., & Tseng, M. L. (2021). The drivers of industry 4.0 in a circular economy: The palm oil industry in Malaysia. *Journal of Cleaner Production, 324*. https://doi.org/10.1016/j.jclepro.2021.129216

Agovino, M., Matricano, D., & Garofalo, A. (2020). Waste management and competitiveness of firms in Europe: A stochastic frontier approach. *Waste Management, 102*, 528–540. https://doi.org/10.1016/j.wasman.2019.11.021

Agyemang, M., Kusi-Sarpong, S., Khan, S., Mani, V., Rehman, S., & Kusi-Sarpong, H. (2019). Drivers and barriers to circular economy implementation. *Management Decision, 57*(4), 971–994. https://doi.org/10.1108/MD-11-2018-1178

Aid, G., Eklund, M., Anderberg, S., & Baas, L. (2017). Expanding roles for the Swedish waste management sector in inter-organizational resource management. *Resources, Conservation and Recycling, 124*(April), 85–97. https://doi.org/10.1016/j.resconrec.2017.04.007

Alesina, A., Spolaore, E., & Wacziarg, R. (2005). Trade, growth and the size of countries. In P. Aghion & S. Durlauf (Eds.), *Handbook of economic growth, 1*(23), 1499–1542. Elsevier. https://doi.org/10.1016/S1574-0684(05)01023-3

Alouini, O., & Hubert, P. (2019). Country size, economic performance and volatility. *Dans Revue de l'OFCE* 2019/4(164), ISSN 1265-9576, pp. 139–163. https://doi.org/10.3917/reof.164.0139

Armstrong, H., De Kervenoael, R. J., Li, X., & Read, R. (1998). A comparison of the economic performance of different micro-states, and between micro-states and larger countries. *World Development, 26*(4), 639–656. https://doi.org/10.1016/S0305-750X(98)00006-0

Bastein, T., Roelofs, E., Rietveld, E., & Hoogendoorn, A. (2013). *Opportunities for a circular economy in the Netherlands*. Contactivity BV.

Bonciu, F. (2014). The European economy: From a linear to a circular economy. *Romanian Journal of European Affairs, 14*(4), 78–91.

Briguglio, L. (1995). Small island developing states and their economic vulnerabilities. *World Development, 23*(9), 1615–1632.

Buzuku, S., & Kässi, T. (2019). Drivers and barriers for the adoption of eco-design Practices in pulp and paper industry: A case study of Finland. *Procedia Manufacturing, 33*, 717–724. https://doi.org/10.1016/j.promfg.2019.04.090

Cainelli, G., D'Amato, A., & Mazzanti, M. (2020). Resource efficient eco-innovations for a circular economy: Evidence from EU firms. *Research Policy, 49*(1). https://doi.org/10.1016/j.respol.2019.103827

Caldera, H. T. S., Desha, C., & Dawes, L. (2019). Evaluating the enablers and barriers for successful implementation of sustainable business practice in 'lean' SMEs. *Journal of Cleaner Production, 218*, 575–590. https://doi.org/10.1016/j.jclepro.2019.01.239

Camagni, R., Capello, R., & Caragliu, A. (2013). One or infinite optimal city sizes? In search of an equilibrium size for cities. *Annals of Regional Science, 51*(2), 309–341. https://doi.org/10.1007/s00168-012-0548-7

Carlin, W., & Soskice, D. (2003). *The open economy—Draft chapter*. http://www.ucl.ac.uk/~uctpa36/ch4march403.pdf

Castellacci, F., & Lie, C. M. (2017). A taxonomy of green innovators: Empirical evidence from South Korea. *Journal of Cleaner Production, 143*, 1036–1047. https://doi.org/10.1016/j.jclepro.2016.12.016

Căutişanu, C., Asandului, L., Borza, M., & Turturean, C. (2018). Quantitative approach to circular economy in the OECD countries. *Amfiteatru Economic, 20*(48), 262–277. https://doi.org/10.24818/EA/2018/48/262

Chen, K. J., Chu, A. C., & Lai, C. C. (2018). Home production and small open economy business cycles. *Journal of Economic Dynamics and Control, 95*, 110–135. ISSN 0165-1889. https://doi.org/10.1016/j.jedc.2018.08.001

Corbo, V., & Di Casola, P. (2022). Drivers of consumer prices and exchange rates in small open economies. *Journal of International Money and Finance*, 122. https://doi.org/10.1016/j.jimonfin.2021.102553

Cullen, J. M. (2017). Circular economy: Theoretical benchmark or perpetual motion machine? *Journal of Industrial Ecology, 21*, 483–486. https://doi.org/10.1111/jiec.12599

Dagilienė, L., Bruneckienė, J., Varaniūtė, V., & Lukauskas, M. (2021). The circular economy for sustainable development: Implementation strategies in advanced small open economies. *International Journal of Environment and Sustainable Development*, pp. 1–26. https://doi.org/10.1504/IJESD.2021.10040657

Dagilienė, L., Bruneckienė, J., Varaniūtė, V., & Lukauskas, M. (2023). The circular economy for sustainable development: Implementation strategies in advanced small open economies. *International Journal of Environment and Sustainable Development, 22*(1), 51–76. https://doi.org/10.1504/IJESD.2021.10040657

Damijan, J. P. (2001). Main economic characteristics of small countries: Some empirical evidence. In D. Salvatore, M. Svetličič, & J. P. Damijan (Eds.), *Small countries in a global economy*. Palgrave Macmillan. https://doi.org/10.1057/9780230513198_4

Euratex Database. (2020). *Facts & key figures of the European textile and clothing industry*. https://euratex.eu/wp-content/uploads/EURATEX-Facts-Key-Figures-2020-LQ.pdf

European Commission. (2018). *Monitoring framework on the circular economy* [online]. https://ec.europa.eu/eurostat/web/circular-economy/indicators. Accessed 12 January 2020.

Eurostat Database. (2021). *Your key to European statistics*. https://ec.europa.eu/eurostat/web/main/data/database. Accessed 28 October 2021.

Fischer, A., & Pascucci, S. (2017). Institutional incentives in circular economy transition: The case of material use in the Dutch textile industry. *Journal of Cleaner Production, 155*, 17–32. https://doi.org/10.1016/j.jclepro.2016.12.038

Frick, S. A., & Rodríguez-Pose, A. (2018). Big or small cities? On city size and economic growth. *Growth and Change, 49*(1), 4–32. https://doi.org/10.1111/grow.12232

Garcia-Bernabeu, A., Hilario-Caballero, A., Pla-Santamaria, D., & Salas-Molina, F. (2020). A process oriented MCDM approach to construct a circular economy composite index. *Sustainability, 12*(2), 618. https://doi.org/10.3390/su12020618

García-Sánchez, I. M., Somohano-Rodríguez, F. M., Amor-Esteban, V., & Frías-Aceituno, J. V. (2021). Which region and which sector leads the circular economy? CEBIX, a multivariant index based on business actions. *Journal of Environmental Management, 297*, 113299. https://doi.org/10.1016/J.JENVMAN.2021.113299

Gavazzi, P., Dobrucka, R., & Przekop, R. (2022). Current trends in the German packaging industry. *Logforum, 18*(1). https://doi.org/10.17270/J.LOG.2022.688

Geerken, T., Schmidt, J., Boonen, K., Christis, M., & Merciai, S. (2019). Assessment of the potential of a circular economy in open economies—Case of Belgium. *Journal of Cleaner Production, 227*, 683–699. https://doi.org/10.1016/j.jclepro.2019.04.120

Giannakitsidou, O., Giannikos, I., & Chondrou, A. (2020). Ranking European countries on the basis of their environmental and circular economy performance: A DEA application in MSW. *Waste Management, 109*, 181–191. https://doi.org/10.1016/j.wasman.2020.04.055

Global Economy. (2018). *Trade openness*. https://www.theglobaleconomy.com/rankings/tradeopenness/European-union/. Accessed 14 January 2020.

Golev, A., Corder, G. D., & Giurco, D. P. (2015). Barriers to industrial symbiosis: Insights from the use of a maturity grid. *Journal of Industrial Ecology, 19*(1), 141–153. https://doi.org/10.1111/jiec.12159

Gusmerotti, N. M., Testa, F., Corsini, F., Pretner, G., & Iraldo, F. (2019). Drivers and approaches to the circular economy in manufacturing firms. *Journal of Cleaner Production, 230*, 314–327. https://doi.org/10.1016/j.jclepro.2019.05.044

Hartley, K., Roosendaal, J., & Kirchherr, J. (2022). Barriers to the circular economy: The case of the Dutch technical and interior textiles industries. *The Official Journal of the International Society for Industrial Ecology (ISIE), 26*(2), 477–490. https://doi.org/10.1111/jiec.13196

Holmes. (1976). Development problems of small countries In L.V. Castle & F. Holmes (Eds.), Co-operation and development in Asia Pacific Region: Relations betweeen large and small countries (pp. 43–66). Japan Economic Research Centre.

Hussain, M., & Malik, M. (2020). Organizational enablers for circular economy in the context of sustainable supply chain management. *Journal of Cleaner Production*, 256. https://doi.org/10.1016/j.jclepro.2020.120375

Ilić, M., & Nikolić, M. (2016). Drivers for development of circular economy—A case study of Serbia. *Habitat International, 56*, 191–200. https://doi.org/10.1016/j.habitatint.2016.06.003

Imbs, J. (2007). Growth and volatility. *Journal of Monetary Economics, 54*(7), 1848–1862. https://doi.org/10.1016/j.jmoneco.2006.08.001

International Monetary Fund List. (2018). *World economic outlook, April 2018: Cyclical upswing, structural change*, 220. https://www.imf.org/en/Publications/WEO/Issues/2018/03/20/world-economic-outlook-april-2018. Accessed 16 December 2019.

Keogh, R., & Brassill, C., & Unit, I. (2018). *Small advanced open economies—A comparative analysis*. https://webcache.googleusercontent.com/search?q=cache:Srfx30_Lhl4J:https://assets.gov.ie/180714/bb20702c-af59-4292-9255-99d76f3759d5.pdf&cd=1&hl=lt&ct=clnk&gl=lt. Accessed 14 January 2021.

Khan, S. A., Mubarik, M. S., & Paul, S. K. (2022). Analyzing cause and effect relationships among drivers and barriers to circular economy implementation in the context of an emerging economy. *Journal of Cleaner Production*, 364. https://doi.org/10.1016/j.jclepro.2022.132618

Kim, Y., Lim, H., & Sohn, W. (2020). Which external shock matters in small open economies? Global risk aversion vs. US economic policy uncertainty. *Japan and the World Economy*, 54. https://doi.org/10.1016/j.japwor.2020.101011

Kuznets, S. (1960). Economic growth of small nations. In E. A. G. Robinson, (Ed.), *Economic consequences of the size of nations*. International Economic Association Conference Volumes, Palgrave Macmillan. https://doi.org/10.1007/978-1-349-15210-0_2

Marino, A., & Pariso, P. (2020). Comparing European countries' performances in the transition towards the Circular Economy. *Science of the Total Environment*, 729. https://doi.org/10.1016/j.scitotenv.2020.138142

Mativenga, P. T., Sultan, A. M., Agwa-Ejon, J., & Mbohwa, C. (2017). Composites in a circular economy: A study of United Kingdom and South Africa. *Procedia CIRP, 61*, 691–696. https://doi.org/10.1016/j.procir.2016.11.270

Mavi, N. K., & Mavi, R. K. (2019). Energy and environmental efficiency of OECD countries in the context of the circular economy: Common weight analysis for Malmquist productivity index. *Journal of Environmental Management, 247*(June), 651–661. https://doi.org/10.1016/j.jenvman.2019.06.069

Mayer, A., Haas, W., Wiedenhofer, D., Krausmann, F., Nuss, P., & Blengini, G. A. (2019). Measuring progress towards a circular economy: A monitoring framework for economy-wide material loop closing in the EU28. *Journal of Industrial Ecology, 23*(1), 62–76. https://doi.org/10.1111/jiec.12809

Mazur-Wierzbicka, E. (2021). Towards circular economy—A comparative analysis of the countries of the European Union. *Resources, 10*, 49. https://doi.org/10.3390/resources10050049

Melo, P. C., Graham, D. J., & Noland, R. B. (2009). A meta-analysis of estimates of urban agglomeration economies. *Regional Science and Urban Economics, 39*(3), 332–342. https://doi.org/10.1016/j.regsciurbeco.2008.12.002

Millar, N., McLaughlin, E., & Börger, T. (2019). The circular economy: Swings and roundabouts? *Ecological Economics, 158*(October 2018), 11–19. https://doi.org/10.1016/j.ecolecon.2018.12.012

Milner, C., & Weyman-Jones, T. (2003). Relative national efficiency and country size: Evidence for developing countries. *Review of Development Economics, 7*(1), 1–14. https://doi.org/10.1111/1467-9361.00171

Mishra, S., Singh, S., Johansen, J., Cheng, Y., & Farooq, S. (2019). Evaluating indicators for international manufacturing network under circular economy. *Management Decision, 57*(4), 811–839. https://doi.org/10.1108/MD-05-2018-0565

Mitrovic, D., & Milan, V. (2018, August). Measuring countries competitiveness in circular economy—Composite index approach. *Quantitative Models in Economics*, 417–436.

Moktadir, M. A., Rahman, T., Rahman, M. H., Ali, S. M., & Paul, S. K. (2018). Drivers to sustainable manufacturing practices and circular economy: A perspective of leather industries in Bangladesh. *Journal of Cleaner Production, 174*, 1366–1380. https://doi.org/10.1016/j.jclepro.2017.11.063

Momete, D. C. (2020). A unified framework for assessing the readiness of European Union economies to migrate to a circular modelling. *Science of the Total Environment, 718*, 137375. https://doi.org/10.1016/j.scitotenv.2020.137375

Moraga, G., Huysveld, S., Mathieux, F., Blengini, G. A., Alaerts, L., Van Acker, K., de Meester, S., & Dewulf, J. (2019). Circular economy indicators: What do they measure? *Resources, Conservation and Recycling, 146*(January), 452–461. https://doi.org/10.1016/j.resconrec.2019.03.045

OECD. (2018) *Population*. https://data.oecd.org/pop/population.html. Accessed 26 January 2020.

Ormazabal, M., Vanessa Prieto-Sandoval, V., Puga-Leal, R., & Jaca, C. (2019). Circular Economy in Spanish SMEs: Challenges and opportunities. *Journal of Cleaner Production, 185*, 157–167. https://doi.org/10.1016/j.jclepro.2018.03.031

Ostermann, C. M., Nascimento, L. D. S., Steinbruch, F. K., & Callegaro-de-Menezes, D. (2021). Drivers to implement the circular economy in born-sustainable business models: A case study in the fashion industry. *Revista de Gestão, 28*(3), 223–240. https://doi.org/10.1108/REGE-03-2020-0017

Päivi, H. M., Kinnunen, A., & Kaksonen, H. (2019). Towards circular economy in mining: Opportunities and bottlenecks for tailings valorization. *Journal of Cleaner Production, 228*, 153–160. https://doi.org/10.1016/j.jclepro.2019.04.171

Paquin, R. L., Busch, T., & Tilleman, S. G. (2015). Creating economic and environmental value through industrial symbiosis. *Long Range Planning, 48*(2), 95–107. https://doi.org/10.1016/j.lrp.2013.11.002

Parente, S. L., Rogerson, R., & Wright, R. (2000). Homework in development economics: Household production and the wealth of nations. *Journal of Political Economy, 108*, 680–687. https://doi.org/10.1086/316102

Piila, N., Sarja, M., Onkila, T., & Mäkelä, M. (2022). Organisational drivers and challenges in circular economy implementation: An issue life cycle approach. *Organization & Environment*. https://doi.org/10.1177/10860266221099658

Pitkänen, K., Antikainen, R., Droste, N., Loiseau, E., Saikku, L., Aissani, L., Hansjürgens, B., Kuikman, P. J., Leskinen, P., & Thomsen, M. (2016). What can be learned from practical cases of green economy?—Studies from five European countries. *Journal of Cleaner Production, 139*, 666–676. https://doi.org/10.1016/j.jclepro.2016.08.071

Politico. (2018). *Ranking how EU countries do with the circular economy?* https://www.politico.eu/article/ranking-how-eu-countries-do-with-the-circular-economy/

Qin, Y., Harrison, J., & Chen, L. (2019). A framework for the practice of corporate environmental responsibility in China. *Journal of Cleaner Production, 235*, 426–452. https://doi.org/10.1016/j.jclepro.2019.06.245

Ranta, V., Aarikka-Stenroos, L., Ritala, P., & Mäkinen, S. J. (2018). Exploring institutional drivers and barriers of the circular economy: A cross-regional comparison of China, the US, and Europe. *Resources, Conservation and Recycling, 135*, 70–82. https://doi.org/10.1016/j.resconrec.2017.08.017

Robaina, M., Villar, J., & Pereira, E. T. (2020). The determinants for a circular economy in Europe. *Environmental Science and Pollution Research, 27*, 12566–12578. https://doi.org/10.1007/s11356-020-07847-9

Robinson, E. A. G. (1960). Economic consequences of the size of nations: Proceedings of a conference held by the International Economic Association. *The ANNALS of the American Academy of Political and Social Science, 333*(1; 1961 January). https://doi.org/10.1177/000271626133300131

Sehnem, S., Jabbour, C. J. C., Pereira, C. S. C. F., de Sousa, L., & Jabbour, A. B (2019). Improving sustainable supply chains performance through operational excellence: Circular economy approach. *Resources, Conservation and Recycling, 149*, 236–248. https://doi.org/10.1016/j.resconrec.2019.05.021

Seth, D., Rehman, M. A. A., & Shrivastava, R. L. (2018). Green manufacturing drivers and their relationships for small and medium (SME) and large industries. *Journal of Cleaner Production, 198*, 1381–1405. https://doi.org/10.1016/j.jclepro.2018.07.106

Škrinjarić, T. (2020). Empirical assessment of the circular economy of selected European countries. *Journal of Cleaner Production*, 255. https://doi.org/10.1016/j.jclepro.2020.120246

Smol, M., Marcinek, P., & Koda, E. (2021). Drivers and barriers for a circular economy (CE) implementation in Poland—A case study of raw materials recovery sector. *Energies, 14*(8), 2219. https://doi.org/10.3390/en14082219

Stanković, J. J., Janković-Milić, V., Marjanović, I., & Janjić, J. (2021). An integrated approach of PCA and PROMETHEE in spatial assessment of circular economy indicators. *Waste Management, 128*, 154–166. https://doi.org/10.1016/J.WASMAN.2021.04.057

Todeschini, B. V., Cortimiglia, M. N., Callegaro-de-Menezes, D., & Ghezzi, A. (2017). Innovative and sustainable business models in the fashion industry: Entrepreneurial drivers, opportunities, and challenges. *Business Horizons, 60*(6), 759–770. https://doi.org/10.1016/j.bushor.2017.07.003

Ünal, E., Urbinati, A., & Chiaroni, D. (2019). Managerial practices for designing circular economy business models. *Journal of Manufacturing Technology Management, 30*(3), 561–589. https://doi.org/10.1108/JMTM-02-2018-0061

Upadhyay, A., Laing, T., Kumar, V., & Dora, M. (2021). Exploring barriers and drivers to the implementation of circular economy practices in the mining industry. *Resources Policy, 72*. https://doi.org/10.1016/j.resourpol.2021.102037

Velenturf, A. P. M., & Purnell, P. (2021). Principles for a sustainable circular economy. *Sustainable Production and Consumption, 27*, 1437–1457. https://doi.org/10.1016/J.SPC.2021.02.018

Vermunt, D. A., Negro, S. O., Verweij, P. A., Kuppens, D. V., & Hekkert, M. P. (2019). Exploring barriers to implementing different circular business models. *Journal of Cleaner Production*, 222. https://doi.org/10.1016/j.jclepro.2019.03.052

Whalen, K. A., Milios, L., & Nussholz, J. (2018). Bridging the gap: Barriers and potential for scaling reuse practices in the Swedish ICT sector. *Resources, Conservation and Recycling, 135*, 123–131. https://doi.org/10.1016/j.resconrec.2017.07.029

Zhang, A., Venkatesh, V. G., Wang, J. X., Mani, V., Wan, M., & Qu, T. (2021). Drivers of industry 4.0-enabled smart waste management in supply chain operations: A circular economy perspective in China. *Production Planning & Control*. https://doi.org/10.1080/09537287.2021.1980909

Zhang, B., & Wang, Z. (2014). Inter-firm collaborations on carbon emission reduction within industrial chains in China: Practices, drivers and effects on firms' performances. *Energy Economics, 42*, 115–131. https://doi.org/10.1016/j.eneco.2013.12.006

Zhu, Q., & Geng, Y. (2013). Drivers and barriers of extended supply chain practices for energy saving and emission reduction among Chinese manufacturers. *Journal of Cleaner Production, 40*, 6–12. https://doi.org/10.1016/j.jclepro.2010.09.017

Chapter 4
Circular Patterns of Manufacturing Companies

Abstract This chapter aims to present key drivers, barriers, challenges, and opportunities for the Lithuanian manufacturing industry in a transition to the circular economy. It starts with an explanation of the importance of circular economy integration in manufacturing companies across value chains. The further focus is on the detailed research methodology by explaining the setting of the sample and the basis of the survey analysis. We then present the results of the original survey of Lithuanian manufacturing companies, as well as unifying drivers, barriers, challenges, and opportunities to encourage Lithuanian manufacturing companies to implement circular activities. Finally, we define a portfolio of relevant circular economy patterns in Lithuanian manufacturing companies and reveal the main differences across manufacturing companies, in terms of both biological and technical cycles.

Keywords Circular patterns · Circular value chain · Manufacturing industry · Vision and strategy · Materials · Eco-design innovation · Cleaner production · Consumption · Waste management

4.1 Manufacturing Companies Moving Towards Circular Value Chains

The pressure from consumers, institutional regulations, and the efforts of individual companies towards circularity (including sustainability) are forcing the transformation of the entire traditional supply chain[1] and an increasing focus on practices and strategies to make the whole value chain[2] environmentally friendly. Thus, the integration of the circular economy (CE) (Farooque et al., 2019) is applied to the traditional value chain, which includes the supply of raw materials, the production process, and the delivery of the product to the final consumer, as well as marketing, research, and

[1] A supply chain is a network of individuals and companies who are involved in creating a product and delivering it to the consumer.

[2] A value chain is a business model that describes the full range of activities needed to create a product or service.

© The Author(s), under exclusive license to Springer Nature Switzerland AG 2023
L. Dagilienė et al., *Circular Business Models in the Manufacturing Industry*, Studies in Energy, Resource and Environmental Economics,
https://doi.org/10.1007/978-3-031-28809-8_4

development, IT, finance, customer service configuration, and coordination within and between business units and organizations (Geissdoerfer et al., 2018).

The CE integration into the value chain occurs mostly through restorative (repair, refurbishing, remanufacturing, and recycling) rather than regenerative options. Hence, there is still a knowledge gap in terms of how to integrate the CE into value chain management (Farooque et al., 2019). In the circular value chain, the primary activities are involved in **materials** (secondary raw materials and primary raw materials) **and eco-design innovation**, **cleaner production**, **consumption** or consumer purchase and use, and **waste management** (see Fig. 4.1). These activities need to be aligned with the company's **vision and strategy**, which should include aspects of circularity related to the business model (Aguiar, 2021; Huynh, 2021), digital technologies (Agrawal et al., 2021), environmental technologies (Isa et al., 2021), adoption of technological innovations (Huynh, 2021), materials and eco-design (Aguiar, 2021), and regenerative resources.

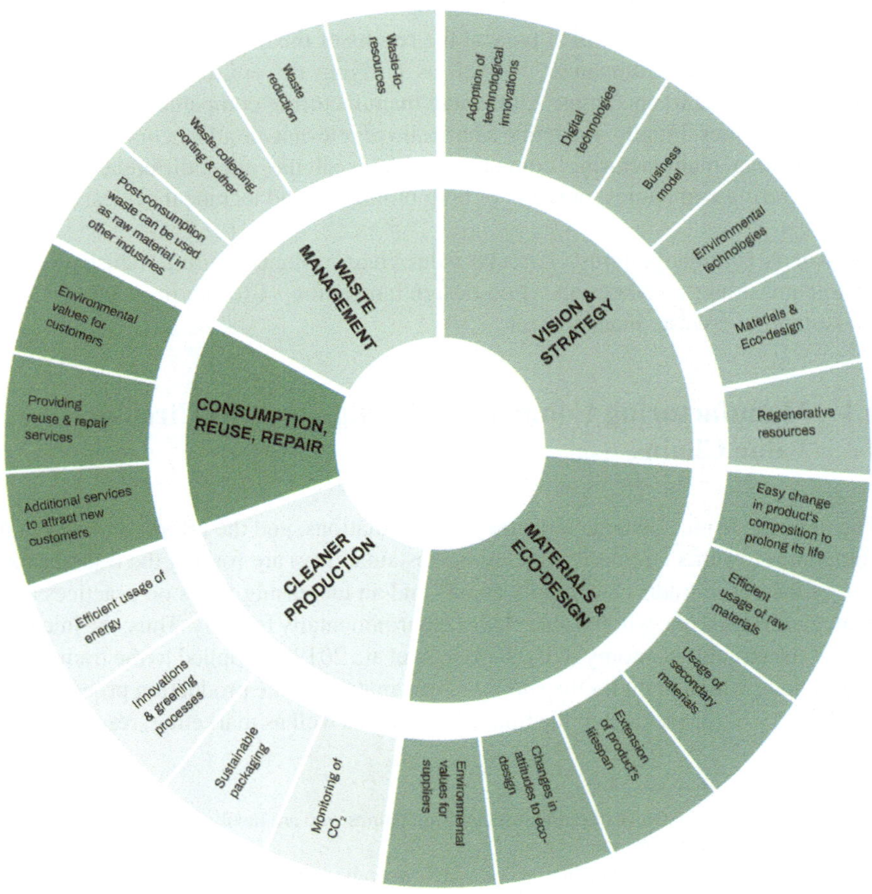

Fig. 4.1 Circular value chain approach

The eco-design approach explains how to design or develop a circular product or service that creates greater value in a sustainable way, but at the same time delivers economic, social, and environmental benefits (Shaharia, 2018). Most scientific research on the CE emphasizes that the successful circular transformation mostly depends on product design that helps to ensure circularity over time, as secondary raw materials form part of the value proposition, value co-creation, and value co-delivery systems, as well as value capture (Biloslavo et al., 2018; Bocken et al., 2014). The focus of the circular value chain is product design, which is focused on circularity, product integrity, product recyclability, close collaboration with suppliers and consumers, biodegradable packaging, green technology, extended producer responsibility, and implementation of green procurement outside the company (Farooque et al., 2019; Masi et al., 2017). Hence, eco-design and product design are critical factors in the functioning of a circular value chain (den Hollander et al., 2017; Sourabh et al., 2018) (Fig. 4.1).

According to the European Commission (EC) (2018), in the value chain, **materials** are either primary or secondary resources. Inputs of raw materials continue, but resources are dwindling, so the aim is to increase the use of secondary raw materials. When choosing a supplier of materials, it is appropriate for the company to assess them in terms of the products they sell (e.g., whether they sell environmentally friendly, certified materials, using secondary raw materials), greener and cleaner production (e.g., what technologies are used, their use of green energy, an ISO 14001:2015 certificate,[3] or if they develop or cooperate with other institutions on eco-innovation), their orientation towards carbon dioxide (CO2) reduction (e.g., recovery and use of residual energy and heat, waste policy, by-product use, CO2 monitoring systems, big data management systems) and, of course, costs, flexibility, and feedback from other customers (Roy et al., 2020), packaging (e.g., using secondary raw materials) and environmentally friendly transport (Shah et al., 2021). Kumar et al. (2012) recommend the selection of suppliers whose raw and secondary materials would allow the company to reduce water and energy consumption and thus contribute to the reduction of environmental pollution, defects, and overproduction.

Based on the literature review, in order to foster and ensure a circular value chain, it is important to analyse such aspects as changes in attitudes to eco-design, efficient usage of raw materials, use of secondary materials, the extension of a product's lifespan, a product composition that can be easily changed to prolong its life, and the environmental values held by suppliers.

Shaharia (2018) notes that, in the **production** process, efficiency in energy and productivity can reduce the price of the final product and helps to maximize utilization, or reduce the input, of raw materials. In the circular value chain, the processing of secondary raw material requires the use of innovative, efficient technology, and human resources. According to the World Trade Organization (2019), in 2015, 57% of the global trade in goods and services consisted of trade in intermediate products,

[3] ISO 14001:2015 specifies the requirements for an environmental management system that an organization can use to enhance its environmental performance. More information: https://www.iso.org/standard/60857.html

which are mostly traded through global supply chains or global networks of products and services. Trade takes place in two ways: firstly, imported raw materials and materials to produce exported goods and services (backward movement in the global supply chain), and secondly, domestically produced products for other companies in the value chain responsible for the later stages of production (forward movement in the supply chain). In addition, production has a special role to play in the value chain, with great potential for reducing resource waste and transportation. Manufacturing companies are encouraged to develop and improve technologies that increase product durability, reuse, and recycling (Shen et al., 2019). In order to implement green value chain measures in production, it is important to optimize production time, minimize the number of defects, reduce waste, minimize or avoid overproduction, reduce downtime, and minimize unnecessary employee movements. Kumar et al. (2012) argue that companies should use information technology to help model more efficient delivery routes by serving multiple customers on a single journey. Based on literature analysis, in order to ensure a circular value chain in terms of production, it is important to analyse such aspects as efficient usage of energy, cleaner production innovations and greening processes, sustainable packaging, and effective monitoring of CO2.

In the circular value chain, **consumption** should lead to socially responsible behaviour. The main challenge is that if repaired, refurbished, and recycled goods or products from secondary raw materials do not become substitutes for newly manufactured goods, the environmental suffers, and the CE effect is not achieved (Zink & Geyer, 2017). In addition, a large part of society still treats recycled products as less desirable (Hazen et al., 2016) and product ownership (rather than functionality) as integral parts of culture and reputation (Tukker, 2016). Thus, building trust and fostering different consumer behaviour through eco-labels and information campaigns is becoming an important tool to ensure the functioning of a circular value chain (Masi et al., 2017). In order to ensure a circular value chain in terms of consumption, the focus must be on such aspects as providing reuse and repair services, providing additional services to attract new customers, and operating according to environmental values.

According to Salmenpera et al. (2021), **waste management** plays a significant role in the transition to the CE (Fellner et al., 2017; Nowakowski & Mrowczynska, 2018), where using design to eliminate waste, regenerating biological materials, and the restoration of technological materials are the key principles (Stahel, 2016). Closed-loop supply chains (which are one type of circular value chain) are the least studied (Masi et al., 2017), despite the fact that, as early as 2003, the electronic and electrical equipment manufacturing industry became the first for which this type of supply chain became mandatory (under Directive 2002/96/EC). The main goal of a closed-loop supply chain is the reuse and recovery of added value and the avoidance of waste, which is possible through reverse logistics and the integrated management of secondary markets (Masi et al., 2017). However, this still generates substantial amounts of waste as it is rarely feasible to reuse/recycle all unwanted items within the same supply chain (Farooque et al., 2019). In addition, a circular supply chain covers the principles of a closed-loop supply chain but adds open-loop supply chain principles around recovering value from waste through collaborating with other organizations within the industrial sector (open-loop, same sector), or with different industrial sectors (open-loop, cross-sector) (Farooque et al., 2019) with the target of producing zero waste. For example, recycled plastic polyethylene terephthalate (PET) bottles may be used for construction, as well as in the textile and apparel industry; recycled textiles could be used in the construction industry as well, while cooking oil can be used for biodiesel production. In terms of waste management, in order to ensure a circular value chain, we need to focus on such aspects as waste-to-resources, waste reduction, waste collecting and sorting, and post-consumption waste that can be used as inputs for other industries.

4.2 Survey Research Methodology

In the literature review, we explore different drivers that may motivate companies to engage in the CE, as well as a number of barriers. The main objective of this research is to determine the key drivers and barriers for the Lithuanian manufacturing industry in circular transition. Therefore, the nature of the research is explanatory by applying deductive access and the description of the research provision is based on subjectivity and personality. Currently, CE research lacks exploratory and confirmatory approaches such as interviews, surveys and experimental studies.

The detailed research methodology is presented as follows: (1) the setting of the sample; and (2) the argumentation of the survey analysis.

4.2.1 The Setting of the Sample

The research focuses on a sample of Lithuanian **manufacturing companies** (C sector, according to the Nomenclature of Economic Activities (NACE)). In 2019, the transport and pipeline transport sector (H49) and the manufacturing sector (C10_TO_C33) emitted the most CO2 (about 60% and 28% of the national total, respectively) other than from biomass (Statistics Lithuania, 2020). On the other hand, in the same year, the manufacturing industry overall created the highest total value-added (€1.987 million, or 19.75% of the national total; Statistics Lithuania, 2020). The description of the setting of the selected industry is critical in the analysis and interpretation of the data. Conducting research on the CE of selected industries becomes very important as these industries are very important in Lithuania. The selection of the industries was based on three criteria:

- Priority industries, according to the strategic EU documents on the CE. The European Green Deal (EC, 2019) focuses on cleaner production processes, giving priority to energy efficiency, sustainable products (eco-design) and to reducing and reusing materials prior to recycling. A focus also remains on reducing waste, in particular highlighting issues in food-related industries. The analysis of energy efficiency highlights important but energy-intensive industries for the European economy, such as steel, chemicals, and cement, as they supply several key value chains. The analysis of sustainable products provides guidance for restructuring in all sectors, but focuses specifically on resource-intensive industries, such as textiles, construction, electronics, and plastics (including rubber). Emphasis is placed on new business models that would allow companies to move faster towards the CE.

- The amount of value-added created. In 2019, the largest value-added in manufacturing was generated by the manufacture of food products (C10), furniture (C31), chemicals and chemical products (C20), wood and products made of wood and cork, except furniture, articles of straw and plaiting materials (C16), fabricated metal products, except machinery and equipment (C25), and rubber and plastic products (C22) (Statistics Lithuania, 2020).
- The largest number of employees. In Q4, 2019, according to Statistics Lithuania (2020), 25% of the workforce worked in the manufacture of furniture (C31); 21% in food products, beverages and tobacco (C10_TO_C12); 14% in wood and paper products, publishing and printing (C16_TO_C18); and 13% in clothing manufacturing (C14).

We focus next on the sample of Lithuanian **manufacturing companies** within the selected industries. These are: furniture (C31); wood and products made of wood and cork, except furniture; articles of straw and plaiting materials (C16_TO_C18); chemicals and chemical products (C20); rubber and plastic products (C22); fabricated metal products (except machinery and equipment) (C25); textiles (including sewing); and wearing apparel (C13_TO_C14).

For the deeper analysis of **sector-specific nature,** we focused on the furniture industry, plastic industry,[4] and textile industry (Fig. 4.2). Argumentation for the selection of these industries for deeper analysis is based on (1) the criteria (mentioned above) showing that these industries are essential for Lithuania's economy; (2) taking an active part in the research (apart from the food industry, these were the most active industries); and (3) cycle similarity, i.e., deploy technical cycle.

By choosing these industries, it is possible to ensure the validity of the data and avoid the risk of having too few results per industry. We exclude companies with a staff headcount of 20 or fewer.

4.2.2 Argumentation of Survey Analysis

This research is aimed at determining the drivers and barriers influencing the CE in companies through a survey. We then conduct a quantitative analysis of the data, based on statistical principles and procedures. The instrument-structured questionnaire was prepared following the literature review and is based on the logic of the circular value chain approach (see Fig. 4.1). The survey covered:

---

[4] Officially (according to the NACE classification) the industry is called rubber and plastics, but in the book we refer to it collectively as the plastic industry.

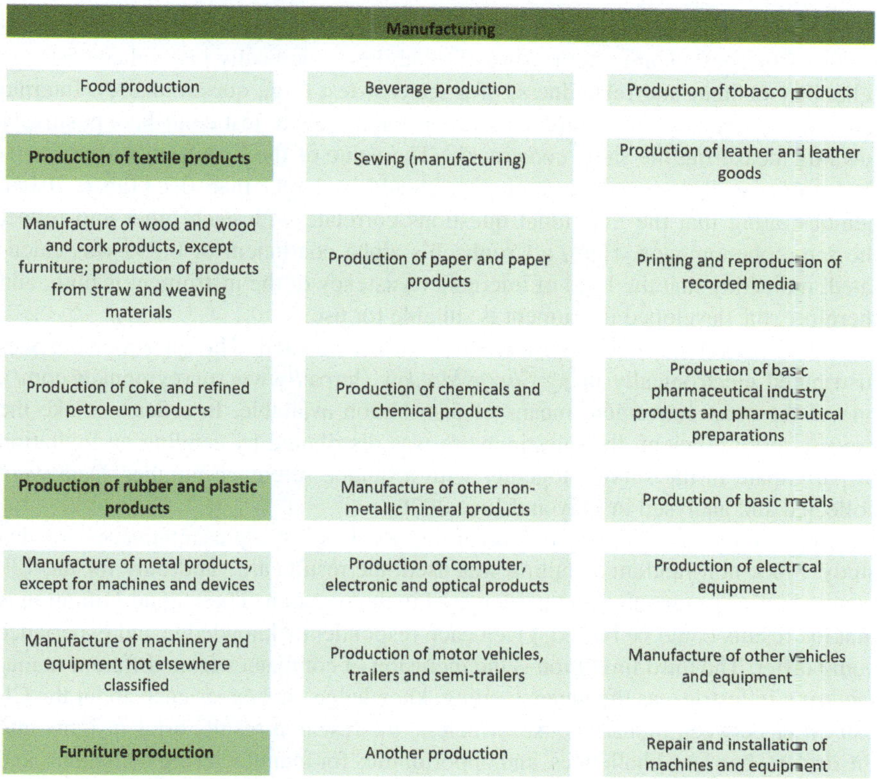

Fig. 4.2 The selected manufacturing industries for the deeper analysis (dark shading)

- a description of the company and its strategy related to CE implementation;
- raw materials, secondary raw materials, and eco-design;
- cleaner production;
- consumption, use, reuse, repair;
- waste management;
- the most important drivers that could shift the companies closer to the CE;
- respondents' position and experience.

Answers were given on a 5-point Likert scale: "strongly disagree" −2; "disagree" −1; "neither agree nor disagree" −0; "agree" +1; and "strongly agree" +2. Each scale included a "N/A" (not applicable) option if the respondent could not answer a question.

In the first step of the quantitative research, a pilot study of five interviews was conducted between February and April 2020, to test the questionnaire. The test respondents were a mix of internal colleagues from within our research group, and external specialists in organizing questionnaires from the Bank of Lithuania. The questionnaire was adjusted according to the results of the pilot study.

The reliability of the quantitative survey was tested using Cronbach's alpha coefficient. This coefficient is "a measure of reliability, specifically internal consistency reliability or item interrelatedness, of a scale or test (e.g., questionnaire). Internal consistency refers to the extent that all items on a scale or test contribute positively towards measuring the same construct".[5] The value of the Cronbach's alpha coefficient of a well-designed questionnaire should be larger than 0.7 (Taber, 2018), demonstrating that the individual questions correlate with each other and reflect the same phenomenon. Here, a Cronbach's alpha coefficient of 0.759 was calculated, indicating that the level of internal consistency of the instrument is high, and therefore, the developed instrument is suitable for use.

In the second step, an empirical study was conducted. The questionnaire was distributed electronically using *SurveyMonkey* (https://www.surveymonkey.com/), one of the most convenient means of distribution available. In order to make the process more efficient, the questionnaire was distributed by sending an invitation to participate in the survey, together with a unique reference number. Data were collected and analysed in May and June 2020.

Limitations. One limitation is regarding the level of representativeness of this study. Since non-random sampling was used, the results are valid only for the 139 manufacturing companies that participated in the research. The second limitation is that the results could be biased, given each respondent's knowledge and experience could differ. The third limitation is the inclusion of companies from different manufacturing industries, as the understanding, knowledge, and experience about the CE can differ between industries. Nevertheless, the research results offer insights into the drivers, barriers, challenges, and opportunities for manufacturing companies and industries to implement circular activities across the value chain, with a particular focus on small open economies (SOEs).

Future research. There is still a great deal of work to be done in researching companies in other nations and in other industries, ideally using a larger sample. Future research could also assess the differences in priorities between different types of organizations in different parts of the value chain.

4.3 Circular Patterns of Lithuanian Manufacturing Companies

4.3.1 Sample Characteristics

A total of 139 manufacturing companies were surveyed to explain the specifics of Lithuania and to identify the main drivers, barriers, challenges, and opportunities leading manufacturing companies to implement circular activities. The final

[5] Introduction to Cronbach's Alpha. https://mattchoward.com/introduction-to-cronbachs-alpha/

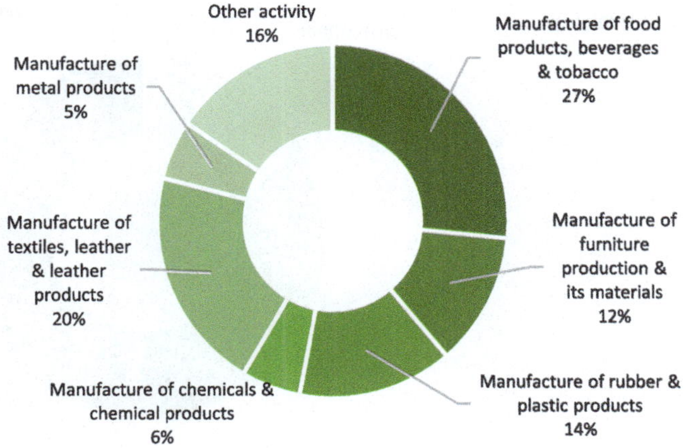

Fig. 4.3 The main activities

response rate was 37%, once the incomplete and non-compliant questionnaires were eliminated.

Main activities and market orientation. The surveyed companies were mainly operating in the food and textile industries, at 27% and 20%, respectively (see Fig. 4.3), and 75% of the companies that provided data were operating in both national and international markets (see Fig. 4.4) because Lithuanian manufacturing companies are largely exporters. Furthermore, 31% of the companies deploy biological cycles[6] and 69% use technical cycles[7] (see Fig. 4.5).

The number of employees. The number of employees is an indicator of the company's size, alongside total revenue. In the research, 58% of the sample have between 50 and 249 employees (see Fig. 4.6), and 90% of the companies that provided data have been operating for more than 10 years (see Fig. 4.7). Start-ups consist only 1% of the sample. To sum up, more mature companies in terms of age, participated in the research.

Revenues and investment. A third indicator for size that is often used is total revenues (also known as total turnover). We find that 42% of the sample have gross revenues in 2019 ranging from €0.700 million to €8.000 million (see Fig. 4.8), though companies in the plastic industry report gross revenues in 2019 from €8.000 million to €50.000 million. Almost a quarter of the companies (24%) do not invest in environmentally friendly technologies, and the least active industries in this regard are the textile and furniture industries. We find that 18% of the companies invest up

[6] The biological cycle is for materials that can biodegrade and safely return to the earth. This cycle mainly concerns products that are consumed, such as food. More information: https://ellenmacarthurfoundation.org/articles/the-biological-cycle-of-the-butterfly-diagram

[7] The technical cycle is relevant for products that are used rather than consumed. More information: https://doi.org/ellenmacarthur foundation.org/articles/the-technical-cycle-of-the-butterfly-diagram.

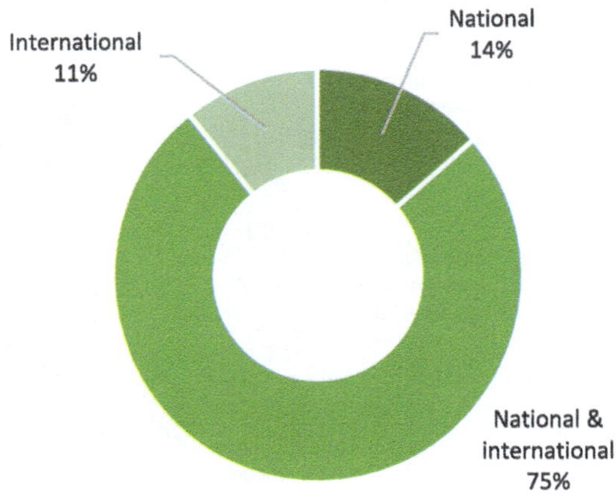

Fig. 4.4 Market orientation

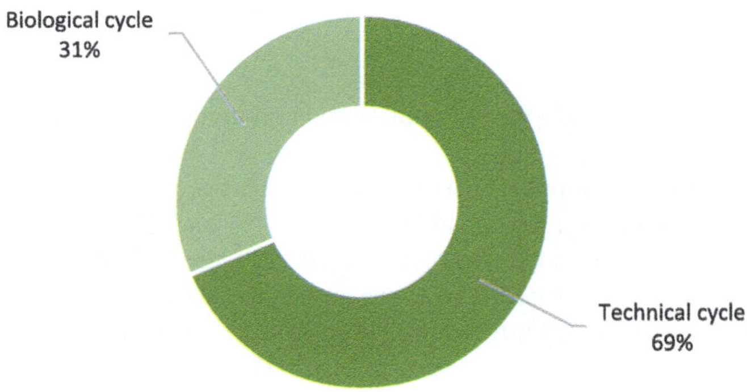

Fig. 4.5 Companies' distribution across different cycles

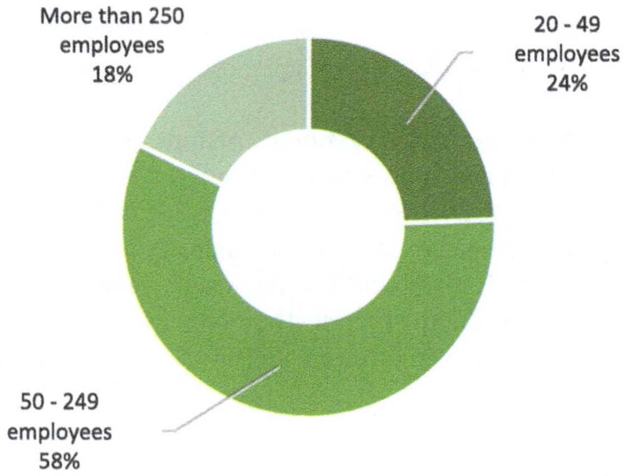

Fig. 4.6 Number of employees (2019)

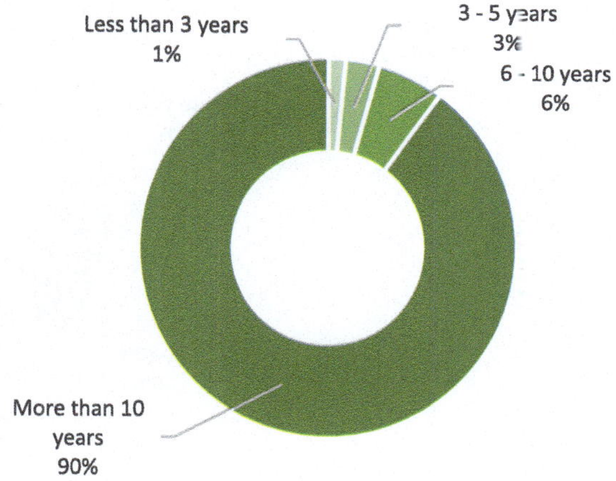

Fig. 4.7 Age of the company (2019)

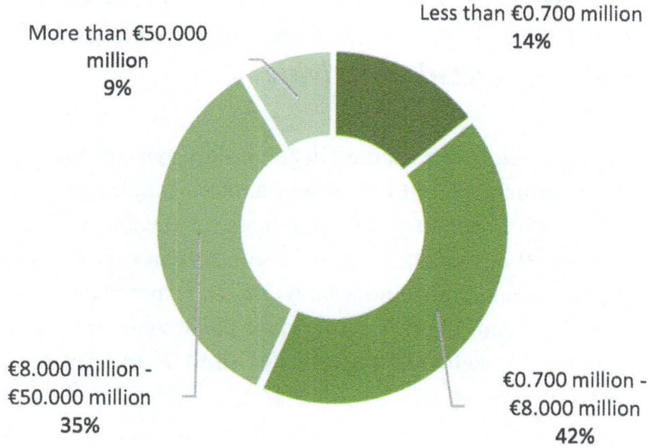

Fig. 4.8 Revenues (2019)

to 5% in environmentally friendly technologies (see Fig. 4.9), while only 4% invest more than 30% in such technologies. The most actively investing industry is the plastic industry.

Most respondents to the questionnaire were managers or company specialists, and their work experience ranged from 1 to 40 years.

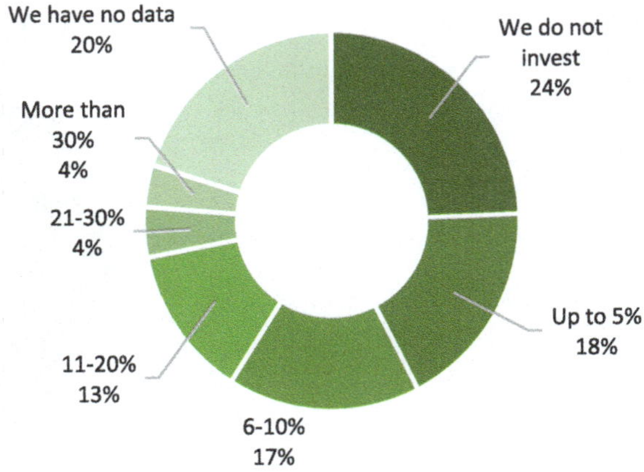

Fig. 4.9 Investment in green technologies as a share of total investment (2019)

4.3.2 Drivers, Barriers, Challenges, and Opportunities Leading Lithuanian Manufacturing Companies to Implement Circular Activities

In this subsection, the results are presented in general from the point of view of Lithuanian manufacturing companies, but in further chapters some results are specified on the focus of industry-level best corporate practices for the CE.

The method of statistical analysis used in this research is descriptive statistics (absolute, percentage, mean, and standard deviation). It must be emphasized that the higher the value of the mean, the more important the statement or category.

Taking into account the **relevant patterns of the CE in Lithuanian manufacturing companies** (see Fig. 4.10), we observe that all parts of the value chain—vision and strategy, materials and eco-design, cleaner production, consumption, and waste management—are important but, in our sample, companies emphasize vision and strategy, and waste management, as the most important patterns in CE implementation. Manufacturing companies show less interest in consumption, reuse, and repair.

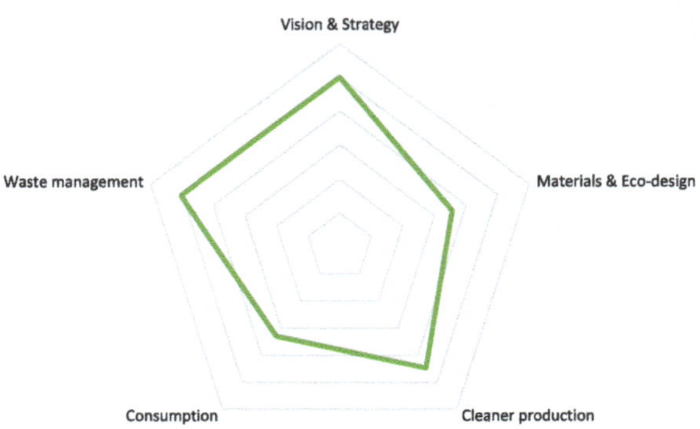

Fig. 4.10 Relevant patterns of the CE in Lithuanian manufacturing companies

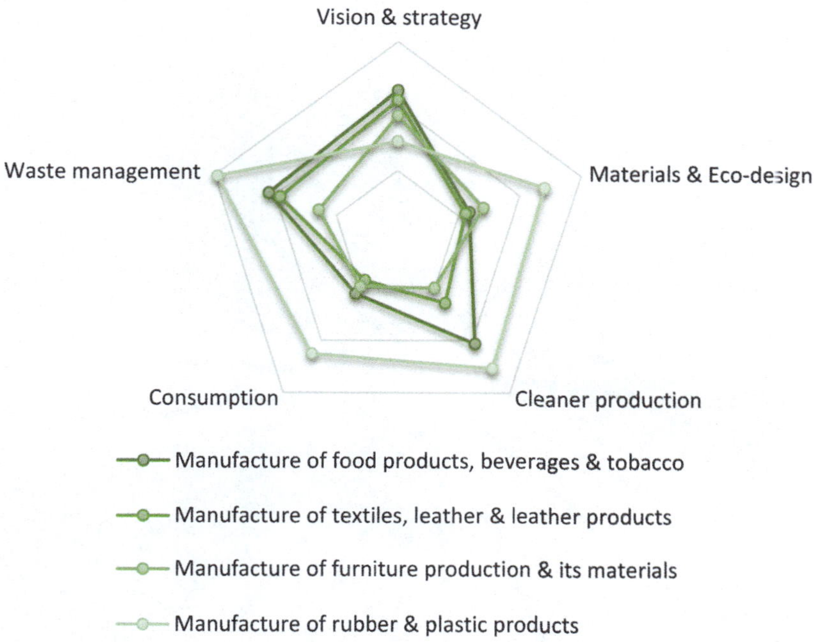

Fig. 4.11 Relevant patterns of the CE in Lithuanian manufacturing companies by different industries

An analysis by industry is shown in Fig. 4.11, where we see that all parts of the value chain are important. As the most important patterns to shift to the CE, the textile and food manufacturers emphasized vision and strategy, and waste management; the furniture industry shared the focus on vision and strategy, plus the role of materials and eco-design, while in the plastic industry, companies mostly struggle with materials (secondary plastic vs primary plastic) and cleaner production techniques.

Lithuanian manufacturing companies are more oriented to the efficient use of raw materials (materials and eco-design) and energy (cleaner production) (see Fig. 4.12). This means that these companies tend to achieve higher productivity rates while potentially cutting cost.

In terms of **vision and strategy,** Fig. 4.12 shows a prioritization of the use of regenerative resources, investment in digital and environmental technologies, and investment in new business models, and yet, paradoxically, the surveyed companies invest little in green technologies. It is interesting to note that companies are more interested in digital, rather than environmental, technologies.

With regard to **materials and eco-design** (see Fig. 4.12), most companies strongly agree that they strive for an efficient use of raw materials, seeing it as important to replace primary raw materials with secondary ones, to invest in extending the life cycle of their products, and to create environmental values for suppliers. On the other hand, the physical composition of many products cannot easily be changed, particularly in the food industry.

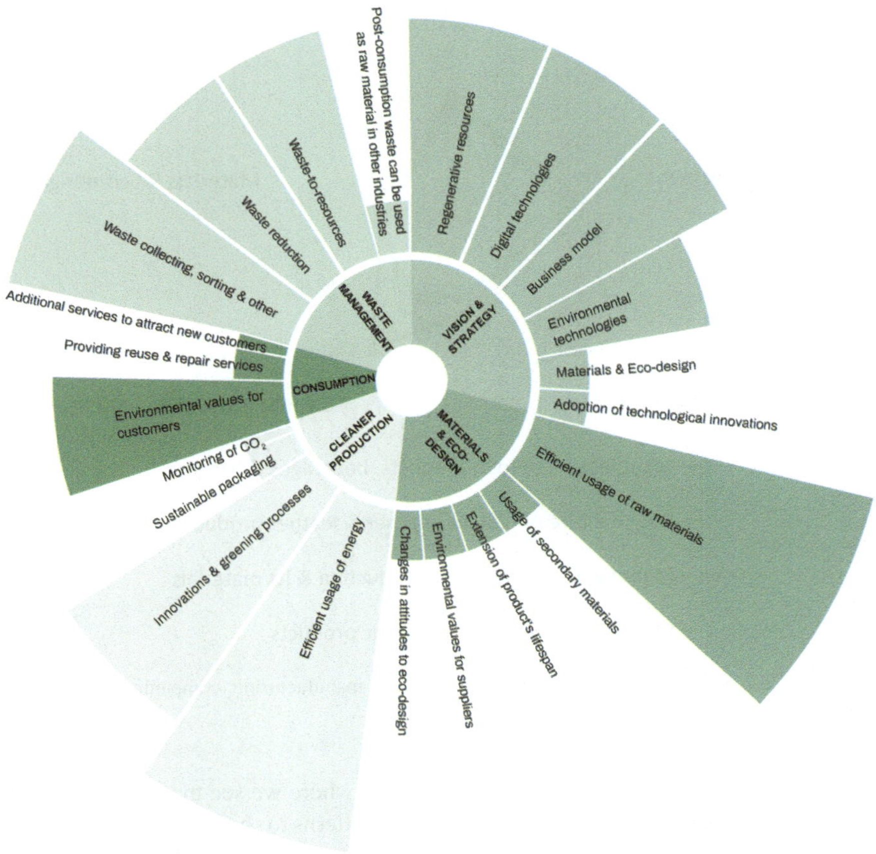

Fig. 4.12 The portfolio of relevant patterns of the CE in Lithuanian manufacturing companies

Our sample largely agrees that increasing energy efficiency is a significant part of moving towards **cleaner production** (see Fig. 4.12), and that it is important to invest in innovations and processes, but they note that the monitoring of environmental pollution is not effective, particularly for small companies.

In the case of **consumption, reuse, repair** (see Fig. 4.12), most respondents agree that it is important for companies to strive to create environmental values to inspire customers, especially since most Lithuanian manufacturing companies are contractual manufacturers or work on a business-to-business (B2B) basis.[8] On the other hand, they doubt whether there is any competitive advantage in eco-design or from the provision of additional services, such as reuse or repair.

[8] Business-to-business (B2B) refers to transactions between businesses, such as manufacturers and wholesalers, or wholesalers and retailers. This business that is conducted between companies is in contrast to business-to-consumer (B2C).

According to Dagilienė et al. (2021), the main gap related to the implementation of the CE in Lithuania is in waste management. Furthermore, Lithuania ranks in the bottom half of EU Member States, according to the EU CE Update (2019). However, companies in our sample agree that **waste management** must be addressed in order to minimize the impact on the environment through waste collecting, sorting, and other methods (see Fig. 4.12). Waste must either be turned into new resources, or the volume produced must be reduced.

Looking deeper, we see that 51% of the companies surveyed report that 76–100% of their products and packaging can be recycled. However, 24% have no information on the recycling potential of their product (see Fig. 4.13). In addition, 39% of the companies surveyed state that more than 50% of their product could be reused if the product were returned at the end of its useful life, but 27% have no information on the reuse potential of their product (see Fig. 4.14).

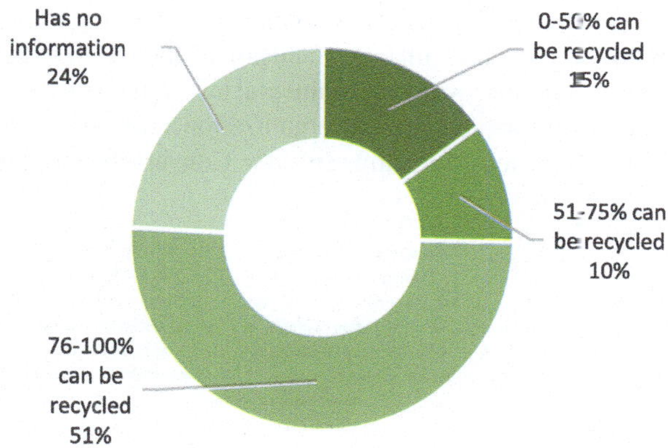

Fig. 4.13 Products and packaging can be partly recycled

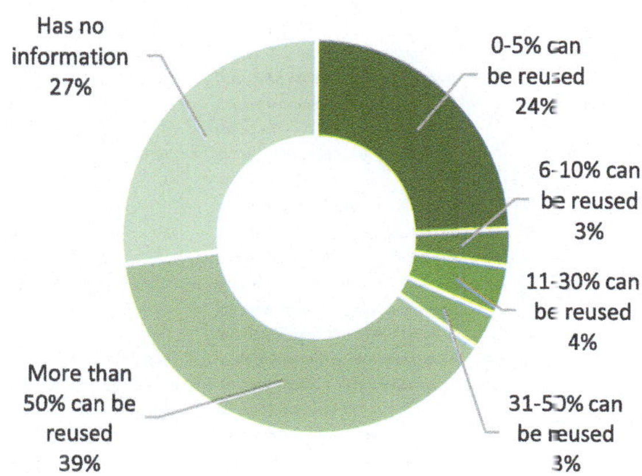

Fig. 4.14 Products can be partly recycled or reused if they are returned at the end of their useful life

4.3.3 Factors Influencing the Transition to the CE

The scientific literature, practical reviews, and feasibility studies find an abundance of factors that promote the CE (see the detailed review in Sect. 2.4).

Analysing the results of the survey with regard to the drivers that encourage the transition of manufacturing companies to circular business models, we find that some factors are more motivating than others (see Fig. 4.15). The most motivating factors are external financial support (e.g., governmental initiatives and financial mechanisms), followed by technological drivers such as production automation and robotization, and the technological transformation of production and business processes. Less relevant factors for the CE are green procurement and reverse logistics.

Besides general analysis of motivating and hindering factors, we also analysed how differ factors for companies, whose activities are related to biological cycles and technical cycles (Table 4.1).

Companies that deploy biological cycles (e.g., companies from food industry) report that legal regulation, inclusion of the CE in strategy documents, penalties for non-compliance with environmental laws, green procurement, copying the behaviour of competitors and/or other organizations, tax policy, initial investments and reverse logistics are less motivating to them. Conversely, they are highly motivated by factors

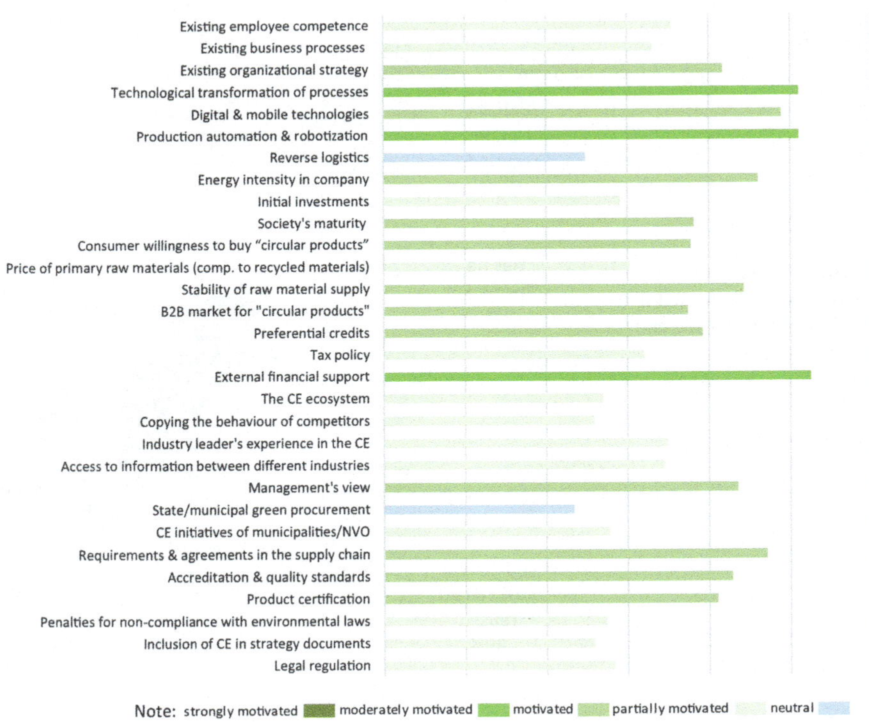

Fig. 4.15 Factors influencing manufacturing companies to shift to the CE

Table 4.1 Factors for CE in Lithuanian manufacturing companies with biological and technical cycles

Factors	Companies with biological cycles	Companies with technical cycles
Legal regulation	neutral	partially motivated
Inclusion of CE in strategy documents	neutral	partially motivated
Penalties for non-compliance with environmental laws	neutral	partially motivated
Product certification	motivated	motivated
Accreditation and quality standards	motivated	motivated
Requirements and agreements in the supply chain	motivated	moderately motivated
CE initiatives of municipalities/ non-governmental organization	partially motivated	partially motivated
State/municipal green procurement	neutral	partially motivated
Management view	motivated	motivated
Access to information between different industries	partially motivated	partially motivated
Industry leader's experience in the CE	partially motivated	motivated
Copying the behaviour of competitors	neutral	partially motivated
The CE ecosystem	partially motivated	partially motivated
External financial support	moderately motivated	moderately motivated
Tax policy	neutral	motivated
Preferential credits	partially motivated	motivated
B2B market for "circular products"	partially motivated	motivated
Stability of raw material supply	moderately motivated	motivated
Price of primary raw materials (comp. to recycled materials)	partially motivated	partially motivated
Consumer willingness to buy "circular products"	motivated	motivated
Society's maturity	motivated	partially motivated
Initial investments	neutral	partially motivated
Energy intensity in company	moderately motivated	motivated
Reverse logistics	neutral	partially motivated
Production automation and robotization	moderately motivated	moderately motivated
Digital and mobile technologies	moderately motivated	motivated
Technological transformation of processes	moderately motivated	moderately motivated
Existing organizational strategy	moderately motivated	motivated
Existing business processes	motivated	partially motivated
Existing employee competence	motivated	partially motivated

Note: strongly motivated ■ moderately motivated ■ motivated ■ partially motivated ■ neutral ■

such as external financial support, stability of raw material supply, energy intensity, production automation and robotization, digital and mobile technologies, technological transformation of processes, and their existing organizational strategy. Hence, manufacturing companies with biological cycles are more interested in technological solutions to increase efficiency and to save resources than the company's strategy and the potential attraction of external funding, and are less motivated by compliance, as this usually leads to additional bureaucratic actions.

For companies that deploy technical cycles (e.g., textile, furniture, plastic industries), all factors are more or less important and motivate companies to undertake actions to implement CE principles. They are highly motivated by requirements and agreements across the value chain, external financial support, production automation and robotization, and the technological transformation of processes. For these manufacturing companies, market compliance, which leads to the stability of raw material supply, means that a B2B market for "circular products", and a consumer willingness to buy "circular products" are very important.

In this section, we discussed the survey results in terms of relevant CE patterns in the value chain and factors influencing a transition to the CE. The detailed information regarding different industries is presented in Chapters 5, 6 and 7.

Key Highlights

- The portfolio of relevant patterns of the CE in Lithuanian manufacturing companies highlights the need for a more developed waste management infrastructure, which many see as the extent of CE. The focus is on waste collection, sorting, and recycling.
- Lithuanian manufacturing companies are oriented to the efficient use of raw materials and energy. The eco-efficiency manifests itself in technological innovations which reduce the amount of raw materials consumed per product, or solar energy.
- Manufacturing companies with biological cycles are more interested in technological solutions to increase efficiency than in the company's strategy and the potential attraction of external funding.
- Those companies with technical cycles are highly embedded into global value chains as contractual manufacturers. Requirements and agreements in the value chain are drivers to improve environmental and circular activities.

References

Agrawal, R., Wankhede, V. A., Kumar, A., Upadhyay, A., & Garza-Reyes, J. A. (2021). Nexus of circular economy and sustainable business performance in the era of digitalization. *International Journal of Productivity and Performance Management*, Vol. ahead-of-print No. ahead-of-print. https://doi.org/10.1108/IJPPM-12-2020-0676

Aguiar, M. F., Mesa, J. A., Jugend, D., Pinheiro, M. A. P., & Fiorini, P. P. D. C. (2021). Circular product design: Strategies, challenges and relationships with new product development. *Management of Environmental Quality*, Vol. ahead-of-print No. ahead-of-print. https://doi.org/10.1108/MEQ-06-2021-0125

Biloslavo, R., Bagnoli, C., & Edgar, D. (2018). An eco-critical perspective on business models: The value triangle as an approach to closing the sustainability gap. *Journal of Cleaner Production, 174*, 746–762. https://doi.org/10.1016/j.jclepro.2017.10.281

Bocken, N. M., Short, S. W., Rana, P., & Evans, S. (2014). A literature and practice review to develop sustainable business model archetypes. *Journal of Cleaner Production, 65*, 42–56. https://doi.org/10.1016/j.jclepro.2013.11.039

Dagilienė, L., Varaniūtė, V., & Bruneckienė, J. (2021). Local governments' perspective on implementing the circular economy: A framework for future solutions. *Journal of Cleaner Production, 310*, 127340. https://doi.org/10.1016/j.jclepro.2021.127340

den Hollander, M., Bakker, C. A., & Hultink, E. (2017). Product design in a circular economy: Development of a typology of key concepts and terms: Key concepts and terms for circular product design. *Journal of Industrial Ecology, 21*. https://doi.org/10.1111/jiec.12610

European Commission. (2018). Monitoring framework on the circular economy. https://ec.europa.eu/eurostat/web/circular-economy/indicators (accessed 11 November 2019).

European Commission. (2019). Reflection paper "Towards a Sustainable Europe by 2030". https://ec.europa.eu/commission/sites/beta-political/files/rp_sustainable_europe_30-01_en_web.pdf (accessed 03 January 2020).

EU Circular Economy Update. (2019, May). EU circular economy update. Overview of circular economy in Europe. Ecopreneur.eu (2019). https://ecopreneur.eu/wp-content/uploads/2019/05/Ecopreneur-Circular-Economy-Update-report-2019.pdf (accessed 22nd Aug 2020).

Farooque, M., Zang, A., Thurer, M., Qu, T., & Huisingh, D. (2019). Circular supply chain management: A definition and structured literature review. *Journal of Cleaner Production, 228*. https://doi.org/10.1016/j.jclepro.2019.04.303

Fellner, J., Lederer, J., Scharff, C., & Laner, D. (2017). Present potentials and limitation of a circular economy with respect to primary raw material demand. *Journal of Industrial Ecology, 21*(3), 494–496. https://doi.org/10.1111/jiec.12582

Geissdoerfer, M., Morioka, S. N., de Carvalho, M. M., & Evans, S. (2018). Business models and supply chains for the circular economy. *Journal of Cleaner Production, 190*, 712–721. https://doi.org/10.1016/j.jclepro.2018.04.159

Hazen, B., Mollenkopf, D., & Wang, Y. (2016). Remanufacturing for the circular economy: An examination of consumer switching behavior. *Business Strategy and the Environment, 26*. https://doi.org/10.1002/bse.1929

Huynh, P. H. (2021). Enabling circular business models in the fashion industry: The role of digital innovation. *International Journal of Productivity and Performance Management, 71*(3), 870–895. https://doi.org/10.1108/IJPPM-12-2020-0683

Isa, N. M., Sivapathy, A., & Adjrina Kamarruddin, N. N. (2021). Malaysia on the way to sustainable development: Circular economy and green technologies, Sergi, B. S. and Jaaffar, A. R. (Ed.), *Modeling economic growth in contemporary Malaysia* (*Entrepreneurship and Global Economic Growth*), Emerald Publishing Limited, pp. 91–115. https://doi.org/10.1108/978-1-80043-806-420211009

Kalmykovaa, Y., Sadagopan, M., & Rosado, L. (2018). Circular economy—From review of theories and practices to development of implementation tools. https://doi.org/10.1016/j.resconrec.2017.10.034

Kinjal, J. S., Shu-Yuan, P., Ingyu, L., Hyunook, K., Zhaoyang, Y., Jian-Ming, Z., & Pen-Chi, C. (2021). Green transportation for sustainability: Review of current barriers, strategies, and innovative technologies. *Journal of Cleaner Production, 326*, 129392, ISSN 0959–6526. https://doi.org/10.1016/j.jclepro.2021.129392

Kumar, S., Teichman, S., & Timpernagel, T. (2012). *A Green Supply Chain is a Requirement for Profitability//INternational Journal of Production Research, 50*(5), 1278–1296. https://doi.org/10.1080/00207543.2011.571924

Masi, D., Day, S., & Godsell, J. (2017). Supply chain configurations in the circular economy: A systematic literature review. *Sustainability, 9*(9), 1602. https://doi.org/10.3390/su9091602

Nowakowski, P., & Mrowczynska, B. (2018). Towards sustainable WEEE collection and transportation methods in circular economy e comparative study for rural and urban settlements. *REsour. Concerv. Recycl, 135*, 93e107. https://doi.org/10.1016/j.resconrec.2017.12.016

Roy, S., Das, M., Ali, S., Raihan, A., Paul, S., & Kabir, G. (2020). Evaluating strategies for environmental sustainability in a supply chain of an emerging economy. *Journal of Cleaner Production, 262*, 121389. https://doi.org/10.10.1016/j.jclepro.2020.121389

Salmenpera, H., Pitkanen, K., Kautto, P., & Saikku, L. (2021). Critical factors for enhancing the circular economy in waste management. *Journal of Cleaner Production, 280*. https://doi.org/10.1016/j.jclepro.2020.124339

Shaharia, P. (2018). Circular economy: The beauty of circularity in value chain. In *Journal of Economics and Business, 1*(4), 584–598. https://doi.org/10.31014/aior.1992.01.04.52

Shen, K., Li., Li, & L., & Wang, J. (2019). Circular economy model for recycling waste resources under government participation: A case study in industrial waste water circulation in China. *Technological and Economic Development of Economy, 26*, 1–27. https://doi.org/10.3846/tede.2019.11249

Sourabh, J., Nikunj, J., & Bhimaraya, M. (2018). Strategic framework towards measuring a circular supply chain management. *Benchmarking: An International Journal, 25*, 00–00. https://doi.org/10.1108/BIJ-11-2017-0304

Stahel, W. R. (2016). The circular economy. *Nature, 531*, 435e438. https://doi.org/10.1038/531435a

Statistics Lithuania. (2020). https://osp.stat.gov.lt/gyventojai1. (accessed 20 May 2020)

Taber, K. S. (2018). The use of Cronbach's alpha when developing and reporting research instruments in science education. *Research in Science Education, 48*, 1273–1296. https://doi.org/10.1007/s11165-016-9602-2

Tukker, A., Bulavskaya, T., Giljum, S., de Koning, A., Lutter, S., Simas, M., Stadler, K., & Wood, R. (2016). Environmental and resource footprints in a global context: Europe's structural deficit in resource endowments. *Global Environmental Change, 40*, 171–181. https://doi.org/10.1016/j.gloenvcha.2016.07.002

World Trade Organization. (2019). World trade statistical review. https://www.wto.org/english/res_e/statis_e/wts219_e/wts2019chapter04_e.pdf

Zink, T., & Geyer, R. (2017). Circular economy rebound. *Journal of Industrial Ecology, 21*, 593–602. https://doi.org/10.1111/jiec.12545

Chapter 5
Circular Transformation of the Textile Industry

Abstract This chapter presents dominant circular business models among textile manufacturers, and challenges and new opportunities in the transition towards a circular economy. The chapter starts with an industry-specific literature review to identify global trends, key barriers, and opportunities for a circular textile industry. The further focus is on statistical circular economy performance within the Lithuanian textile industry in the context of small open economies. We then present the results of the original survey of Lithuanian textile manufacturers on their priorities towards the circular economy, as well as drivers and barriers. Finally, the chapter ends with the best circular business models and practices.

Keywords Textile industry · Global trends · Circular performance · Circular patterns · Textile circular business models

5.1 Global Trends in the Textile Industry

The textile industry is one of the most essential consumer goods-based sectors and an **economically important** part of the European manufacturing industry. Based on the Euratex database (2020), the textile and clothing industry consists of 160,000 companies (9% of all European Union (EU) manufacturing companies), employs 1.5 million people (5% of all those employed in the EU manufacturing sector), and generates a turnover of €162 billion (2% of EU manufacturing turnover). The textile industry is characterized by **intense competition** that is forcing companies to look for solutions to stay competitive and operate profitably under considerable **cost and innovation pressure**. Producers located in other countries, especially in Southern Europe, Asia, and North Africa, drain market share away from mature industrial countries, not only due to the cheaper labour in these regions, but also due to their relatively low environmental and emission standards. New high-quality rivals emerge regularly, and customers become increasingly demanding (Fromhold-Eisebith et al., 2021).

The textile industry is **a diverse industry** and is characterized by **a variety of products**. The textile industry covers a range of activities from the transformation of natural fibres, such as cotton, flax, and wool, or synthetic ones like polyester and

© The Author(s), under exclusive license to Springer Nature Switzerland AG 2023
L. Dagilienė et al., *Circular Business Models in the Manufacturing Industry*, Studies in Energy, Resource and Environmental Economics,
https://doi.org/10.1007/978-3-031-28809-8_5

polyamide, into yarns and fabrics, to the production of a wide variety of products, such as fashion and clothing, home furnishings, and industrial and technical products such as ropes, nettings, parachutes, medical textiles, synthetic grass, sunblind, and smart textiles. Textile production is firmly embedded in the value chains of other sectors, supplying intermediate goods mostly to the automotive, medical technology, and aircraft and aerospace industries (Fromhold-Eisebith et al., 2021).

The textile industry **is highly globalized** with lengthy, multi-layered, geographically dispersed supply chains (Malik et al., 2021), and it lacks transparency, as there are many different economic entities performing different functions all over the world. It also involves a **very complex network of industries**, including clothing or apparel, interior textiles, and technical textiles (Franco, 2017). Typically, the textile and clothing supply chain begins in the EU or the USA, where the major brands or retailers are located, controlling almost the entire supply chain and responsible for research and development, design, marketing, distribution, and sales (Fernandez-Stark et al., 2011). Production, on the other hand, is often relocated to developing countries, mostly in Asia, where costs are lower and the environmental regulations tend to be more lax, too. There is a tendency for developed countries to focus on higher value-added activities and developing countries on labour-intensive activities. While apparel producers could reduce their costs by shifting labour-intensive processes abroad, fabric and technical textile producers are rationalized by substituting labour with capital (Fromhold-Eisebith et al., 2021), which is concentrated in more developed countries such as Germany, Italy, the UK, as well as the Netherlands, Spain, Belgium, France, the Czech Republic, Sweden, and Poland. As textile and clothing manufacturers in most developing countries do not have their own brand or distribution channel to give them direct access to the global consumer markets, they are highly dependent on the large Western retailers and/or brands. This is usually **a buyer-driven chain**, where greater bargaining power and, at the same time, change-maker leadership falls on the brands or the retailers. For example, if a brand declares that it is working on the principles of circularity, it demands the same from the manufacturer which, in turn, demands the same from their suppliers of raw materials. This puts pressure on the rest of the supply chain to follow suit and meet the quality standards or requirements set for them. This encourages the simultaneous implementation of the principles of the circular economy (CE) throughout the supply chain, which involves many and varied economic actors. The power of brands to make systemic changes throughout the supply chain is an important feature of the textile and clothing sector.

The specificity of the textile and clothing supply chain means that each country, depending on its role in the supply chain, **faces a different set of environmental and social challenges**. Most of the pressures and impacts related to textile production occur beyond the European borders, mostly in Asian countries, where the majority of production takes place. In 2017, the EU produced 7.4 kg of textiles per person, while consuming nearly 26 kg. The EU is, therefore, a net importer of textiles, mainly as finished products from Asia, and EU consumers discard about 11 kg of textiles per person per year. EU producers are dependent on the resource market as there is a lack of domestically grown natural resources such as cotton

(Fromhold-Eisebith et al., 2021). Meanwhile, the export of used clothes—mainly to Eastern European countries, Asia and Africa—is significant and increasing, while those that are not exported are mostly incinerated or landfilled in these countries (European Environment Agency, 2020). Of course, every country faces the challenges of post-consumer textile waste, as well as industrial waste.

Due to population growth, economic development, and prosperity, the demand for textile products is steadily **increasing**; however, these products are associated with **high environmental and social impacts** throughout the value chain (Lacy et al., 2020; Provin et al., 2021; Sandin & Peters, 2018). The textile industry is accused of being one of the most polluting industries, where not only the production but also the consumption of textiles produces waste (Manickam & Duraisamy, 2019). The fashion industry accounts for around 10% of global CO_2 emissions (Lacy et al., 2020). The production of textiles generates 1.2 billion tonnes of global greenhouse gas emissions annually, more than those of all international flights and maritime shipping combined (Staicu & Pop, 2018), and consumes significant volumes of natural resources, fuel, and a variety of chemicals used in processes such as spinning, bleaching, dyeing (Parisi et al., 2015), as well as producing large volumes of industrial waste. Furthermore, 20% of global industrial water pollution is attributed to textile dyeing and treatment (Lacy et al., 2020). Textile and clothing production is also very wasteful in itself, with up to 30% of textiles remaining unused (Bruneckienė et al., 2021).

According to the International Labour Organization (2021), the textile industry is under pressure to improve working conditions across the supply chain and to end the use of child labour. In addition, industrial accidents, including fatalities, occur regularly (European Environment Agency, 2020). Due to the severe negative impacts related to the textile industry, one of the main concerns is to achieve sustainability in the textile supply chain, thus mitigating greenhouse gas emissions, resource use, and the pressure on nature (Europe Environmental Agency, 2020) as well as social problems (Neto et al., 2019).

The textile and fashion industries are mainly built on a "**take, make, consume, dispose**" pattern of growth, which is exacerbated by the "buy-and-throw-away" culture of fast fashion (Ellen McArthur Foundation, 2017; Riba et al., 2020; Siderius & Poldner, 2021). This has led to a fall in prices (Koszewska, 2018) so that, between 1996 and 2018, clothing prices in the EU dropped by over 30%, relative to inflation. Economic growth now largely depends on the ongoing promotion of new products and the disposal of old ones, which were branded useless simply because the stylistic norms emphasized their obsolescence (Koszewska, 2018). Such market trends promote increased textile production, consumption, reduced lifespans, and increased levels of industrial pre- and post-consumer waste (Shirvanimoghaddam et al., 2020), which are usually sent to landfill. Ninety-two million tonnes of clothing (mostly cotton and polyester) become waste every year, and half a million tonnes of microfibres end up in the ocean every year, equal to over 50 billion plastic bottles (Lacy et al., 2020).

The textile industry is still characterized by **low recycle rates**. Only 20% of clothing waste is collected globally for reuse or recycling (Koszewska, 2018) and less than 1% is recycled at the end of use (Lacy et al., 2020). The remaining 80%

is landfilled or incinerated, which results in a great loss of energy and raw materials (Koszewska, 2018). This is due to a lack of collection systems for post-consumer textile waste, the technical features of certain types of garments (Koszewska, 2018), the complexity or impossibility of separating the fibres (Franco, 2017), the high costs associated with sorting and recycling (Riba et al., 2020) or even the absence, expense or technological risk of sorting and recycling technology. Pal et al. (2019) identify these technical barriers as **technological unreadiness**. Infrastructure issues are the most fundamental barriers that handicap circular textile innovation (Huang et al., 2021). In addition, increasing environmental taxes and competition in the sector have a direct impact on the level of implementation of greener and cleaner production technologies in the supply chain of the textile and clothing sector.

There are various factors slowing down the transformation of the textile and clothing supply chain towards a green supply chain. Complexity of green process and system design (technological barriers), lack of consumer support (market barriers), lack of support from regulatory authorities (legal barriers), and high implementation and maintenance cost (economic barriers) are the basic barriers of green textile supply chain management. Lack of green suppliers is the barrier which is influenced by most of the other barriers (Majumdar & Sinha, 2019).

Significant **changes are starting to occur** in the textile industry at unexpected speed, so at the end of the first quarter of this century, the sector will be very different from the one we know today (Gazzola et al., 2020). The most important changes affecting the textile industry are attention to sustainability and the CE; digitalization and automation of operations; development of e-commerce; fast fashion; personalization; the use of artificial intelligence in the entire supply chain; importance of social media and influencers; and a developing preference to rent clothes rather than buy them (Fromhold-Eisebith et al., 2021; Gazzola et al., 2020; Koszewska, 2018; Shirvanimoghaddama et al., 2020). Among the changes mentioned above, the attention to sustainability and the CE has undoubtedly become a fundamental driver in the development of the textile industry in recent years (Gazzola et al., 2020). Some textile companies intensively implement cleaner production practices by reducing water and electric power consumption, minimizing the volumes of residual water and gas emissions, as well as by changing to less toxic or more biodegradable products in the production processes by means of new processes or technological innovation (Neto et al., 2019). The shift in business model, accompanied by automation and internationalization of labour-intensive tasks, has helped the German textile industry to survive (Fromhold-Eisebith et al., 2021). Fashion companies redefine their business models according to the deep transformation in the lifestyles and behaviours of their final consumers (Gazzola et al., 2020). Companies are starting to change the raw materials employed in manufacturing by using: (1) materials from renewable resources, with an acquisition rate below the growth rate; (2) recycled materials, obtained from reprocessing resources that have already been incorporated into other products; and (3) revived materials, that is, those comprised of resources discarded from industrial production flows, such as agricultural waste (Provin et al., 2021). These transformations in the textile and apparel sector contribute directly to Sustainable Development Goals 9, 12, and 15.

The possibilities to recycle the textile products, the growing consumer sustainability, cooperation among companies, and legal regulation (e.g., CE Action Plan [2020]) create the conditions for **closed and open loops** in the industry. There are a number of innovations that hold promise for more effective open-loop and closed-loop recycling within the textile industry in the future (Payne, 2015; Sandin & Peters, 2018). In some cases, circularity in the textile industry is economically beneficial (Manickam & Duraisamy, 2019). However, the technical nature of some products creates the conditions for **recycling, usually downcycling, and some cases for upcycling.** According to H&M, the downcycling of natural fibres, like cotton and wool, is currently the most scalable recycling technology for post-consumer textiles, but the result is shorter fibres of a lower quality than virgin fibres. To increase their quality, recycled fibres must be blended with virgin fibres. When it comes to upcycling, only polyester and certain nylons can currently be reprocessed. However, technological developments in the recycling, reuse, or repurposing of textile waste are being made all the time, and recycled fibres could be just around the corner (Manickam & Duraisamy, 2019). Recycled textiles could be used in various industries and products (Shirvanimoghaddam et al., 2020): the building industry and the construction sector; the paper industry; carpets; agriculture; automobiles; toys; as well as the textile and fashion industry themselves. The **displacement effect** is also seen in the textile and apparel industry, related to both textiles and garments that will not be bought or produced as a result of efficient use of existing items (Manickam & Duraisamy, 2019). The various cloth rent services, second-hand shops have been popular for many years, and are now being joined by companies renting clothing and platforms allowing consumers to sell their unwanted clothing.

Despite the markedly positive developments in the textile and clothing sector, and the fact that the textile and clothing sector is **not technically constrained to be circular**, this sector still faces significant challenges that need to be overcome in order to ensure a rapid and systematic transformation of its territory, both inside and beyond the EU boundaries.

The textile supply chain **lacks a life-cycle approach** in that product design and sourcing lack focus on the environmental footprint, longevity, and recyclability; producers are mostly oriented towards efficiency; there is limited waste collection and reverse logistics infrastructure; and consumers fail to make an impact through their purchasing choices. Environmental costs (externalities) are not considered (Huang et al., 2021), and supply chain coordination mechanisms are a necessity to transition towards a CE (Fischer & Pascucci, 2017). The main issue is the uncertainty regarding previously used materials in terms of quality, price, and availability (Franco, 2017), leading to supply chain ineffectiveness (Pal et al., 2019). Nimbalker et al. (2015) analysed more than 200 fashion brands selling clothing in the Australian market, and found that 75% of them did not know where the raw materials, including fabrics, zippers, and threads, came from. Neither consumers nor employees knew how the value chain works, from fibre production to the final product, nor did they know what would happen to the clothes after they were thrown away. A weak circular ecosystem in the textile and apparel sector in Romania is determined by poor interactions among the stakeholders. There is a low visibility of what social entrepreneurship stands for in this industry, and where they are situated in the value chain (Staicu & Pop, 2018).

Given that 80% of product environmental impacts are determined at the design stage, mandatory **minimum eco-design** requirements for textiles, supported by robust technical standards, is an essential step to begin the transformation of the textile sector towards circularity. According to Ertz et al. (2019), if the use of clothes was extended, on average, by nine months, the overall footprint could be reduced by 20–30%. Entities in different countries have issued "green labels" and other schemes for certification of sustainable textiles; however, they are far from able to transform the current linear fast fashion model into a circular one. An analysis by Environmental Coalition on Standards (ECOS) (2021) of current certification schemes and reports shows that their requirements overlook reuse and repair. They are ineffective mainly because they lack requirements for a minimum desired lifespan of products; lack definitions of what "high-quality fabrics" are; contain only limited references to recycled or natural fibre content of fabrics; only marginally address chemical additives and material composition; and include no methods to address the problem of the shedding of microplastics by synthetic fibres.

Designers and engineers face a real challenge in **combining optimal recycling options with product desirability**, because designing sustainable, fully recyclable products that no one wants would be pointless (Koszewska, 2018). Since the sustainability of textiles is a relatively recent concern for mainstream firms, the range of green component parts presently available to manufacturers is extremely low (Franco, 2017). Recycled textiles are usually more expensive and, in some cases, of lower quality compared to virgin textiles. They are mostly sorted manually, which is expensive and slow, and it is impossible to automate, which would be required to process huge volumes of materials (Riba et al., 2020). The scale of the recycling industry is smaller than that of the primary raw material industry, making secondary raw materials more expensive than newly produced textiles (Euratex, 2017). It is difficult to reconcile the high quality, complexity, or technical requirements of a product with the use of secondary raw materials. Recycled cotton, for example, has shorter fibres and is of lower quality (Ütebay et al., 2019), which can shorten the useful life of a product, so it is thrown away quicker. Complexity in basic materials and component parts, complexity in product architecture, and complexity in product functionality and aesthetics may limit the range of circular products (Franco, 2017).

The textile industry faces **severe image problems**. The wider public is neither aware of the successful restructuring of the industry, nor the rising innovative drive towards high-quality products, nor the special role in value chains of various other sectors. The image problem entails demographics of industry employees: 52% them in Germany are at least 50 years old, compared to only 37% in all industries. Hence, all firms risk losing a great deal of people-bound know-how in the next decade (Fromhold-Eisebith et al., 2021).

The current market still **does not accept CE textile products** (Pal et al., 2019). The growing consumer willingness to pay more for a "sustainable or green" product is motivating companies to adopt the principles of a CE, but the critical mass that would be willing to pay more is still lacking. In a survey, 55% of global Internet users from 60 countries indicated that they are willing to pay more for products and services that commit to having a positive social and environmental impact, though this overall number hides regional differences; 40% in Europe, 42% in North America, 63% in Latin America, Central, and East Asia (Nielsen, 2014). In Lithuania, sustainability is quite important to local consumers, but it is still overshadowed by price; only 25% of all residents are willing to pay more for a sustainable product (Bruneckienė et al., 2021). Although there is a widespread perception that demand for sustainable products, in general, is on the rise, the efforts of some proactive firms have not scaled up as much as expected (Franco, 2017).

Finally, the cost of textile repairs is high due to the need for manual labour, and repair prices sometimes exceed the price of a new product, which encourages the purchase of new products.

Key Barriers to a Circular Textile Industry:

- Product design and materials-related (supply):
  - Product-specific requirements.
  - Lack of recycled textile solutions.
  - Lack of industrial waste solutions.
  - Intensive natural resources, energy, and water use.
  - Use of toxic chemicals.
- Supply chain-related (supply):
  - Lack of life-cycle approach in the whole textile supply chain.
  - Severe industry image problems.
  - Limited post-use waste collection and reverse logistics infrastructure.
  - Technological unreadiness for recycling.
  - Lack of high-quality recycled materials.
  - Price of recycled materials higher than virgin materials.
  - High cost of repairs.
- Environmental regulation:

  No mandatory eco-design requirements.
- Consumer-related (demand):
  - Demand for cheaper and new products (fast fashion).
  - Insufficient demand for circular textile products.
  - Poor consumer awareness about responsible consumption ("buy-and-throw-away" culture).

Opportunities for a Circular Textile Industry

Eco-design and novel business models, as well as a focus on cleaner production, are the most commonly used CE strategies for textile manufacturers (Huang et al., 2021). However, looking through the whole textile industry, strategies related to textile recycling technologies and infrastructure, as well as textile supply chain platforms are developing rapidly (Huang et al., 2021; Lacy et al., 2020) (Table 5.1).

Eco-efficiency through energy and material optimization is quite characteristic of the EU textile industry. From the CE point of view, the textile industry still lacks eco-design solutions and novel business models orientated to product life-cycle extension. The technological and realization possibilities of repurposing textile waste into new

Table 5.1 Opportunities for a circular textile industry

Strategy Currently dominates—eco-efficiency (narrow the loops)	– Direct to consumer (D2C) models (Lacy et al., 2020) – Emerging technologies for process innovation and efficiency (e.g., digital tracking of garments) (Lacy et al., 2020) – Eco-textile clusters and collaborative R&D alliances or manufacturing unions (Huang et al., 2021) – Industrial symbiosis (Ellen McArthur Foundation, 2017) – Application of recycled textiles in various industries and products (Shirvanimoghaddam et al., 2020) – Information exchange platforms for textile supply chain networking (Huang et al., 2021)
Product design and materials	– Circular materials that use waste as raw inputs (Lacy et al., 2020) – Reusable and recyclable products (Shirvanimoghaddam et al., 2020) – Fully biodegradable textiles (Shirvanimoghaddam et al., 2020) – Increase product quality and functionality (smart textile)
Cleaner production	– Intelligent and circular operations that reduce waste in production (Lacy et al., 2020) – Reduce the energy consumption in the manufacturing process (Shirvanimoghaddam et al., 2020) – Decrease the use of natural resources and materials (Shirvanimoghaddam et al., 2020) – Use renewable resources and green energy
Usage and product life-cycle extension	– Models for fractional ownership, rental, subscription, and resale that increase use and extend clothing life (Lacy et al., 2020) – Models for reinventing the product's purpose: reuse, including repair and refurbishment (Keßler et al., 2021) – Good maintenance of the product – Repair services or development of do-it-yourself repairs
Waste management	– Breakthroughs in textile recycling technologies and innovations in materials science (Lacy et al., 2020) – Energy recovery (heat or electricity) via incineration (Shirvanimoghaddam et al., 2020) while there is technological unreadiness for recycling

products have not yet been sufficiently explored. According to Lacy et al. (2020), true circularity in the textile industry demands greater pull from consumers and an increased push from regulators to incentivize brands to work with suppliers to make fundamental changes to their business models. To achieve a real shift in the textile and apparel sector, the CE would demand unprecedented levels of alignment in terms of the need for change and collaboration. A system-level change approach is required, including rallying key industry players to set ambitious joint commitments, kick-starting cross-value chain demonstrator projects, and orchestrating complementary initiatives (Manickam & Duraisamy, 2019).

5.2 Circular Performance of the Lithuanian Textile Industry

The analysis of the CE indicators of the textile sector is done by comparing macroeconomic indicators that could help to evaluate circularity. Five areas are distinguished to present the results, which can be found in the methodology section (see Chapter 3).

The textile industry carries the Nomenclature of Economic Activities (NACE) classification code C13. Due to the limited statistical information about some specific indicators of the textile industry, we take aggregated information of the C13–C15 sectors, where C14 represents the manufacture of wearing apparel, and C15 is the manufacture of leather and related products.

Vision and strategy. Vision and strategy reveal the motivation of textile companies to implement environmental innovations. We select two indicators for analysis: environmental protection expenditure and environmental protection investment.

The results of the analysis show that the total amount of environmental protection expenditure varies significantly in the period 2014–2018. As presented in Fig. 5.1, protection expenditure on ambient air and climate, and on waste management, is growing steadily. The amount of expenditure for waste-water management accounts for 62–72% of total expenditures in 2014–2016, but decreased to 29–39% of total expenditures in 2017–2018. Expenditure on other environmental protection activities is very volatile throughout the period. Environmental protection investment remains very low, from 0 to 0.37% of total investment, showing that the motivation of Lithuanian textile manufacturers (C13) to implement environmental innovations is still very weak. The highest amount of environmental protection investment is found in 2016 (€77,600) but decreased to zero in 2018. The total amount of environmental protection investment is targeted at environmental protection activities, yet there is no investment in environmentally friendly production processes.

According to the Eurostat database, Belgium, the Netherlands, Austria, and Slovenia are the countries investing most heavily among the SOEs, while the Lithuanian textile industry (C13) are modest investors in pollution control.

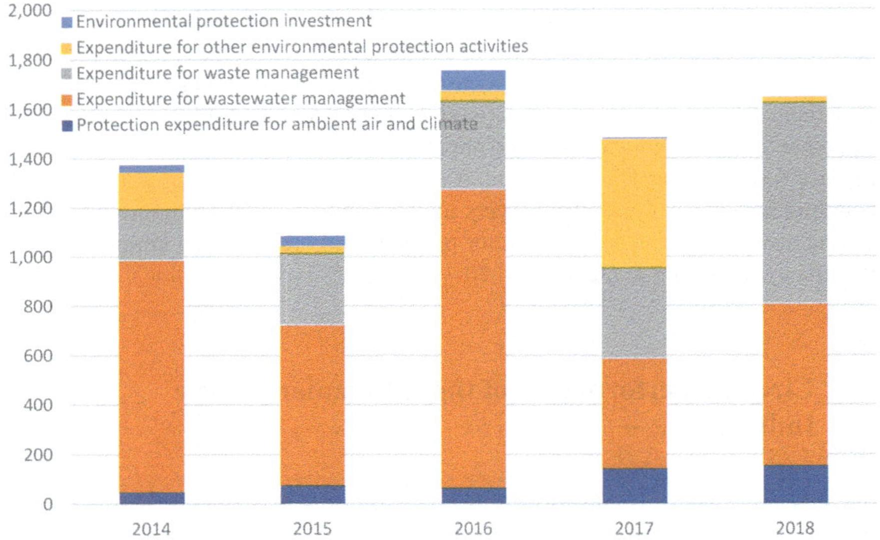

Fig. 5.1 Environmental expenditure and investment in equipment and plant for pollution control of the Lithuanian textile sector (C13) in 2014–2018 (€'000)

Raw materials, secondary raw materials, and eco-design. The usage and complexity of raw materials are best described by the input structure in the Lithuanian C13–15 sectors, though there is limited data to help us analyse the use of secondary raw materials in particular industries, as well as eco-design changes. However, eco-design structure is partly reflected by input complexity.

As presented in Fig. 5.2, the value-added at basic prices has more than half of the C13–15 sector input. While analysing the structure of value-added in different economic sectors, such a high rate of value-added is common in the service sector in Lithuania and for IT products. About one-fifth of the input is used to purchase products from other companies in the same sector. Expenses for both wholesale and retail account for a relatively large share of the sector's input, at 9%.

Products from the chemical and pharmaceutical industries account for 3%, whereas energy, water, and environmental services only account for 1% of the input structure. Despite that, from the environmental point of view, it is important to evaluate structural changes in water and energy usage as a part of cleaner production.

Cleaner production. While analysing the Lithuanian textile, wearing apparel, leather, and related products (C13–15) industry, the indicators of energy and emissions related to cleaner production were selected for review.

According to Fig. 5.3, CO_2 emissions grew slightly from 2014 and reached 31,922 tonnes generated in 2018, or 11.42 kg per capita, whereas in other SOEs, CO_2 emissions per capita were almost constant, or decreasing, and most rapidly in Estonia, Sweden, and Malta.

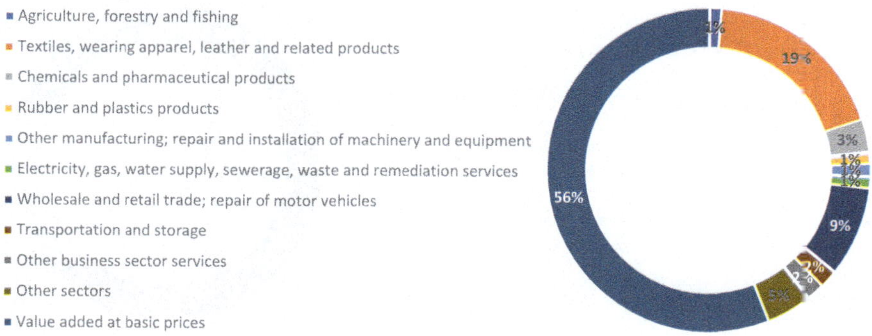

Fig. 5.2 Input structure of the C13–15 sectors in Lithuania

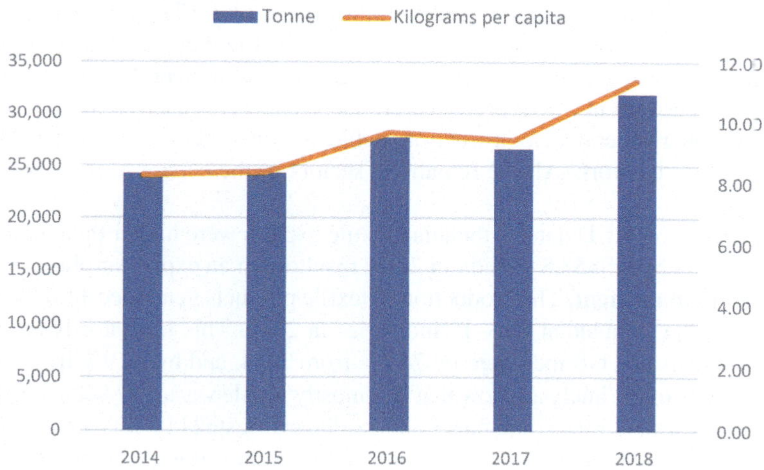

Fig. 5.3 CO_2 emissions of the C13–15 sectors in Lithuania

The analysis of energy use shows the increasing demand for energy in the Lithuanian textile, wearing apparel, leather and related products sector. The average growth in energy use was 4.6% from 2014 to 2018. In 2018, energy was consumed mainly from natural gas (39.5%) and electricity (35.4%). A further 10% is transport diesel, and heating takes up 7% of the energy picture. All these are similar to other SOEs, though diesel use is higher than average, as it is in Cyprus and Slovenia. Ireland and Malta have completely different structures; in Malta, electricity use is 98.4%, and in Ireland, 75.4% of energy is from electricity, and 7.6% is from natural gas.

Consumption, reuse, repair. The consumption analysis is done by analysing output measures in 2015 from the OECD database. The results show that the main consumers of Lithuanian textile, wearing apparel, leather, and related products (C13–15) were households (52%) (see Fig. 5.4).

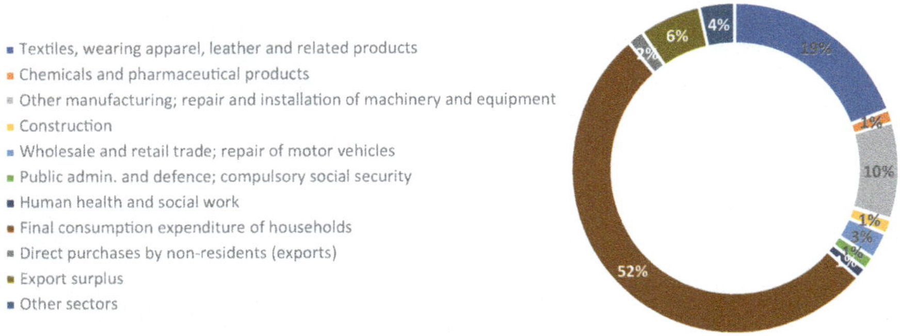

Fig. 5.4 Use structure of the output of the C13–15 sectors in Lithuania in 2015

About 19% of the output produced by Lithuanian C13–C15 sectors is used within the same industry, whereas 10% of production goes to other manufacturing areas, including the repair and installation of machinery and equipment. The wholesale and retail sectors use about 3% of produced products, and 1% is used by sectors such as chemicals, pharmaceutical, construction, public administration and defence, human health, and social work. All the remaining sectors of the economy consume about 4%.

According to OECD data, Lithuanian textile exports were higher than imports of these products by US$58.8 million in 2015, resulting in an export surplus of 6%.

Waste management. The production of textile products generated 11,078 tonnes of waste in the Lithuanian C13–15 industries in 2018. This indicator is measured every two years and has increased by 74.1% from 2014, and by 34.9% from 2016.

The results of the analysis show that it is mostly textile waste (47.9%), household and similar waste (13.9%), and paper and cardboard waste (11.3%) (see Fig. 5.5).

A comparison of the structure of waste generated in Lithuania with other SOEs shows that only Finland has a higher share of textile waste (53%). Denmark, Luxembourg, and Malta appear to have zero textile waste from the industry, but it is probably included in other classification fields, based on the fact that, in Malta, 98% of the waste stream is classified as household and similar wastes.

5.3 Circular Patterns of Lithuanian Textile Manufacturing Companies

The Lithuanian textile industry is increasingly focusing on **technological progress** and **material efficiency** as means to reduce costs and increase productivity, as most manufacturers are working for prominent foreign brands. The Lithuanian clothing and textile industries export about 85% of production (in some companies it's as high as 95–100%). Manufacturers focus on technological progress, innovation, and adaptation which, together with the long-term competence of employees, enable them

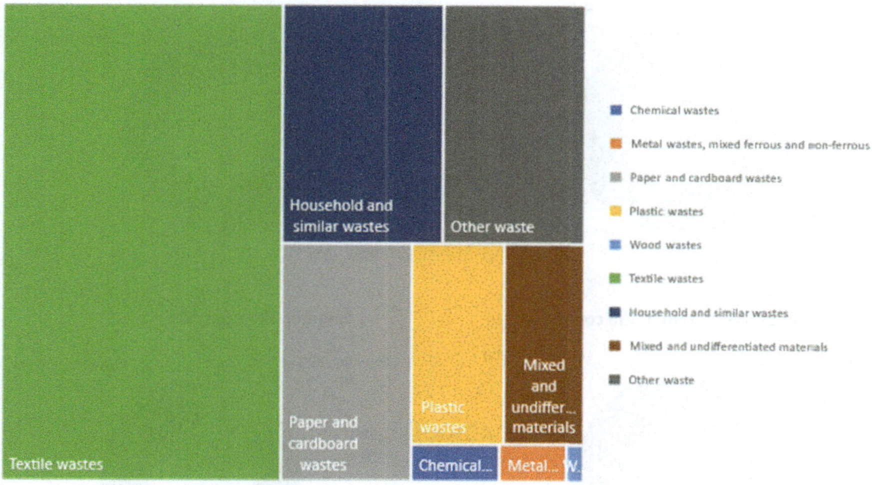

Fig. 5.5 The structure of generated waste from the C13–15 sectors in Lithuania in 2018

to focus on higher added value, i.e., more expensive and technologically sophisticated products. The textile and clothing companies themselves see their main competitive advantages arising from quality, innovation, technology, employee competence, and a world-class reputation.

In order to explain CE specifically within the Lithuanian textile industry, 30 textile companies were surveyed, mainly operating in both international and national markets. The survey was dominated by large companies in terms of both number of employees and revenues (see Fig. 5.6). It is noticeable that 60% of the textile companies that participated in the survey do not invest in green technologies or have no data on such investments. On the other hand, we see that at least 30% of them invest up to 10% in green technologies.

The surveyed textile manufacturers prioritize the efficient use of resources (narrowing the loop strategy) that could be achieved mainly by investment in digital technologies, technological innovations (mainly adoption), and the use of regenerative resources (mostly renewable energy) (see Fig. 5.7). The visions and strategies with regard to CE are mainly oriented towards production and technological innovations, and investment in environmental technologies are not among the key strategic priorities.

The textile companies mainly focus on the **efficient use of raw materials and supplies,** which enables more efficient production processes, and minimal quantities of industrial waste. The surveyed companies look positively at the replacement of primary raw materials with secondary replacements, product life extension, and the creation of environmental values for suppliers to meet the eco-design challenges. However, the main challenge arises from the peculiarities of subcontracted manufacturing: the contractor (a brand name) is responsible for product design and marketing,

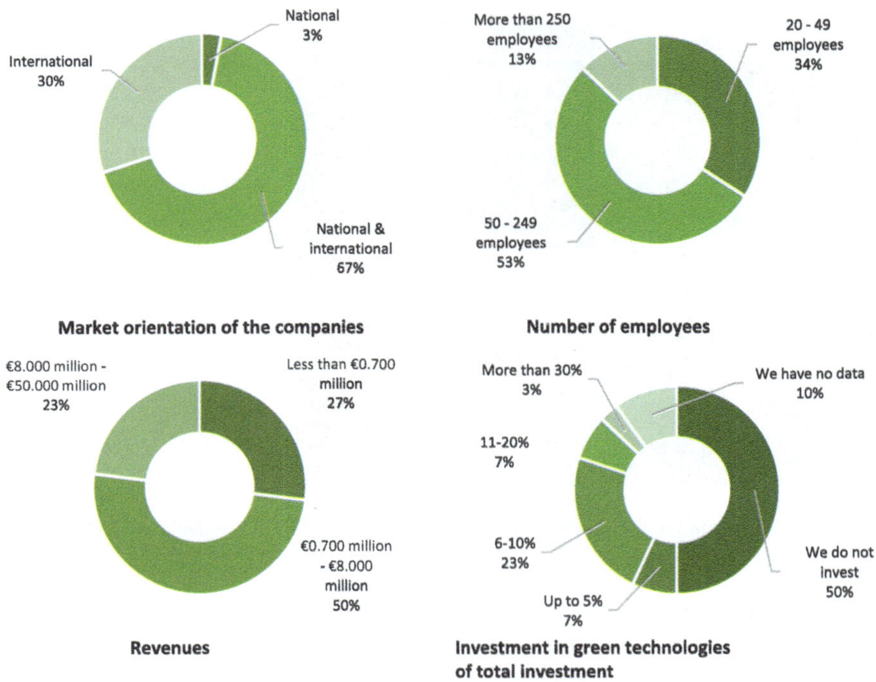

Fig. 5.6 Surveyed textile companies' characteristics (2019)

and specifies the product requirements, which usually call for the use of virgin materials. There are also technical challenges around replacing virgin raw material with a recycled version, and it is unlikely that a garment can be made to high-quality specifications using secondary raw material. Product life extension is related to quality: if the product is high quality, it can be used for longer and the repair of such products may be cheaper than buying a new one.

Textile companies see the **efficient use of energy** as an important issue for CE, which is part of their focus on, and investment in, innovations and processes for cleaner production. Sustainable packaging still lacks attention from textile manufacturers; however, there is an increase in the use of recyclable and recycled packaging. Basically, companies are still faced with serious challenges regarding cleaner production, which shows that there are moves towards cleaner production and tangible progress is visible. In addition, the companies do not tend to measure their negative environmental impacts, such as CO_2 emissions.

Lithuanian textile manufacturing companies, most of which are exporters and contractual manufacturers, are part of a global (usually European) value chain and are under pressure from environmental requirements regarding product quality and manufacturing processes by the contractor (Brand Name) and the specific regulations in each of their export markets. For example, the Scandinavian markets are very oriented towards sustainability. Textile companies strive to **create environmental**

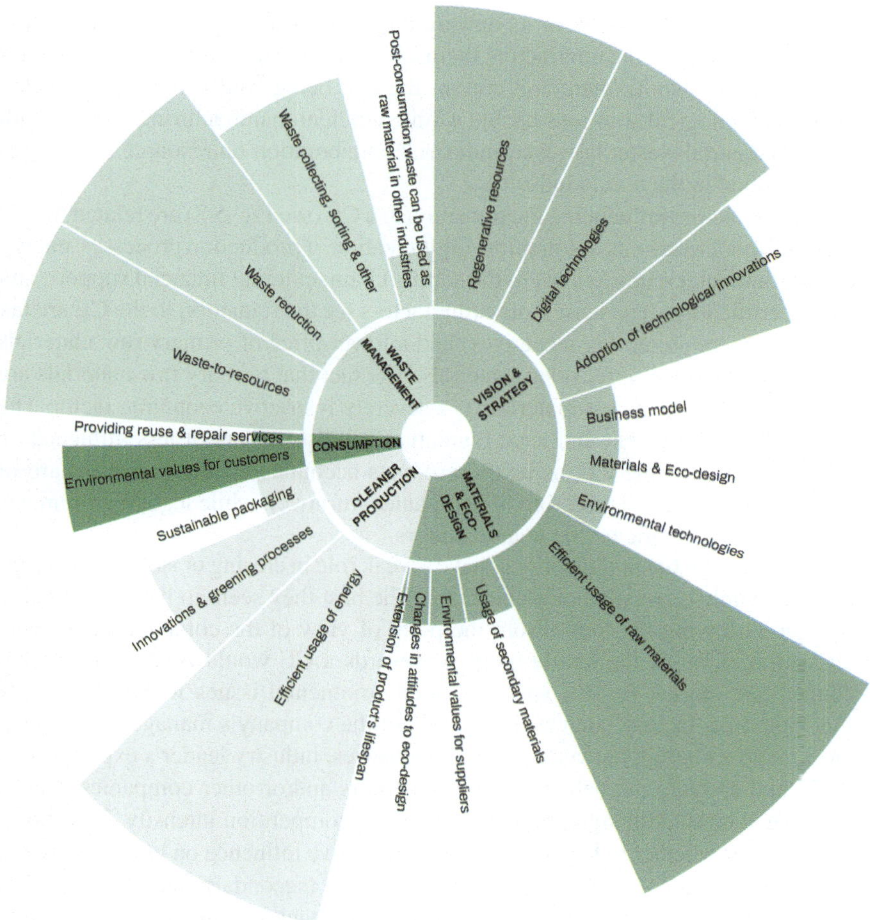

Fig. 5.7 The portfolio of relevant patterns of the CE in Lithuanian textile companies

values for customers (mainly by stressing the use of ecological and natural fabrics such as linen, cotton, bamboo, and wool, and product durability), but the challenge is to meet these requirements at a price that is acceptable to the end user. Given that manufacturers are specialized in the production process, additional services (such as repairs) are usually in the future plans. Eco-design is still challenging for textile companies and is not yet popularly employed to gain a competitive advantage.

The manufacturer is in the middle of the value chain and does not have a connection with the products at the end of their life. They do not face waste management challenges within the company as most of them collect, sort, and transfer to waste management companies but, from the perspective of the life-cycle approach, there are significant national challenges around how to best handle industrial waste, as well as post-use textile waste. The manufacturer transfers its industrial waste to the waste manager, who is responsible for its onward disposal. In some rare cases, the industrial waste is taken by the contractors themselves, who extract from its pure natural material, namely wool, linen, and cotton, the rest being sold to a waste recycler. Modern technological solutions enable a quite efficient manufacturing process with minimal industrial waste; however, industrial collaboration on resource recovery is weakly applied in the textile industry.

The main factors influencing the transition to a CE (see Fig. 5.8) are related to efficiency and modernization, automation, digitalization of production processes, energy use, environmental requirements in the supply chain, external financial support, and product certification. The least motivating factors for the transition to the CE are tax policy (i.e., there are no tax incentives) and a lower price of primary raw materials compared to the price of recycled materials. The fact that primary raw materials are often cheaper than recycled materials is a severely restrictive economic factor. The green public procurement and legal regulation are also factors of less influence on a transition towards the CE, as textile products account for only a small share of public procurement, and therefore of companies' turnover, while legal requirements are already strict for the textile manufacturers.

In summary, textile manufacturers have a weak role in closing or slowing the loops across the whole ecosystem or value chain. The best they seem to have achieved to date is in narrowing the loop. From the point of view of the companies surveyed, the transformation of the textile industry towards a CE would be driven by technological and market factors, specifically environmental issues within the supply chain. Cognitive factors, such as the attitude of the company's management, access to information, sharing between different industries, industry leader's experience in the CE, and copying the behaviour of competitors and/or other companies, have a slightly smaller but still significant impact due to competition intensity. The choice of the end user whether to buy, however, has a decisive influence on brand behaviour and, at the same time, on the manufacturer's orders (secondary demand). The fact that the textile manufacturer does not have direct contact with the final user has less direct influence on the manufacturer transformation towards CE, but the consumer impact is reflected in the supply chain requirements.

5.4 Best Practices of Textile Circular Business Models

Statistical analysis and the survey results indicate that business models embedded in the Lithuanian textile industry (manufacturers) are mostly orientated to narrow the flows, according to Bocken et al. (2016), which are also common in a linear economy. Technological unreadiness for recycling is also a feature in Lithuania: post-use waste collection infrastructure is underdeveloped and there is a lack of recycling technologies. The most common model for the implementation of a circular business model, according to Geissdoerfer et al. (2020), is the diversification of the existing model into a circular one, so that the main business model remains, supplemented by a circular business model. From an ecosystem-wide perspective, circular business models are

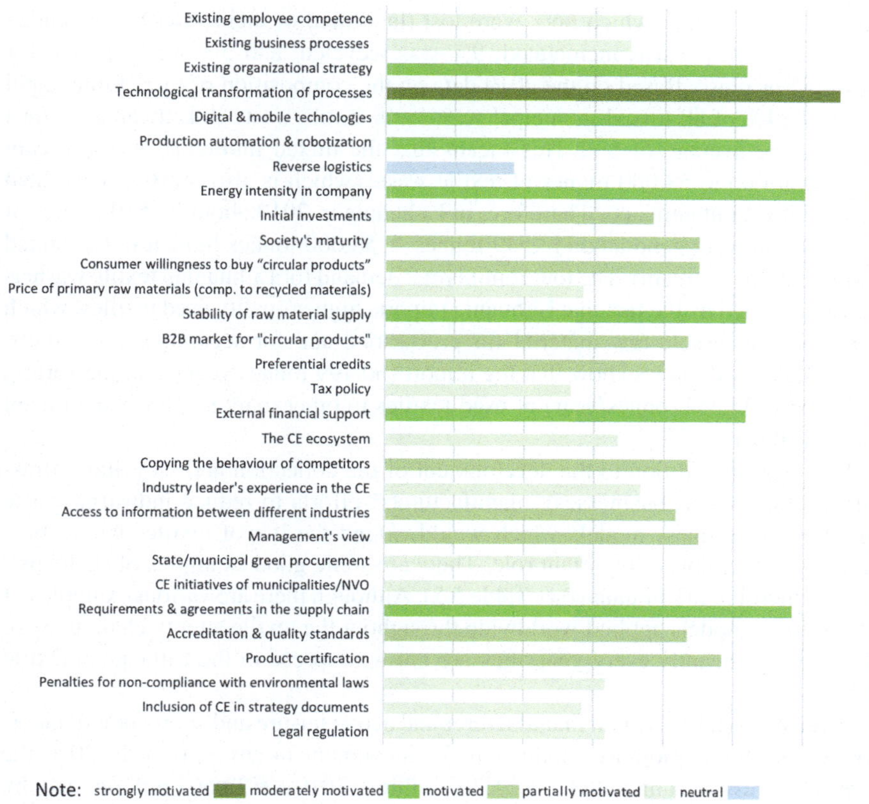

Fig. 5.8 Factors influencing the textile industry transition to the CE

patchily adopted, dominating a few individual firms that then fail to collaborate. Manufacturing companies treat the CE business model as experimental. There is more active cooperation between producers and the remaining supply participants in the production of waste natural and homogeneous fibres (linen, cotton, wool) production than there is in other production waste (synthetic, composite), which is still dominated by a linear supply chain, where waste is mostly incinerated.

For the circular textile industry, it is important to analyse the entire supply chain, not only the manufacturers. The analysis of textile waste streams allows us to state that, up to now, the Lithuanian goal is aligned with the EU target for 2025, which is to collect textiles separately so that they do not enter the mixed municipal waste stream. This means that, throughout the supply chain, the largest initiatives (in terms of flow volumes) are focused on collection infrastructure development, paid for with public finance. However, technological unreadiness for recycling means that the dominant (in terms of waste volume) CE initiative in the textile supply chain is lowest in the waste hierarchy pyramid, namely recovery and sub-optimal disposal options. According to official statistics, 13,549 tonnes of textile waste were generated in

Lithuania in 2019, of which 66% were lost (landfilled or incinerated); 44% ended up in landfill; 31% was incinerated; 9% was recycled; and 5% was exported for recycling or reuse. Based on the 2019 data on the composition of mixed municipal waste, 7.84% of all mixed municipal waste was textile waste in Lithuania, against an EU-wide average of 5%. This means that the mixed municipal waste stream can contain up to 58,000 tonnes of textile waste, which is also mostly incinerated because it is contaminated. Therefore, in Lithuania in 2019 about 71,549 tonnes of textile waste were generated (13,549 tonnes + 58,000 tonnes hidden in the mixed municipal waste stream). The low commercial demand for Lithuanian textile waste is also determined by the fact that Lithuania imports higher quality used textiles, which is a more favourable raw material for processors, and for secondary use outlets. Lithuanian textile flows show that the import (60,499 tonnes/year), and the sorting and export (36,354 tonnes/year) of used textiles to other markets play a significant role in Lithuania.

However, in addition to the development of the collection and recycling infrastructure (as well as businesses), manufacturers' efforts to reduce industrial waste and develop business models which would extend the life of textiles before they become waste play an important role. There are some good examples of such businesses emerging in Lithuania (see Table 5.2). Although there are various examples of CE business models applied worldwide throughout the textile supply chain that are growing significantly every year, they are not widespread in the Lithuanian textile industry.

Audimas is a Lithuanian manufacturer and active leisure and sports brand, incorporated in 1997. Audimas' clothing is for movement in any season. In 2020 the company's revenue amounted to €21.263 million (2019—€23.667 million) and, by the end of 2021, the company had 367 employees. Around 30% of their revenue is generated in their domestic Lithuanian market, and the other 70% from exports, mainly to Sweden, Norway, Switzerland, Italy, and Germany.

Vision and strategy. Their main competitive advantage is quality, innovation, technology, employee experience, and social and environmental responsibility. From the middle of 2021, the reconstruction of the management began, where production and trade activities were separated, and a new real estate management company was established. The outsourced business will be conducted by Audimas Supply, and the brand business will be conducted by Audimas Brand. Sustainability as a company's priority is established more than 10 years.

Materials and eco-design. The company focus is on quality products made of durable and non-crease fabric, with the functional characteristics of sports clothing, and are attractive and stylish. To ensure functionality, the company use the most advanced fabric printing or seamless technologies that make them suitable to wear under various conditions. One of the collections—"Conscious"—is environmentally friendly as it combines experimental eco-design with sustainable production techniques using recycled materials.

Cleaner production. Old production facilities have been replaced by more efficient ones, consuming less electricity and being more efficient, as well as a number of energy-saving solutions.

Table 5.2 Lithuanian sustainable textile cases

Case company	Product features	Business model	CE aspects
Manufacturers and brand names			
Audimas[1] Sports and leisure clothing	Durability Functionality	Efficient use of resources (narrow the loops) Experimental eco-design ("Conscious" sustainable collection) High-quality products Cooperation with TEXTALE	– Some products are made from recycled polyester material – The energy used to produce the products is from renewable sources – Packaging and labels recycled – The water is purified and reused – The used and unworn Audimas clothes are collected from customers in the stores and send to TEXTALE
Utenos trikotažas[2] Casual wear, jerseys, and underwear	Durability Functionality	Efficient use of resources (narrow the loops) Experimental Eco-design (sustainable collection) High-quality products	– Compliance with Greenpeace-approved textile production standards – Orientation towards natural, naturally degradable organic fibres that do not have a negative impact on the environment – Collection from industrial leftovers

(continued)

[1] Audimas. https://www.audimas.com/about-us/about/

[2] Utenos trikotažas. https://www.ut.lt/en/

Table 5.2 (continued)

Case company	Product features	Business model	CE aspects
Brand names			
Ūkai[3] Socks (also, scarves, beanies)	Durability Functionality (long-lasting comfort and freshness)	Efficient use of resources (narrow the loops) Eco-design (full) High-quality products Networking Social impact (inside, outside)	– Sustainability requirements for suppliers – Eco-packaging, green delivery – The use of recycled materials – The products are recyclable – Collaboration with Plastic Bank and "Kickstarter" – Decent workplaces – Sustainable values of the buyer
Digital sharing platforms			
Vinted[4] Online marketplace for sell/purchase/exchange items	Convenience	Access model Social impact (inside, outside)	– Technological conditions for sale—purchase of used textiles – Sustainable office interior

(continued)

[3] Ūkai. https://www.ukai.eu/sustainability/we-are-more-than-sustainable-socks/

[4] Vinted. https://www.vinted.lt/how_it_works.

Table 5.2 (continued)

Case company	Product features	Business model	CE aspects
Digital sharing platforms + physical swap places			
Mamų mugė and MAINAI[5] A technological mechanism that allows trading days to be organized on the basis of a temporary commission	Convenience	Access model Social impact (outside)	– Technological conditions and physical places to sell—to buy used textiles – Donation and charity, volunteering
Resursai tvariai plėtrai (social business TEXTALE)[6] Platform and network	Complexity	Access model Classic long-life model Social impact (outside)	– Sharing platforms (online resale platform, physical store, repair studio (competencies) – Upcycling – Collection, sorting, preparing for reuse, recreating, and recycle – Workshop studio/repair cafe – Social inclusion and volunteer – Community education for sustainability – Expertise, consultancy activities, advocacy – Partnership for student internship

[5] MAINAI. https://www.mainai.eu/.

[6] TEXTALE. https://textale.lt/wp-content/uploads/2021/03/10.png.

a. In 2013, two solar power plants were installed on the roof of the production units, and they reached payback in 2019. They have so far generated more than 380,000 kWh of electricity. In addition, the company purchases the other necessary energy from an independent electricity supplier, which guarantees the supply of exclusively green electricity.
b. Old light sources were replaced with LED bulbs. Specifically, 65-watt lamps were replaced with 28-watt LEDs and, by 2019, about 580 lamps and more than 280 luminaires had been renewed, saving the company more than €11,000 in two years. The changes also helped to avoid the additional costs of maintaining the conventional lamps. The company's goal is to replace every light system with LED, together with the implementation of IT solutions for energy-saving in various areas. An energy audit confirmed the savings and motivated the company to focus even more on environmentally friendly solutions.

Furthermore, the company was awarded ISO 9001 in 2001 and is currently implementing the ISO14001 environmental standard. It also applies the REACH regulations in its activities.

When the branded products are sold, mainly in Lithuanian stores, recycled plastic packaging is used. Paper packaging and less packaging, in general, are also encouraged. Large boxes are used for export customers, while small boxes are used as little as possible.

Waste management. The company sorts industrial waste, based on technical specifics and sorting possibilities, and business or operating waste, such as paper and plastic.

Utenos trikotažas is the Lithuanian manufacturer whose core B2B activity provides a full production cycle, from product design to finished products. The Utenos trikotažas factory started operating in 1967 and currently operates two in-house fashion brands, offering innovative underwear and jersey made-for-all clothing collections. The "UTENOS" brand stands for comfortable and quality casual wear for the entire family, whereas "ABOUT" presents innovative jersey underwear and leisure clothing.

Vision and strategy. Environmental and social responsibility commitments cover all areas of Utenos trikotažas' production and operations, from organically farmed natural fibres, the minimal use of chemicals in production, to fair pay for employees and absolute transparency in their production processes.

Materials and eco-design. Since 2012, the company's priority has been to use natural, naturally degradable, environmentally friendly organic fibres. One of the company's latest innovations is a material made with soybean fibre, which is produced using soybean husks and food industry waste. No raw materials are especially grown for the production of this part of the yarn. Another innovation is a material using mint fibre, which is also environmentally friendly. The ABOUT brand has been supplemented with a new line of clothing made from industrial textile leftovers.

Cleaner production. In 2017, Utenos trikotažas became the first company in Lithuania to officially join the Detox campaign by Greenpeace and, in 2020 and 2021, it was the first and only company in the world to work entirely according to the stringent requirements of the standard, and the only Greenpeace textile production partner on a global scale. The Greenpeace Global Textile Procurement Standard covers a wide range of environmental and social responsibility requirements which apply throughout the production process, from naturally grown fibres, the use of chemicals in production and their environmental impact, and the characteristics of the garment, to fair remuneration and complete transparency of the production process. This is ensured through complex certification tools and testing throughout the production process.

Waste management. The company sorts industrial waste, based on technical specifics and sorting possibilities, and business or operating waste, such as paper and plastic.

Ūkai is a relatively new socks brand, which uses yarns made from recycled plastic bottles to make socks.

Vision and strategy. The brand is collaborating with Plastic Bank[7] by helping to recycle 50 plastic bottles from each pair of socks made. Brands such as "Henkel", "IDW", "Logitech", and "Marks & Spencer" work with this organization. The Kickstarter crowdfunding platform was chosen to finance the Ūkai business model. Right now, Ūkai is working with scientists in order to make other products from socks at the end of their useful life. In addition, Ūkai is planning to make shoes from recycled materials, to have collaborations with water sports teams and museums, to participate in eco events, and to educate. In terms of a decent workplace, employees are valued, are safe, and are paid fair salaries.

Materials and eco-design. The focus is on minimal and aesthetic design. The plastic bottle becomes recycled plastic yarns and is part of the sock's material. It goes together with upcycled cotton, organic cotton, polyamide, and elastane. The socks are recyclable.

Cleaner production. The recycled plastic bottle yarns are made into fabric without the use of water or chemicals, and in a way that reduces their CO_2 emissions and energy use. Polyethylene terephthalate (PET) yarns are made at a factory that is trusted worldwide and are certificated to meet the Global Recycled Standard (GRS), the Global Compact, and OEKO-TEX Standard 100. All packaging, postcards, labels, and other details are made from recycled materials. The standard shipping is sustainable, too, rather than using express shipping.

Waste management. The company sorts industrial waste, based on technical specifics and sorting possibilities, and business or operating waste, such as paper and plastic.

Vinted is the first Lithuanian unicorn and the largest online international C2C marketplace in Europe, dedicated to second-hand fashion. Vinted grew from a local website into a mobile-first community of 45+ million people in 15 markets (Vinted, 2021). On December 31, 2021, the company employed 844 people and was seeking a €250 million investment.

[7] Plastic Bank® empowers the regenerative society. They build ethical recycling ecosystems in coastal communities, and reprocess the materials for reintroduction into the global supply chain as Social Plastic®.

Sharing platforms (e-platforms). The main idea of Vinted is to help people sell used clothes in the easiest possible way and, at the same time, to find clothes for themselves without falling into the fast fashion trap. Every second, Vinted members list clothes, which they sell, buy, or exchange with each other. The company's operations are based on a simple operating model and, since Vinted has no sales taxes, the seller is left with the full amount from the transaction.

> We are approaching an inflection point in the market for second-hand fashion; consumers around the world are becoming increasingly conscious of their buying choices. We're grateful to our new and existing backers who believe in our mission to make second-hand the first choice worldwide. Today's investment is an endorsement of the future market opportunity and of our approach to maximise value generation for our members. —Thomas Plantenga, CEO at Vinted.[8]

The company's office uses second-hand furniture and the interior uses only durable, natural materials that can be renewed over time, such as real wood floors, metal industrial stairs, carpets made from recycled fibres, and unpainted walls.

Mamų mugė (The Mothers' Fair) is a social project that unites around 20,000 families and encourages family-to-family sharing. It is the largest seasonal 10-day charity fair, for children up to 14 years old and pregnant women, in the Baltic States. Individuals are encouraged to exchange items such pets' goods, Christmas goods, books, school materials for a symbolic price. Most of the unsold items are donated to charity. The fair has been held twice a year since 2012, and it is estimated that a total of 2 million items were presented at the fair, 1.1 million of which were sold and 350,000 donated to charity. The fair was initially held in Vilnius, and since 2019 it has expanded to other cities started: the autumn–winter fair took place in Kaunas (the second largest town in Lithuania), organized by a new, independent company that rents an IT system for the event and uses the name of the Mothers' Fair, all based on a separate agreement.

Sharing platforms (e-platforms and physical exchange sites). **MAINAI** is an innovative and convenient online platform for organizing "live" trading days. The business fair exchange model is based on IT accounting technology, which allows "live accounting" when a participant registers their items at home, prints labels, and presents the items before the event. They can then monitor sales live in the IT system. The same IT technology enables the exchange of large-scale items and can be used for other events of a similar nature. The most convenient feature of this platform is that the sellers, who have priced and printed product labels at home and presented their good-quality items to the fair, do not participate in the trade themselves. These "live" trading days are highly anticipated by buyers, so up to 70% of goods delivered are sold.

In 2020, 129,500 items found a new home during the Mothers' Fair events. According to the organizers, this included around 54.4 tonnes of textiles—almost

[8] Togoh, I. (2019). A used-clothing marketplace is Europe's newest and trendiest tech-unicorn. https://www.forbes.com/sites/isabeltogoh/2019/11/28/a-used-clothing-marketplace-is-europes-newest-and-trendiest-tech-unicorn/?sh=634d4ee94d9e.

as much as the volume of textiles simply thrown into mixed waste containers in the country per year.

Resursai tvariai plėtrai (social business TEXTALE) started in 2016. They take a systemic approach to maximizing environmental and social impacts throughout the textile supply chain, from education, resources collection, sorting, preparing for reuse, to repair, recreating, upcycling, and recycling.

Sharing platforms (e-platform and physical exchange and competencies). TEXTALE accepts wearable clothing, footwear, accessories, and home textiles, sorts them, prepares them for use, distributes them for support and sales, repairs parts, upcycles them, or uses them as secondary raw materials for remodelling projects. TEXTALE collaborates with designers and enthusiasts to upcycle and sell secondary design products.

Networking. For community inclusion and consumer education, TEXTALE organizes style, repair, and upcycling workshops, celebrations, and other educational activities on sustainability topics, focusing on the power of personal choice, raising consumer awareness, and introducing environmentally friendly (zero waste) alternatives. Working on national and international projects, TEXTALE is constantly looking for the best solutions for the development of the CE in the textile sphere, including the development of a sustainable textile collection and waste management system, the improvement of the sharing platform, the development of innovative sorting and recycling innovations, and building the market competitiveness of recycled products.

TEXTALE is run by volunteers and is open for student internships. Free activities carried out in TEXTALE include the distribution of support items to social organizations, and the integration of vulnerable groups in textile sorting, clothing preparation, repair, and upcycling activities, thereby giving them the opportunity to acquire new skills and participate in creative projects.

Based on TEXTALE info,[9] in three years, the company collected and prepared for reuse, repair, recreating, upcycling, and recycling 7,4 tonnes of used textiles, saved 21,1 tonnes of CO_2, organized employment for 45 persons from socially vulnerable groups, and ran almost 100 educational events with more than 1,800 participants.

Key Highlights

- Lithuanian textile manufacturers are part of the international (mostly European) supply chain.
- The Lithuanian textile industry is mainly based on subcontract production.
- The customer (brand) plays a critical role in eco-design solutions.
- Lithuanian manufacturers are highly technologically developed with an increasing focus on digitalization and adoption of technological innovations.
- Business models are mostly oriented to eco-efficiency.
- Lithuanian textile manufacturers have a weak role in eco-design because of subcontracted production specifics; however, eco-design is gaining importance.

[9] TEXTALE. https://textale.lt/wp-content/uploads/2021/03/10.png

- Textile manufacturers are advanced in waste management, at least internally.
- Manufacturing companies still treat circular business models as experimental.
- Consumers lack direct contact with manufacturers.
- National manufacturers, which sell their products directly to final customers (as well as retail companies), are fragmented in their implementation of reverse logistics.
- The Lithuanian textile industry suffers from technological unreadiness for recycling, much like the rest of Europe.
- The largest challenges in waste management are in sorting and recycling at the level of the whole ecosystem.
- Industrial textile waste collection infrastructure is developing in Lithuania.
- Post-use textile waste collection infrastructure is under development and characterized by interregional development differences.
- The dominant CE waste initiative in the textile supply chain is recovery (the lowest in the waste hierarchy pyramid) and disposal (which is undesirable).
- The most active CE initiatives are found in the post-consumption part of the textile supply chain, namely waste collection, rent, repair, reuse, and repurpose. The exchange of second-hand clothes between private consumers (C2C) is intensive.
- Niche remanufacturing is an undeveloped area in Lithuania.
- Lithuania is characterized by relatively large volumes of imported, sorted, and exported flows of second-hand textiles
- The potential of the CE has not yet been fully explored, discovered, and exploited by the Lithuanian textile industry.

References

Bocken, N. M. P., de Pauw, I., Bakker, C., & van der Grinten, B. (2016). Product design and business model strategies for a circular economy. *Journal of Industrial and Production Engineering, 33*(5), 308–320. https://doi.org/10.1080/21681015.2016.1172124

Bruneckienė, J., Dagilienė, L., Varaniūtė, V., Zykienė, I., Stasiškienė, Ž., Kliaugaitė, D., & Gurauskienė, I. (2021). *Žiedinės ekonomikos iššūkiai ir galimybės Lietuvoje: mokslo studija* (191 p.). Technologija. eISBN 9786090217382. https://doi.org/10.5755/e01.9786090217382

Ecos. (2021). *Durable, repairable and mainstream How ecodesign can make our textiles circular*. https://ecostandard.org/wp-content/uploads/2021/04/ECOS-REPORT-HOW-ECODESIGN-CAN-MAKE-OUR-TEXTILES-CIRCULAR.pdf

Ellen MacArthur Foundation. (2017). *A new textiles economy: Redesigning fashion's future*. https://www.ellenmacarthurfoundation.org/publications/a-new-textiles-economy-redesigning-fashions-future

Ertz, M., Leblanc-Proulx, S., Sarigöllü, E., & Morin, V. (2019). Advancing quantitative rigor in the circular economy literature: New methodology for product lifetime extension business models. *Resources, Conservation and Recycling, 150*, 104437. https://doi.org/10.1016/j.resconrec.2019.104437

Euratex. (2017). *Prospering in the circular economy*. Retrieved from: http://pr.euractiv.com/sites/default/files/pr/SB-26-2017_A1_EURATEX_CE_

European Commission. (2020). *Circular Economy Action Plan*. https://environment.ec.europa.eu/strategy/circular-economy-action-plan_en

European Environment Agency. (2020). *Textiles in Europe's circular economy*. Retrieved from: https://circulareconomy.europa.eu/platform/sites/default/files/briefieng-textiles-in-europe-s-circular-economy_1.pdf

Fernandez-Stark, K., Frederick, S., & Gereffi, G. (2011). *The Apparel Global Value Chain: Economic upgrading and workforce development*. https://gvcc.duke.edu/wp-content/uploads/2011-11-11CGGC_Ex.Summary_Apparel-Global-Value-Chain.pdf

Fischer, A., & Pascucci, S. (2017). Institutional incentives in circular economy transition: The case of material use in the Dutch textile industry. *Journal of Cleaner Production, 155*, 17–32. https://doi.org/10.1016/j.jclepro.2016.12.038

Franco, M. A. (2017). Circular economy at the micro level: A dynamic view of incumbents' struggles and challenges in the textile industry. *Journal of Cleaner Production, 168*, 833–845. https://doi.org/10.1016/j.jclepro.2017.09.056

Fromhold-Eisebith, M., Marschall, P., Peters, R., & Thomes, P. (2021). Torn between digitized future and context dependent past—How implementing 'Industry 4.0' production technologies could transform the German textile industry. *Technological Forecasting and Social Change, 166*. https://doi.org/10.1016/j.techfore.2021.120620

Gazzola, P., Pavione, E., Pezzetti, R., & Grechi, D. (2020). Trends in the fashion industry. The perception of sustainability and circular economy: A gender/generation quantitative approach. *Sustainability, 12*, 2809. https://doi.org/10.3390/su12072809

Geissdoerfer, M., Pieroni, M. P. P., Pigosso, D. C. A., & Soufani, K. (2020). Circular business models: A review. *Journal of Cleaner Production, 277*, 123741. https://doi.org/10.1016/j.jclepro.2020.123741

Huang, Y., Garrido, S., Lin, T., Cheng, C., & Lin, C. (2021). Exploring the decisive barriers to achieve circular economy: Strategies for the textile innovation in Taiwan. *Sustainable Production and Consumption, 27*. https://doi.org/10.1016/j.spc.2021.03.007

International Labour Organization. (2021). *Greener clothes? Environmental initiatives and tools in the garment sector in Asia ILO Asia-Pacific report*. https://www.ilo.org/wcmsp5/groups/public/---asia/---ro-bangkok/documents/publication/wcms_800026.pdf

Keßler, L., Matlin, S., & Kümmerer, K. (2021). The contribution of material circularity to sustainability—Recycling & re-use of textiles. *Current Opinion in Green and Sustainable Chemistry, 32*, 100535. https://doi.org/10.1016/j.cogsc.2021.100535

Koszewska, M. (2018). Circular economy—Challenges for the textile and clothing industry. *Autex Research Journal, 18*(4), 337–347. https://doi.org/10.1515/aut-2018-0023

Lacy, P., Long. J., & Spindler, W. (2020). *The circular economy handbook: Realizing the circular advantage* (p. 363). Springer, ISBN 978-1-349-95967-9. https://doi.org/10.1057/978-1-349-95968-6

Majumdar, A., & Sinha, S. K. (2019). Analyzing the barriers of green textile supply chain management in Southeast Asia using interpretive structural modeling. *Sustainable Production and Consumption, 17*. https://doi.org/10.1016/j.spc.2018.10.005

Malik, A., Lafortune, G., Carter, S., Li, M., Lenzen, M., & Kroll, C. (2021). International spillover effects in the EU's textile supply chains: A global SDG assessment. *Journal of Environmental Management, 295*. https://doi.org/10.1016/j.jenvman.2021.113037

Manickam, P., & Duraisamy, G. (2019). *3Rs and circular economy*. https://doi.org/10.1016/B978-0-08-102630-4.00004-2

Neto, O., Correia, J., Silva, J., Sanches, A., & Wagner, J. (2019). Cleaner Production in the textile industry and its relationship to sustainable development goals. *Journal of Cleaner Production, 228*. https://doi.org/10.1016/j.jclepro.2019.04.334

Nielsen, N. (2014). *Global consumers are willing to put their money where their heart is when it comes to goods and services from companies committed to social responsibility*. http://www.nielsen.com/us/en/press-room/2014/global-consumers-arewilling-to-put-their-money-where-their-heartis.html

Nimbalker, G., Mawson, J., Cremen, C., Wrinkle, H., & Eriksson, E. (2015). *The truth behind the barcode: Australian Fashion Report 2015, Baptist World Aid Australia.* Retrieved from: https://apo.org.au/sites/default/files/resource-files/2015-04/apo-nid54298.pdf

Pal, R., Shen, B., & Sandberg, E. (2019). Circular fashion supply chain management: Exploring impediments and prescribing future research agenda. *In Journal of Fashion Marketing and Management: An International Journal, 23*(3), 298–307. https://doi.org/10.1108/jfmm-07-2019-166

Parisi, M., Fatarella, E., Spinelli, D., Pogni, R., & Basosi, R. (2015). Environmental impact assessment of an eco-efficient production for coloured textiles. *Journal of Cleaner Production, 108.* https://doi.org/10.1016/j.jclepro.2015.06.032

Payne, A. (2015). Open-and closed-loop recycling of textile and apparel products. In *Handbook of life cycle assessment (LCA) of textiles and clothing* (pp. 103–123). https://doi.org/10.1016/B978-0-08-100169-1.00006-X

Provin, A., Dutra, A., Gouveia, I., & Cubas, A. (2021). Circular economy for fashion industry: Use of waste from the food industry for the production of biotextiles. *Technological Forecasting and Social Change, 169.* https://doi.org/10.1016/j.techfore.2021.120858

Riba, J., Cantero, R., Canals, T., & Puig, R. (2020). Circular economy of post-consumer textile waste: Classification through infrared spectroscopy. *Journal of Cleaner Production, 272,* 123011. https://doi.org/10.1016/j.jclepro.2020.123011

Sandin, G., & Peters, G. (2018). Environmental impact of textile reuse and recycling—A review. *Journal of Cleaner Production, 184.* https://doi.org/10.1016/j.jclepro.2018.02.266

Shirvanimoghaddam K., Motamed B., Ramakrishna S., & Naebe M. (2020). Death by waste: Fashion and textile circular economy case. *Science of the Total Environment, 718,* 137317. https://doi.org/10.1016/j.scitotenv.2020.137317

Siderius, T., & Poldner, K. (2021). Reconsidering the circular economy rebound effect: Propositions from a case study of the Dutch Circular Textile Valley. *Journal of Cleaner Production, 293.* https://doi.org/10.1016/j.jclepro.2021.125996

Staicu, D., & Pop, O. (2018). Mapping the interactions between the stakeholders of the circular economy ecosystem applied to the textile and apparel sector in Romania. *Management & Marketing. Challenges for the Knowledge Society, 13*(4), 1190–1209. https://doi.org/10.2478/mmcks-2018-0031

Ütebay, B., Celik, P., & Cayb, A. (2019). Effects of cotton textile waste properties on recycled fibre quality. *Journal of Cleaner Production, 222,* 29–35. https://doi.org/10.1016/j.jclepro.2019.03.033

Chapter 6
Circular Transformation of the Furniture Industry

Abstract This chapter presents dominant circular business models among furniture manufacturers, as well as challenges and new opportunities in the transition towards the circular economy. The chapter starts with an industry-specific literature review to identify global trends, key barriers, and opportunities for a circular furniture industry. The further focus is on statistical CE performance of the Lithuanian furniture industry in the context of small open economies. Then, we present the results of the original survey of Lithuanian furniture manufacturers regarding their priorities towards the CE, as well as drivers and barriers. Finally, the chapter ends with the best practices of furniture circular business models.

Keywords Furniture industry · Global trends · Circular performance · Circular patterns · Furniture circular business models

6.1 Global Trends in the Furniture Industry

The global furniture market is well developed. Furniture products are usually used for a long time and are quite expensive. A growing world population and a growing demand for cheaper and more accessible items are driving the use of **lower-quality materials** and **unsustainable design** standards that do not consider product durability, reusability, and extension of use (Lacy et al., 2020).

The European Union (EU) Member States produce 28% of the furniture sold worldwide, amounting to an €84 billion market which employs approximately one million European workers.[1] The furniture industry is dominated by small and medium-sized enterprises (Forrest et al., 2017). Although the EU furniture industry has so far managed to remain reasonably competitive globally, it is facing escalating problems with the quality and sustainability of furniture products in its domestic market (Forrest et al., 2017). The cost of energy, raw materials, and labour are

[1] Circular Economy in the furniture industry. Overview of current challenges and competencies needs. https://circulareconomy.europa.eu/platform/sites/default/files/circular-economy-in-the-furniture-industry.pdf

© The Author(s), under exclusive license to Springer Nature Switzerland AG 2023
L. Dagilienė et al., *Circular Business Models in the Manufacturing Industry*, Studies in Energy, Resource and Environmental Economics,
https://doi.org/10.1007/978-3-031-28809-8_6

increasing, challenging business as usual. In the domestic market, the **demand for cheap furniture products** is increasing, and it is difficult for companies that focus on long-lasting and quality products to compete. Evidence also shows that most furniture is destined for landfill at the end of its useful life (Vanacore et al., 2021).

In the academic and grey literature, it is suggested that the circular economy (CE) can open new opportunities for the furniture industry. Research mostly concentrates on manufacturing companies (Bjørnbet et al., 2021; Lieder & Rashid, 2016; Parida et al., 2019), whereas furniture manufacturers are usually included in the multiple-case studies and are analysed together with other sectors. Notably, the mode of CE implementation in different sectors helps in understanding the current trends, along with the future scope of CE development (Mhatre et al., 2021) and the peculiarities of circular business models.

In their handbook about the CE, Lacy et al. (2020) examine the role of ten different industries and how they can upscale significant value through implementing the CE principles. Regarding the furniture industry, the authors propose a heatmap of waste analysis, which shows that the largest challenges for furniture companies globally are **resource-intensive production** and **toxic chemical use**, followed by **unsustainable design choices** and **end-of-use products going to landfill**. Moving from solid wood and metal furniture to cheaper materials leads to unsustainable designs because such materials limit the possibilities of products being sold on into the second-hand market.

The CE is a systemic and multi-perspective concept based on the principle of resource conservation (Bjørnbet et al., 2021). One recent, comprehensive study is the research by Pieroni et al. (2021), which explores sectorial patterns of circular business model innovation within manufacturing companies. Among 180 case studies, the authors explored 42 home and office furnishings companies across Western Europe and America. The authors identify **circular patterns** for furniture products, such as modular, durable, biomaterials-based, locally made, refurbished or remanufactured, idle or second hand, repurposed or based on recycled materials, and equipped with monitoring devices. The best cases in the furniture sector reveal ambitious efforts from companies in changing not just to eco-efficient strategies, but transforming into more circular business models that are more promising in fighting overconsumption (e.g., offering products or functions as a service). **Product-Service Systems** (PSSs) are only now **emerging** in the furniture industry, and consumer preferences over ownership still hinder the broader development. For example, furniture manufacturing companies might experiment with various business model innovations such as the Furniture-as-a-Service subscription model for users with a nomadic lifestyle. Hence, it is crucial that product developers, together with marketing professionals, understand consumers' needs for services (Vermunt et al., 2019).

Circular business model innovations in the furniture industry could also be developed through **sufficiency** circular business models (Bocken et al., 2020). One example could be the Swedish furniture retailer IKEA[2] where the company sells furniture in small, easy-to-transport boxes, which encourages the consumer to

[2] How is IKEA embracing circular design? https://ellenmacarthurfoundation.org/podcasts/how-is-ikea-embracing-circular-design

assemble furniture at home. Although this was considered a huge loss of user convenience at the time, it now appears to be a positive experience for users (Bocken et al., 2020).

A **classic long-life** circular business model (Bocken et al., 2016) might be quite typical for furniture manufacturers. Usually, the implementation strategies encompass integrated take-back systems, and refurbishment and resale services for furniture and appliances (Santa-Maria et al., 2021). Furniture products with life extension services (Pieroni et al., 2020), eco-design, and product durability provide good opportunities to downstream the customer value proposition and interface. Modularity, as part of furniture design, is also attracting the attention of furniture manufacturers who produce products that are easy to disassemble, reuse, and recycle. However, Vermunt et al. (2019) note that business models orientated towards long-life life-cycle extension might be less attractive in the market because consumers embrace fashion, and this usually implies more diverse products over time.

Another promising opportunity for fostering circular business models in the furniture industry is **remanufacturing**. Jensen et al. (2019) investigate how an integrated perspective can promote sustainable (and at the same time circular) value creation in remanufacturing products, based on the case of the UK furniture industry leader. This integrated perspective considers remanufacturing activities across the product's life cycle: product design and development, remanufacturing processes, value chain management, and consumer/user relationship (Jensen et al., 2019). Stumpf et al. (2021) also find that the remanufacture principle is mostly related to manufacturing and slow-moving goods sectors, such as home furnishing, machinery and equipment, transport, information, and communication technologies. Remanufacturing favours product design based on modularity and timelessness (Linder & Williander, 2017). Meanwhile **reuse** activity in the furnishing industry is low, mostly conducted through commercial second-hand shops, social enterprise companies, and charities (Forrest et al., 2017). Similar to the long-life or product's life-cycle extension models, consumer's non-acceptance of these models is a challenge (Vermunt et al., 2019), due to a wide resistance to second-hand furniture.

The barriers to circular business model innovation that are identified by Guldmann and Huulgaard (2020) are often general, such as the institutional environment, a lack of recycling technology and infrastructure, or a lack of financial resources. These barriers were described in Chapter 2. We summarize key barriers that are particularly important to the furniture industry below.

Key Barriers to a Circular Furniture Industry:

- Product design and materials-related (supply):
  - Use of lower-quality materials.
  - Unsustainable product design and specification (lack of modular and durable designs).
  - Intensive energy and water use.
  - Toxic chemical use.

- Supply chain-related (supply):
  - High cost of repair and refurbishment.
  - Lack of reverse logistics infrastructure and collection systems.
  - Limited recycling infrastructure.
- Environmental regulation:
  - REACH regulation.
  - Weak overarching policy drivers.
- Consumer-related (demand):
  - Low demand for second-hand furniture (usually because of consumer non-acceptance).
  - Low demand for refurbished furniture (usually because of higher price).
  - Low demand for recycled, secondary materials.
  - Demand for cheaper, more accessible furniture products.
  - Poor consumer information and availability of spares.
  - Poor consumer information of how to maintain, repair, or recycle responsibly.

Opportunities for a Circular Furniture Industry
There are plenty of opportunities that could be implemented to enhance circularity for furniture products. Eco-design and design for disassembly are the most commonly used CE strategies for furniture (Mhatre et al., 2021; Rieckhof & Guenther, 2018). The furniture industry involves a resource-intensive manufacturing process, constantly requiring millions of tonnes of raw materials. Therefore, design choices for durability, second-use options, and material recovery (Lacy et al., 2020) are extremely welcome.

In order to shift towards a more circular furniture industry, the focus should be on the higher levels of the waste hierarchy (Bjørnbet et al., 2021), starting with sustainable design standards and enabling business model innovation to prolong product life cycles. Various eco-efficiency strategies are oriented towards narrowing resource loops through eco-design and higher-quality materials. Apparently, the most promising CE strategies used in the furniture industry are customization, eco-design & eco-labelling, materials recovery, functional recycling, materials reduction, remanufacture, and take-back/trade-in structures (Mhatre et al., 2021) (Table 6.1).

Although eco-efficiency through energy and materials optimization is quite characteristic of the EU furniture industry, as this also creates a competitive advantage, from the CE point of view, the furniture industry lacks business model innovation orientated to self-sufficiency and reducing overconsumption. Furniture PSSs are not widely adopted, even though they can offer promising opportunities for the furniture industry.

Table 6.1 Opportunities for a circular furniture industry

Strategy	- Furniture PSSs (Pieroni et al., 2021; Tukker, 2015) (especially for office furniture) - Use of digital technologies (e.g., platforms for accessing furniture on a temporary basis) - Sharing of furniture/furnishing solutions
Product design and materials	- Modular furniture to allow customizations and multiple assembles (Pieroni et al., 2021) - User-centred design to develop function/activity-based furniture - Use of secondary materials from other value chains (Lacy et al., 2020)
Cleaner production	- Reduce material waste and toxicity in production (Lacy et al., 2020) - Reduce the use of energy and water
Usage & product life-cycle extension	- Leasing model (Vermunt et al., 2019) - Refurbishment/remanufacturing facilities (Jensen et al., 2019; Stumpf et al., 2021) - Collaboration with designers/design firms and local workshops/craftsmen to prolong product life (Pieroni et al., 2021) - Collaboration with redistributors for the commercialization and reuse of second-hand furniture - Repair services or development of do-it-yourself repairs
Waste management	- A clearer definition of when a material is considered waste would improve the end-of-life options for furniture materials - Upcycling of discarded furniture - Recycling of materials to produce new furniture - A landfill ban on furniture disposal (Forrest et al., 2017)

6.2 Circular Performance of the Lithuanian Furniture Industry

The analysis of the CE indicators is done by comparing macro-economic indicators that could help to evaluate the circularity. Five areas are distinguished to present the results, which are presented in the methodology section (see Chapter 3).

The furniture industry bears the Nomenclature of Economic Activities (NACE) classification code C31. Due to the limited statistical information about some specific indicators, we take aggregated information of C31–C32 or C31–33 sectors, where code C32 covers other manufacturing (jewellery, musical instruments, toys) and C33 is the repair and installation of machinery and equipment.

Vision and strategy. The vision and strategy chapter presents the motivation of furniture companies to implement environmental innovations. We select two indicators for analysis: environmental protection expenditure and environmental protection investment.

The results of the analysis show that the total amount of environmental protection expenditures varies from €1.9 million to €2.5 million in the period 2014–2018. As presented in Fig. 6.1, protection expenditure on ambient air, climate, and wastewater management grew in the period 2014–2016 and decreased between 2016 and 2018, whereas expenditure for waste management shows growth throughout the period under investigation. Expenditure on waste management was 68–76% of the total expenditures and this grew steadily from 2015 to 2018. The expenditure for other environmental protection activities was very volatile throughout the period. Overall, the statistical tendencies show that C31 companies buy external environmental services and corporate external environmental services accounted for 99% of the total amount of environmental protection expenditures over the period.

Investment in environmental protection was quite low at between 0.7% and 6.6% of the total although in 2017–2018, there was growth to the point where environmental investment exceeded environmental expenditure. The highest level of environmental protection investment is seen in 2017 €4.8 million but decreased to €2.6 million in 2018. Investments were targeted mainly at environmental protection activities (87%), with the remainder invested in production processes. Thus, this data shows the motivation of Lithuanian furniture manufacturing companies (C31) to implement environmental innovations in 2017–2018.

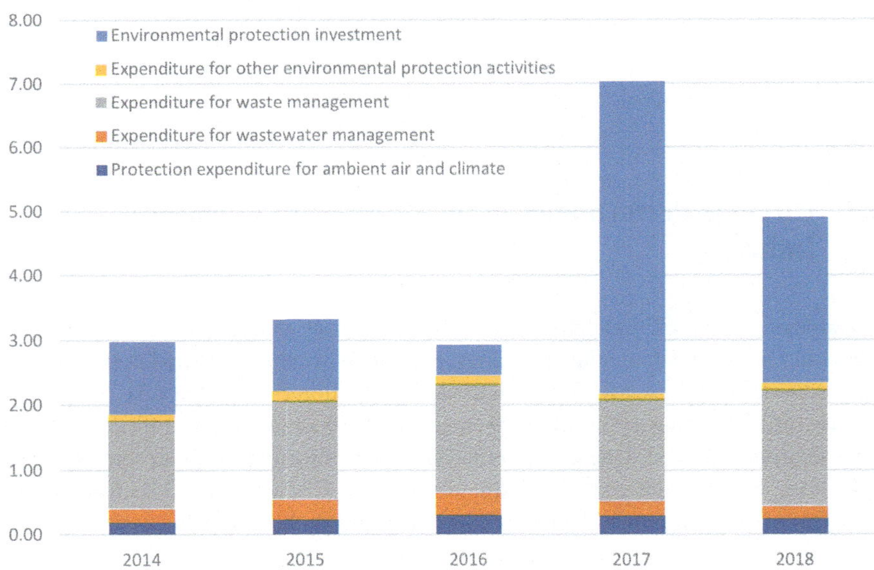

Fig. 6.1 Environmental expenditure and investment in plant and equipment for pollution control in the Lithuanian furniture manufacturing sector (C31) in 2014–2018 (€ million)

According to the Eurostat database, the Lithuanian furniture industry (C31) is the most motivated to invest in plant and equipment for pollution control (€4.8 million in 2017, €2.2 million in 2018) compared with other SOEs. Austria is in second place with investment of €0.7 million, Belgium and Slovenia at €0.1 million each, whereas the Netherlands, Czech Republic, and Sweden are investing more in clean technology.

Raw materials, secondary raw materials, and eco-design. The use and complexity of raw materials are best described by the structure of the inputs into the C31–33 industries. However, there is a lack of data to analyse the use of secondary raw materials and eco-design changes in particular industries, although eco-design is partly reflected by input complexity. Compared to the Lithuanian textile, wearing apparel, leather and related products (C13–15) industries, the inputs into furniture manufacturing are much more complex.

As presented in Fig. 6.2, the value-added at basic prices has less than half that of the C31–33 sector input. Expenses for wholesale and retail account for a relatively large share of the sector's input, at 9%. Both wood and products of wood and cork and other manufacturing, repair, and installation of machinery and equipment each have an 8% share of the total input, while textiles, wearing apparel, leather and related products, rubber and plastics products, and other business sector services all reach 3%.

Products from the chemical and pharmaceutical, fabricated metal products, and transportation and storage industries account for 2%, whereas paper products and printing; coke and refined petroleum; basic metals; electrical equipment; machinery and equipment; electricity, gas, and water supplies and environmental services financial and insurance activities; and real estate activities only account for 1% each of the input structure.

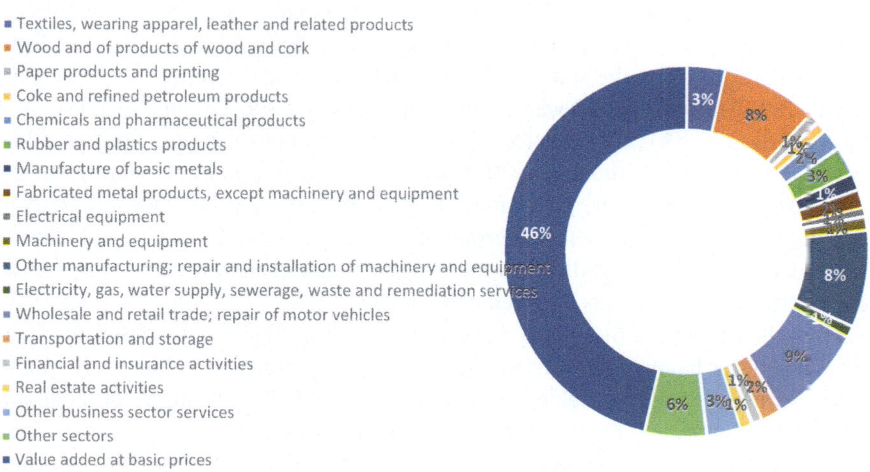

Fig. 6.2 Input structure of Lithuanian C31–33 industries

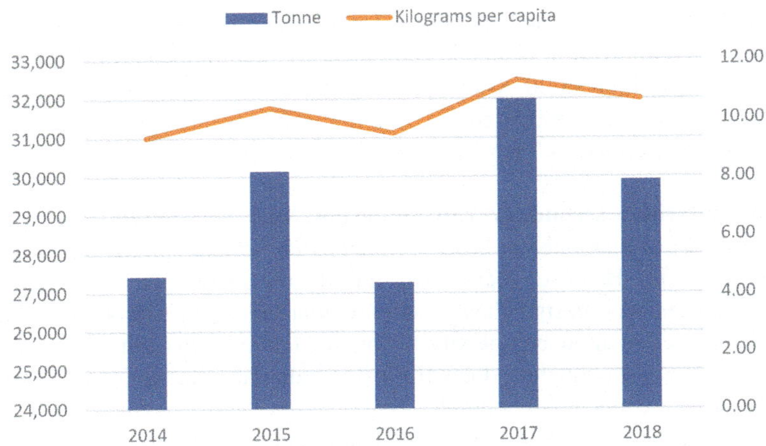

Fig. 6.3 CO2 emissions from the Lithuanian C31–33 industries

Cleaner production. We now review the energy and emissions indicators related to cleaner production.

According to Fig. 6.3, CO2 emissions rise from 27,280 tonnes in 2016 to 32,003 tonnes in 2017. During the analysed period, the average value of CO2 emissions was 29,362 tonnes or 10.25 kg per capita. In 2018, the C31-33 industries in Lithuania emitted 10.68 kg of CO2 per capita, compared to 0.6 kg in Finland (the lowest of the SOEs) and 29.9 kg in Ireland (the highest). This indicator was decreasing in Belgium (4.9 kg in 2018), Malta (16.1 kg in 2018), and Sweden (3.7 kg in 2018), and was increasing in Czech Republic, Denmark, Estonia, Cyprus, Austria, Slovenia, and Slovakia.

The analysis of energy use shows an increasing demand for energy in the Lithuanian C31–33 manufacturing sector, averaging an increase of 4.2% per year from 2014 to 2018. In 2018, the sources of consumed energy are biomass (65.0%), electricity (18.9%), wood, wood waste, charcoal, and other solid biomass (6.6%), and transport diesel (3%). Of the selected SOEs, the amount of energy used in C31–33 was the highest in Lithuania in 2018, as was the use of renewable natural energy sources (64.99% of total energy sources). Considering the use of renewable energy in these industries across the selected group of SOEs, only Latvia (42.1%) and Estonia (64.3%) use a similarly significant amount of renewable energy, while in other SOEs, renewable energy input was between zero and 4%.

From the analysis of the energy use structure in the C31-33 industries, four countries stand out as having completely different energy structures to Lithuania. In Malta, electricity use is 91.4%; in Ireland, transport diesel is 95.8% of the total energy input; in the Netherlands, it is 86.1%; and in Slovakia, it is 82.4%.

Consumption, reuse, repair. The consumption analysis was done by analysing output measures in 2015 from the OECD database. The results show that the main

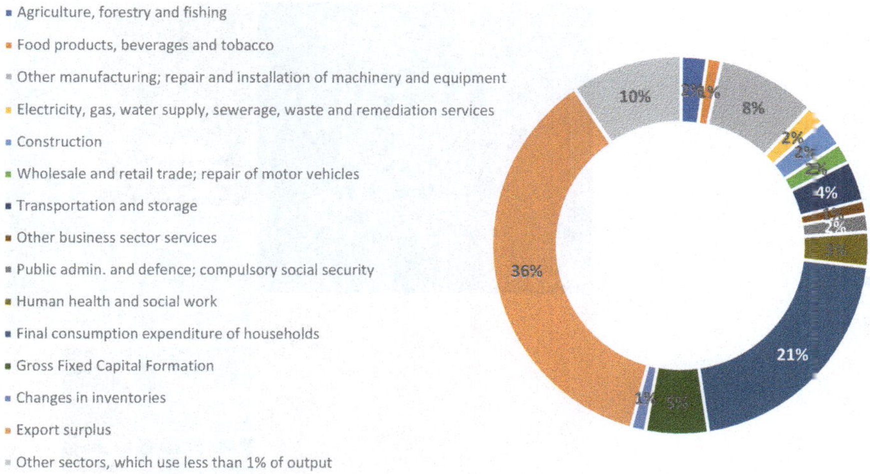

Fig. 6.4 Use structure of the output of Lithuanian (C31-33) industries in 2015

consumers of Lithuanian furniture, other manufacturing, repair, and installation of machinery and equipment (C31–33) products were foreign users (36%) and households (21%) (see Fig. 6.4).

According to OECD data, exports of Lithuanian manufacture of furniture, other manufacturing, repair, and installation of machinery and equipment (C31–33) were worth US$979.8 million more than imports of these products in 2015, representing an export surplus of 36%.

Waste management. The C31-C33 industries generated 56,127 tonnes of waste in Lithuania in 2018. This is measured every two years and decreased by 0.5% from 2016, whereas it has increased significantly by 38% from 2014 to 2016.

The results of the analysis show that the main waste from the sector consists of wood waste (32.0%), metal ferrous waste (23.8%), and mixed and undifferentiated materials (10.6%) (see Fig. 6.5). Paper and cardboard wastes make up 5.9% of the total, household and similar wastes 5.6%, and plastic wastes 5.2%. About 3.5% of the generated waste is chemical, 3.2% is mineral waste from construction and demolition, 3.0% is textiles, and 3% is mixed metal.

A comparison of the structure of waste generated in Lithuania with other SOEs shows that Denmark, the Netherlands, and Slovakia generate higher shares of wood waste (41.7%, 43.4%, and 54.6%, respectively). Moreover, each country has a very specific waste structure and it is very difficult to find similarities. The exceptional waste structures are found in Malta, Finland, and Latvia, where the largest proportions consist of household and similar waste in Malta (90.8%), other waste in Finland (60.6%), and industrial effluent sludge in Latvia (59.0%).

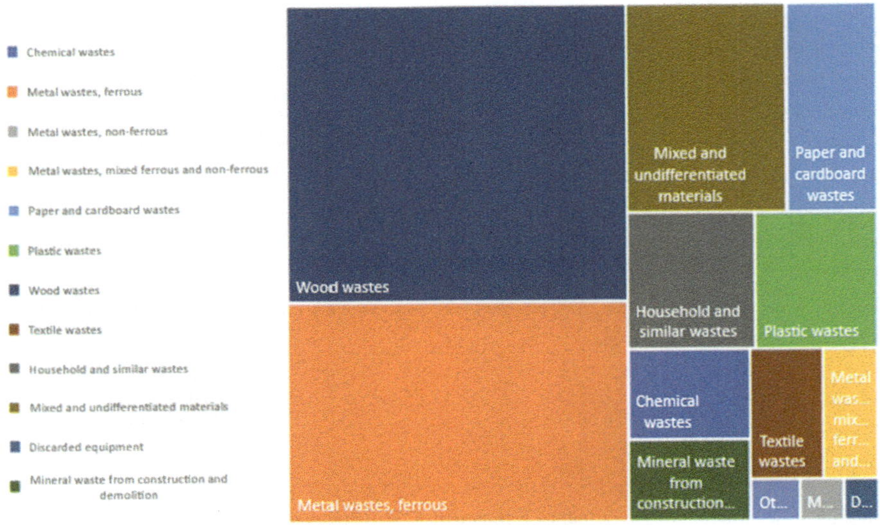

Fig. 6.5 The structure of generated waste from Lithuanian C31–33 industries in 2018

6.3 Circular Patterns of Lithuanian Furniture Manufacturing Companies

Details of our survey are given in Chapter 4. This chapter presents the results for the furniture companies surveyed. The furniture companies are mainly operating in both national and international markets (see Fig. 6.6). It is noticeable that 61% of the furniture companies that participated in the survey do not invest in green technologies, or have no data on such investments, though at least 22% of them invest up to 5% in green technologies of total investments.

Lithuania had the best-performing market in Europe in the last five years for furniture production growth, with almost 900 companies now active in the industry.[3] It is a priority sector for the country's economy, with an export intensity of 88% and an export value of €1.4 million a year.[4] The survey results on the relevant CE patterns in Lithuanian furniture companies are visualized in Fig. 6.7.

The Lithuanian furniture industry is strongly focusing on material and energy efficiency as a means of reducing costs, and because of sustainability demands from important foreign retailers, like IKEA. Evidence suggests that digitalization practices are emerging in this sector, for IKEA producers and others who use, for example, integrated design tools that minimize input materials and keep account of residues for future use.

The surveyed furniture manufacturers prioritize investments in digital technologies, followed by effective use of regenerative resources (mostly renewable energy

[3] Lithuania furniture outlook. worldfurnitureonline.com.

[4] Lithuania in focus. https://www.kcci.lt/file/manual/Lithuania%20in%20Focus.pdf

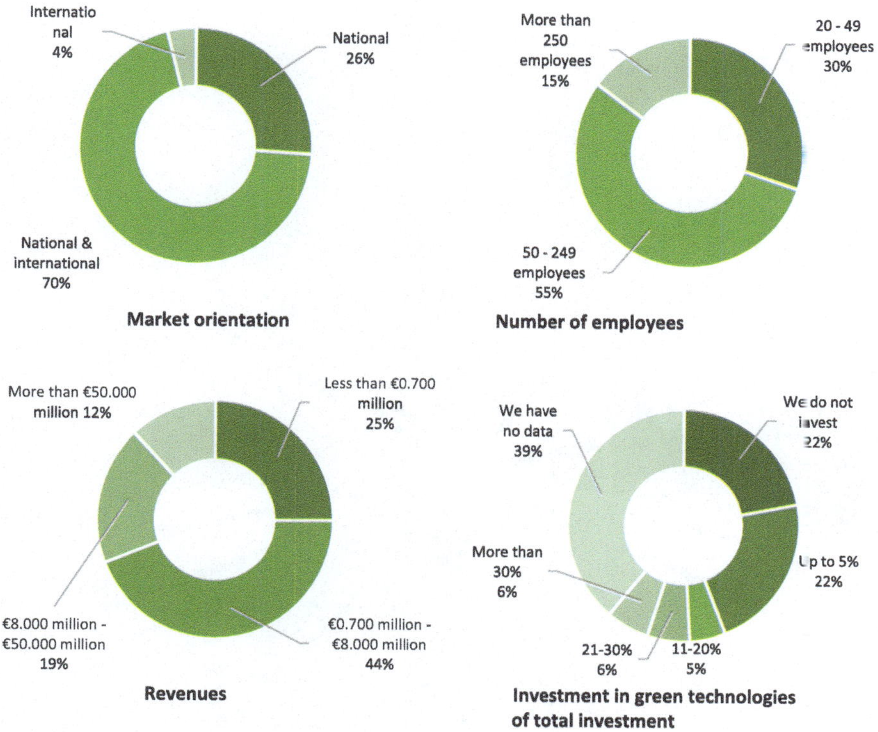

Fig. 6.6 Surveyed furniture companies' characteristics (2019)

for production systems), sustainable materials, and creating long-lasting products. As regards technological solutions for the CE, they mainly cover manufacturing technologies, followed by robotic process automation (RPA), mobile and digital technologies, process innovation, and platforms. Investments in environmental or green technologies are not among the key strategic priorities, though the national statistics show the Lithuanian furniture manufacturers' intention is to implement environmental innovations over the coming years. This may be related to the specifics of the survey sample, which largely consisted of small and medium-sized enterprises. Research shows that, for the most part, leaders of industrial companies are digitizing essential functions within their internal vertical value chains, as well as with their horizontal partners. In addition, they are enhancing their product portfolio with digital functionalities and introducing innovative, data-based services.[5]

The furniture companies strongly focus on narrowing the resource flows as part of the efficient use of input materials, which indicates the prevalence of eco-efficient strategies. However, the use of secondary materials is slightly less common and is more related to packaging than with the product itself. This means that resource efficiency is usually achieved through eco-efficient production processes and the

[5] PwC. Industry 4.0: companies worldwide are investing over $US900 billion per year until 2020.

Fig. 6.7 The portfolio of relevant patterns of the CE in Lithuanian furniture companies

minimization of industrial waste. It is important to note that the surveyed companies are still not proactive in creating environmental values for their suppliers, or experimenting with product composition. Changes in attitudes to eco-design are taking place, but very slowly.

Sustainable packaging is another important pattern for furniture manufacturers. Recyclable and recycled packaging are becoming prevalent, along with light, biodegradable materials that reduce the energy used in transportation, and waste at the end of use. Basically, companies do not perceive serious challenges regarding cleaner production processes because they constantly use renewable energy inputs, such as solar. Furthermore, the companies do not measure the negative environmental impact of CO2 emissions. This might be explained by the fact that only the largest companies have the legal obligation to monitor and report on emissions, meanwhile, small and medium-sized enterprises often have simplified requirements and pollution monitoring systems.

It is important to note that the Lithuanian furniture manufacturers are well interconnected in the European value chains and export markets. Since most Lithuanian furniture companies are exporters and contractual manufacturers, their key customers are foreign companies, some of whom are retailers that place additional environmental requirements on product quality and clean production processes. On the other hand, those companies, which also sell to local consumers, still face challenging customer attitudes to second hand and recycled furniture. To enhance effective collaboration across the supply chain, manufacturing companies apply different certification and accreditation schemas dealing with environmental improvement, traceability, quality of raw materials, and effective process management.

Overall, the surveyed companies do not face huge challenges in waste management, because this area is more mature from legislation point of view, especially in terms of waste collection & sorting systems. This can be explained by the fact that the largest challenge to transition to a circular furniture value chain is end-of-life furniture products, which quite often go to landfill. These companies are in the middle of the furniture value chain and usually have no direct connection with the furniture after its market life, especially as most of them are exporters. On the other hand, manufacturers apply modern technological solutions and already have an efficient manufacturing process with minimal industrial waste. However, circular material recovery and closing the loop are weakly applied in the furniture industry. The results also indicate that, currently, manufacturers do not see any significant value in closing the loops, as production and consumption systems are treated separately.

The analysis of factors motivating furniture manufacturers towards the CE is presented in Fig. 6.8. The results indicate the importance of RPA, digital and mobile technologies, and the technological transformation of production and business processes. Intensive adoption of innovative technological solutions results in a strongly competitive furniture industry and might also contribute to a higher circularity. Collaboration-related factors, such as market requirements around quality and certification, and agreements in the supply chain, also foster manufacturers' intentions to move towards the CE.

6.4 Best Practices of Furniture Circular Business Models

As mentioned in previous chapters, Lithuanian furniture companies are also important players at the EU level. Before presenting some of the best practices we have identified, we start with some well-known business cases from around the world.

Steelcase,[6] the leading manufacturer of office furniture, has 50 + Cradle-to-cradle Certified products. The company has a strategy for sustainable design and has adopted

[6] The future is a circle. How the Circular Economy is making what's old new again. https://www.steelcase.com/research/articles/topics/sustainability/steelcase-named-circulars-finalist/.

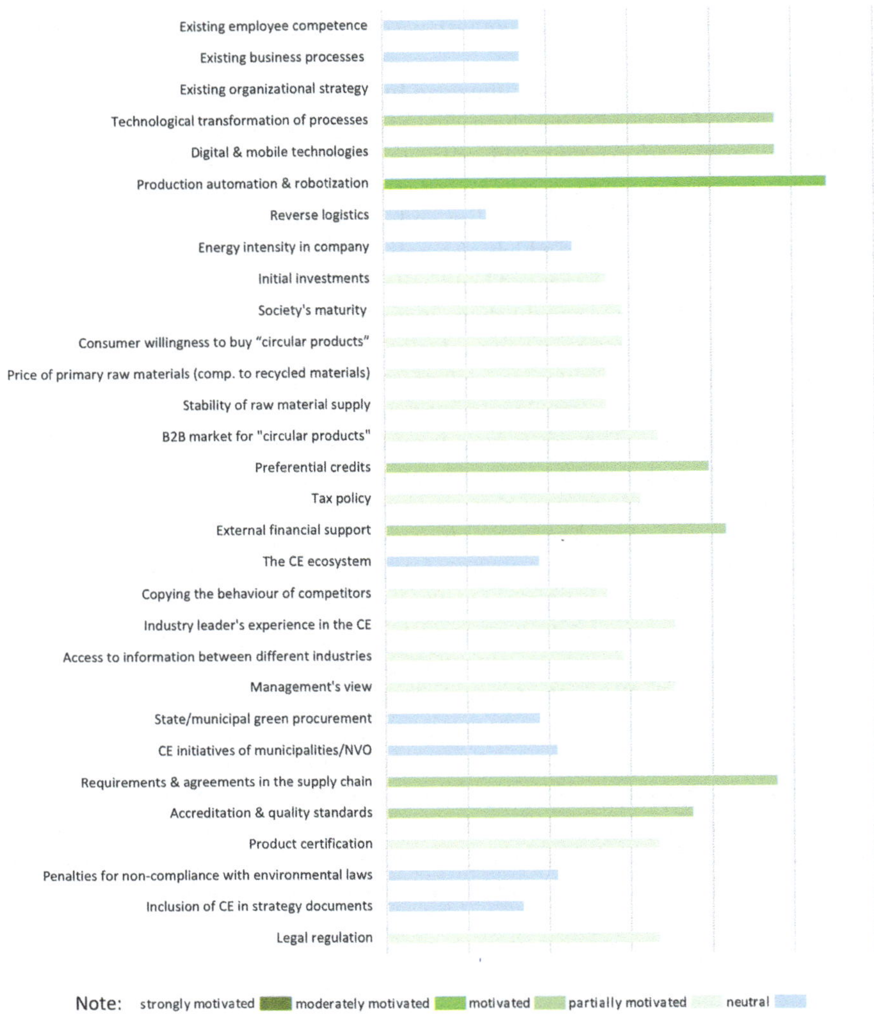

Fig. 6.8 Factors influencing the furniture manufacturers transition to the CE

a circular product-service business model which includes asset recovery and furniture redeployment programmes.

As was identified earlier, new business models for repair and remanufacture also have huge potential in the furniture industry. The Swedish giant, IKEA,[7] aims to encourage consumers to repair furniture products, rather than throwing them away when they break. In 2018, IKEA received more than one million orders for spare parts from customers who were able to perform do-it-yourself repairs. This is in line with

[7] IKEA to begin renting furniture as part of wider sustainability push. https://www.dezeen.com/2019/02/20/ikea-rental-furniture-circular-economy-design/.

the core IKEA premise of producing modular, customizable, affordable furniture that can be easily repaired, reused, or redesigned with relatively little effort.[8]

Ahrend[9] is a Dutch office furniture company that designs timeless products for life. Their strategic focus is on modular and durable design and includes CE strategies for slowing the loops, such as Furniture-as-a-Service, revitalizing, and maintenance.

Prevailing circular business models are focused on extending product life cycles through modular design, product-service systems, and repair and refurbishment. However, this development is more common for office furniture, which is largely a business-to-business (B2B) market.

A few exemplary Lithuanian companies that have formulated a sustainability strategy are presented in Table 6.2. Lithuanian companies focus on high-quality durable products with high environmental performance, which is characterized by the use of renewable energy and responsible management of resources (raw and secondary materials).

Narbutas has a responsible approach to the use of materials for production and constantly invests in cutting-edge technology, which positively affects operational and energy performance. The responsible management of resources (both energy and materials) is at the core of the company's strategy.

Energy. The company aims to use solar, wind, and water energy to develop ergonomic and durable products. The company's factory roof is covered with 6000m^2 of solar panels, which generate 15% of the total electricity used in the factory. An expansion of the solar panels is planned.

Materials. The boards are compliant with the US regulation CARB phase II and, while no equal unified regulation exists in Europe, the boards also comply with the strictest regulation currently, which was adopted in Germany in 2020.

Waste. All production waste is sorted and handed over to waste management companies, which is a legal requirement. However, Narbutas also donates furniture and left-over production materials of satisfactory quality to various institutions engaged in social causes. Furthermore, they take an active role in consumer education by encouraging their clients to shape new habits and reduce paper waste by using online product assembly instructions instead of the paper versions.

Ergolain. The CE mindset is at the heart of the Ergolain group of companies and is embedded into every stage, from design to production.

The company's sustainability policy has been developed and continuously improved for over 20 years by employees who believe in the benefits of sustainability. By carefully reviewing and managing processes, the company is moving towards a more sustainable future. The goal of Ergolain is to reduce pollution and manage the impact of manufactured furniture and production technologies on the environment.

Materials. Ergolain creates long-lasting furniture that can not only be used continuously, but can also be easily disassembled, refurbished, or reused in new products.

---

8 What can design engineers learn from IKEA? https://www.designnews.com/design-hardware-software/what-can-design-engineers-learn-ikea.

9 Ahrend https://www.ahrend.com/en/about-ahrend/sustainability/.

Table 6.2 Lithuanian furniture best practices cases

Company	Product features	Business model	CE aspects
Own brands manufacturers			
Narbutas[10] Office furniture	Ergonomic Durability (supported by warranties) Adaptability	**Efficient and responsible use of resources (narrow the resource flows)**	- Self-sufficiency and reducing consumption - Long service life - 100% of the energy is sourced from renewable energy sources - Controlled emission levels - Donation of furniture and left-over production material - Customer education—to reduce paper waste by using online product assembly instructions instead of the paper versions
Ergolain[11] Ergonomic furniture	Ergonomic Long-lasting Adaptable Modular	**Pollution reduction and management of the impact of manufactured furniture and production technologies on the environment (narrow the resource flows, slow the loops)**	- User-centric design - Use of cutting-edge technologies - Collaboration with architects and well-known furniture manufacturers - Easily disassembled, refurbished, or reused - Sustainable materials - Recycled materials (e.g., wool and polyester)

(continued)

[10] Narbutas https://www.narbutas.com/about-us/social-responsibility/.

[11] Ergolain https://www.ergolain.lt/en/sustainability/.

Table 6.2 (continued)

Company	Product features	Business model	CE aspects
Baldai Jums[12] Solid wood furniture	Eco-friendly Resistant and functional Long-lasting	**High-quality products and innovative, energy-efficient production technologies (narrow the resource flows)**	- User-centric design - Energy efficiency - Sustainable and certified materials - Renewed raw materials, without toxic substances
Sub-contractual manufacturers			
Freda[13] Living room and hallway furniture		**Cost-efficiency, product quality, and maximized production capacity**	- High environmental performance (key client—IKEA) - Energy efficiency - Use of cutting-edge technologies
Platforms for furniture rent/secondary furniture			
Ofisas prabangiai Office furniture rent	Additional services: rent, lease, purchase of used furniture	**Furniture rent and lease, purchase of second-hand furniture**	- Digital platform - Rent/lease options - Warranties - Opportunity to take back after the furniture is no longer required
Baldų turgus Furniture rent	Additional services: rent, lease, purchase of used furniture	**Furniture rent and lease, purchase of second-hand furniture**	- Digital platform - Rent/lease options - Warranties

[12] Baldai Jums https://baldaijums.lt/en/musu-kokybe/.

[13] Freda https://www.efsen.dk/wp-content/uploads/2020/01/Breakthrough-in-furniture-coating-with-UV-LED-curing_compressed.pdf.

The company carefully selects and considers the origin of the sustainable materials used in the production processes. The wood is sourced from Forest Stewardship Council (FSC) and/or Programme for the Endorsement of Forest Certification (PEFC) certified, sustainably managed forests. They also choose sustainable materials in the production of their upholstered furniture. Fabrics include natural wool, recycled wool, and recycled polyester, which is extracted from plastic collected from the sea and turned into yarn.

Waste. Waste from the production process is carefully sorted and transported for recycling. Their clients have the opportunity to contribute to their corporate sustainability policy by renovating worn-out furniture and giving it a new life. The furniture that is no longer in use is donated to institutions organizing social activities, thus contributing to the well-being of the whole society. Both production waste and obsolete furniture are collected by the company and handed over for recycling.

Recycling. The most common materials sent for recycling are plastics, cardboard, wood (furniture wood, panels, solid wood, etc.), and metal. All furniture produced in the factory is packed with easily recyclable materials, which can be sorted responsibly after assembling the furniture.

One more national company **Baldai Jums** uses only ecological and certified materials. In order to meet their customers' expectations, furniture products are sustainable, recyclable, free from prohibited chemicals, and made from safe materials. The entire production cycle is located in one area, including the sawmill, drying kilns, production, and product finishing, which ensures control of each production stage. The focus is on value-added products due to synergies between existing capabilities. **Baldai Jums** seeks to compete by providing durable products, eco-designed, using ecologically sound materials.

Key Highlights

- Business models embedded in industrial furniture systems are orientated towards eco-efficiency through input material optimization and cleaner production.
- Furniture manufacturers are advanced in industrial waste management, but post-consumption waste is problematic. Reuse and refurbishment activities are quite weakly developed.
- Eco-design is gaining importance, although there is much room for improvement because there is demand for cheaper and more accessible items.
- The Lithuanian furniture industry is highly technologically developed, with an increasing focus on digitalization, and provides a significant proportion of economic value-added.
- Lithuanian furniture manufacturers are quite well integrated into international (mostly European) supply chains.
- There is little opportunity for Lithuanian manufacturers to close the loop because they sell furniture to other furniture retailers and do not contribute to reverse value chains. They usually work as subcontractors and have to fulfil the requirements of famous brands such as IKEA.

- Lithuania also has local brands, such as Narbutas and Baldai Jums, which are known to both national and international consumers.
- Business models are mostly orientated towards eco-efficiency and high quality. Furniture companies invest in cutting-edge technologies to optimize the use of raw materials and drive towards zero industrial waste, as well as to minimize energy use.
- All sustainable brands emphasize the high quality of their products. Key features of the best eco-design practices are functional, long-lasting, ergonomic, and durable.
- Final consumers have no direct contact with manufacturers through value creation. Other services related to prolonging furniture life cycle are not prevalent, such as repair, refurbish, redesign.
- So far, activities such as the donation of furniture and left-over production materials, and consumer education, are still not widespread.
- IKEA is a major foreign buyer requiring certification and can be seen as a leverage opportunity to increase environmental sustainability and certification expertise. The sustainability of business processes and the necessary certificates might strengthen the competitiveness of the furniture industry.
- Product-service business models (e.g., rental and maintenance of office furniture) are not developed across Lithuanian furniture manufacturers, and there is significant potential to adopt such models, particularly in the office furniture market.

References

Bjørnbet, M. M., Skaar, C., Fet, A. M., & Schulte, K. Ø. (2021). Circular economy in manufacturing companies: A review of case study literature. *Journal of Cleaner Production, 294*, 126268. https://doi.org/10.1016/j.jclepro.2021.126268

Bocken, N. M. P., Pauw, I., Bakker, C. A., & van der Grinten, B. (2016). Product design and business model strategies for a circular economy. *Journal of Industrial and Production Engineering, 3*(5), 308–320. https://doi.org/10.1080/21681015.2016.1172124

Bocken, N., Morales, L. S., & Lehner, M. (2020). Sufficiency business strategies in the food industry-the case of oatly. *Sustainability (Switzerland), 12*(3). https://doi.org/10.3390/su12030824

Circular Economy in the Furniture Industry. Overview of Current Challenges and Competences Needs. Report. https://circulareconomy.europa.eu/platform/sites/default/files/circular-economy-in-the-furniture-industry.pdf

Forrest, A., Hilton, M., Ballinger, A., & Whittaker, D. (2017). Circular economy opportunities in the furniture sector. *European Environmental Bureau (EEB)*, 55. https://eeb.org/library/circular-economy-opportunities-in-the-furniture-sector

Guldmann, E., & Huulgaard, R. D. (2020). Barriers to circular business model innovation: A multiple-case study. *Journal of Cleaner Production, 243*, 118160. https://doi.org/10.1016/j.jclepro.2019.118160

Jensen, J. P., Prendeville, S. M., Bocken, N. M. P., & Peck, D. (2019). Creating sustainable value through remanufacturing: Three industry cases. *Journal of Cleaner Production, 218*, 304–314. https://doi.org/10.1016/j.jclepro.2019.01.301

Lacy, P., Long. J., & Spindler, W. (2020). *The circular economy handbook: Realizing the circular advantage* (p. 363). Springer, ISBN 978-1-349-95967-9. https://doi.org/10.1057/978-1-349-95968-6

Lieder, M., & Rashid, A. (2016). Towards circular economy implementation: A comprehensive review in context of manufacturing industry. *Journal of Cleaner Production, 115*, 36–51. https://doi.org/10.1016/j.jclepro.2015.12.042

Mhatre, P., Panchal, R., Singh, A., & Bibyan, S. (2021). A systematic literature review on the circular economy initiatives in the European Union. *Sustainable Production and Consumption, 26*, 187–202. https://doi.org/10.1016/j.spc2020.09.008

Parida, V., Burström, T., Visnjic, I., & Wincent, J. (2019). Orchestrating industrial ecosystem in circular economy: A two-stage transformation model for large manufacturing companies. *Journal of Business Research, 101*, 715–725. https://doi.org/10.1016/j.jbusres.2019.01.006

Pieroni, M. P. P., McAloone, T. C., & Pigosso, D. C. A. (2020). From theory to practice: Systematising and testing business model archetypes for circular economy. *Resources, Conservation and Recycling, 162*(March), 105029. https://doi.org/10.1016/j.resconrec.2020.105029

Pieroni, M. P. P., McAloone, T. C., & Pigosso, D. C. A. (2021). Circular economy business model innovation: Sectorial patterns within manufacturing companies. *Journal of Cleaner Production, 286*, 124921. https://doi.org/10.1016/j.jclepro.2020.124921

Rieckhof, R., & Guenther, E. (2018). Integrating life cycle assessment and material flow cost accounting to account for resource productivity and economic- environmental performance. *International Journal of Life Cycle Assessment, 23*, 1491–1506. https://doi.org/10.1007/s11367-018-1447-7

Santa-Maria, T., Vermeulen, W. J. V., & Baumgartner, R. J. (2021). Framing and assessing the emergent field of business model innovation for the circular economy: A combined literature review and multiple case study approach. *Sustainable Production and Consumption, 26*, 872–891. https://doi.org/10.1016/j.spc.2020.12.037

Stumpf, L., Schöggl, J.-P., & Baumgartner, R. J. (2021). Climbing up the circularity ladder? – A mixed-methods analysis of circular economy in business practice. *Journal of Cleaner Production, 316*(128158). https://doi.org/10.1016/J.JCLEPRO.2021.128158

Tukker, A. (2015). Product services for a resource-efficient and circular economy—A review. *Journal of Cleaner Production, 97*, 76–91. https://doi.org/10.1016/j.jclepro.2013.11.049

Vanacore, E., Rex, E., & Wickman, T. (2021). *Circular economy & the furniture industry : The state-of-the-art in the EU & Sweden* (Issue June).https://doi.org/10.1016/j.jclepro.2019.03.052

Vermunt, D. A., Negro, S. O., Verweij, P. A., Kuppens, D. V., & Hekkert, M. P. (2019). Exploring barriers to implementing different circular business models. *Journal of Cleaner Production, 222*, 891–902. https://doi.org/10.1016/j.jclepro.2019.03.052

Chapter 7
Circular Transformation of the Plastic Industry

Abstract This chapter presents dominant circular business models across the plastic industry, as well as challenges and new opportunities in the transition towards a circular economy. The chapter starts with an industry-specific literature review to identify global trends, key barriers, and opportunities for circular transformation in the plastic industry. The further focus is on the statistical circular performance of the Lithuanian plastic industry in the context of small open economies. We then present the results of our original survey of Lithuanian plastic manufacturers regarding their priorities towards the circular economy, as well as drivers and barriers. Finally, the chapter ends with a summary of best practices of plastic circular business models.

Keywords Plastic industry · Global trends · Circular performance · Circular patterns · Plastic circular business models

7.1 Global Trends in the Plastic Industry

The circular economy (CE) aims to fundamentally change the business logic of plastics, with increasing bans on single-use plastics and ambitious recycling targets. Negative public perceptions, caused by the marine plastics crisis, became a disruptive change driver for the industry that resulted in a series of strict regulations and pressures from environmental and social groups around the world (Mah, 2021).

Plastics are widely used. Some are the end products in and of themselves such as garden furniture, household items, packaging (e.g., bags and bottles), and some are part of a larger product, appearing in cars, for example, or electronic devices. The statistics highlight the **scale of plastic production and consumption**. At the end of their life, end user products become waste that is collected and processed. In 2018, 9.4 million tonnes of plastic post-consumer waste were collected in Europe to be recycled (inside and outside the European Union [EU]) (Plastics Europe, 2019), meanwhile, generation of plastic packaging waste alone accounted for 14.82 million tonnes in the EU in 2018 (27).[1] In 2018, global production of plastic reached almost

[1] Generation of plastic packaging waste in the European Union (EU-27) from 2005 to 2019. https://www.statista.com/statistics/881996/plastic-packaging-waste-generated-eu/.

© The Author(s), under exclusive license to Springer Nature Switzerland AG 2023
L. Dagilienė et al., *Circular Business Models in the Manufacturing Industry*, Studies in Energy, Resource and Environmental Economics,
https://doi.org/10.1007/978-3-031-28809-8_7

360 million tonnes, and the production of plastic in Europe reached almost 62 million tonnes, accounting for 17.2% of global plastic production (Plastics Europe, 2019).

The world is facing a plastic crisis because plastic pollution is a serious global problem that requires an urgent international response, involving all relevant actors at different levels. The plastic crisis caused a great resonance in the actions of governmental institutions, supranational bodies, business enterprises, and non-governmental organizations. Major plastics enterprises have responded to the crisis, and to social pressures, by reallocating money for ocean clean-ups, developing new recycling technologies, and joining voluntary alliances with other industry stakeholders (Mah, 2021).

The European Commission (EC) has introduced a **European strategy for plastic** in the CE (European Commission, 2018) that aims to transform the way plastic products are designed, produced, used, and recycled in the EU. This strategic approach outlines the challenges, strategies, and opportunities for a more circular production and use of plastic products (Paletta et al., 2019). From the bottom-up approach, "The New Plastics Economy" report by the Ellen MacArthur Foundation (2016, 2019) provides a "transition strategy" for the plastics industry, to redesign packaging and implement new business models that enable better use of packaging and increase the recycling rate up to 70%. The report makes six key aims[2]:

- Prioritize the elimination of problematic or unnecessary plastic packaging through design, innovation, and new delivery models.
- Reuse models are applied where appropriate, reducing (or eliminating if possible) the need for single-use packaging.
- All plastic packaging is 100% reusable, recyclable, or compostable.
- All plastic packaging is practically reused, recycled, or composted.
- The use of plastic is completely decoupled from the consumption of primary (virgin) resources.
- All plastic packaging is free of hazardous chemicals; therefore the health, safety, and rights of everyone involved are respected.

The study by Paletta et al. (2019) revealed importance of **legislative** factors such as the REACH Regulation[3] and the RoHS Directive[4] in some detail. Another important piece of legislation, the European Directive on Single-Use Plastics,[5] aims to make plastics manufacturers take more responsibility and ban single-use plastics by 2021. Single-use plastic plates, cutlery, straws, balloon sticks, and cotton buds can no longer be sold in any of the EU Member States. This a good way to show how it is possible

[2] The New Plastics Economy: Rethinking the future of plastics. https://ellenmacarthurfoundation.org/the-new-plastics-economy-rethinking-the-future-of-plastics

[3] REACH Legislation. https://echa.europa.eu/regulations/reach/legislation.

[4] Restriction of the use of certain hazardous substances (RoHS) https://single-market-economy.ec.europa.eu/single-market/european-standards/harmonised-standards/restriction-use-certain-hazardous-substances-rohs_en.

[5] This legislation was introduced in June 2019. More information: https://environment.ec.europa.eu/topics/plastics/single-use-plastics/eu-restrictions-certain-single-use-plastics_en.

to eliminate problematic single-use plastic products through proper regulation and design.

Although there are significant regulatory attempts and initiatives for plastic reduction and recycling at the global level, definitional issues and a call for more standardized product declarations and security regarding material composition are needed in the plastic industry (Stumpf et al., 2021). Industrial waste can circulate without mandatory requirements, but the boundary between waste and non-waste status is still unclear. Other constraints relate to incompatible legislation on chemicals, wastes, and products, as well as a lack of eco-design guidelines and support for the development of circular models (Paletta et al., 2019).

With regard to the **technological and recycling challenges**, the key structural and material challenges are related to the multiple types of plastics, contamination issues in the waste stream, proper quality for recycling, and cost (Mah, 2021). Research targeted at plastic manufacturers, and partially at other related industries (Khan et al., 2020; Paletta et al., 2019; Rossi et al., 2020) stress the importance of technological solutions, including digital technologies (Lacy et al., 2020). Interestingly, most organizations have positive intentions towards industrial plastic waste management, yet they seem to be failing in implementing best practices in plastic recycling due to a number of critical barriers such as access to recycling facilities, transport and storage issues (Mhatre et al., 2021), and a lack of recycling technologies and skilled personnel to sort plastic waste (Khan et al., 2020).[6]

In line with general reviews about drivers and barriers for the CE (Guldmann & Huulgaard, 2020), Paletta et al. (2019) also emphasize possible trade-offs between the **quality of plastic products** and the **use of recycled materials**. In particular, the presence of certain impurities can cause problems in relation to the correct processing temperature, also causing a reduction in mechanical performance. Finally, Paletta et al. (2019) mapped different barriers in plastic production, namely compound, conversion, distribution & use, and finally, recycling. Depending on the requirements for the manufacture of specific plastic products, compounders add chemicals to improve the properties of the polymers, such as flexibility and strength (Paletta et al., 2019). Therefore, one of the technical–technological barriers is the lack of information on the composition of recycled plastics, including hazardous substances.

In the literature, examples of business models from the plastics industry are often associated with the **resource recovery business model** (Vermunt et al., 2019). The value proposition of this business model revolves around exploiting the residual value of plastic waste by converting it into new forms of value (Bocken et al., 2016). Rossi et al. (2020) analyse existing circular business models for the plastic manufacturing industry, among others. By using a case study, the authors identify such features as the recovery of secondary raw materials/by-products and the use of reverse logistics to close the loops in agrochemicals and packaging. Lacy et al. (2020) also emphasize

---

[6] Khan et al. (2020) surveyed 637 organizations from different industries, investigating behaviours and attitudes towards industrial plastic waste. Only 14% of respondents reported that their organizations are successfully reusing plastic waste, and 23% are reducing it.

the need to develop technologies and business models to circulate molecules through reuse and recycling, and through renewable feedstock.

It is important to note that most research that focuses on circular business models usually explores **sustainable plastic packaging** as an integral part of other industries, e.g., the food and beverages industry and the fast-moving consumer goods (FMCG) industry. For example, in a study of companies that apply CE principles (namely fully circular, upstream circular, and downstream circular), Urbinati et al. (2017) present the case of Replenish, operating in the FMCG and packaging industries. The so-called upstream circular company seeks to eliminate plastic bottle waste by providing brands and businesses with reusable, refillable bottles for liquid concentrate that can be added to water by the end user. Upstream circular companies operate more on the internal and networking aspect of the CE, and most of their efforts are invisible to the customer (Urbinati et al., 2017).

FMCG (glass, packaging, ceramics, food and drinks, textiles, apparel and leather, plastics, and rubber) are not related to remanufacturing, and rather are orientated towards recycling, reducing, or reuse (Stumpf et al., 2021). Processed foods, refined sugars, additives, and preservatives, with little nutritional value and addictive qualities, are not only unhealthy but are usually sold in single-use packaging and so are a major contributor to the global problem of plastic packaging waste (Bocken et al., 2020). **Discarded plastic packaging** is increasingly recognized as a major global issue requiring, at minimum, the organization of take-back systems or reverse logistics.

The academic and grey literature clearly gives a great deal of attention to the plastics problem and various ways of solving it. However, a number of these measures are still aimed at eliminating the consequences through recycling, rather than essentially reducing the amount of material produced. As pointed out by Mah (2021, p. 122), "while the petrochemical industry commits to the aspiration of a circular economy with less waste and maximal efficiency, it continues to invest in unsustainable projects with environmental justice and climate change consequences".

The barriers to circular business model innovation, according to Guldmann and Huulgaard (2020), include a lack of definitions, a lack of recycling technology and infrastructure, and insufficient financial resources, as described in Chapter 2. Below, we summarize key barriers that are particularly important to the plastics industry.

Key Barriers to a Circular Plastic Industry:

- Product design and materials (supply):
  - High use of non-renewable resources for energy and feedstock.
  - Possible trade-offs between product quality and the use of recycled materials (Paletta et al., 2019).
  - Hazardous by-products and high energy use (Lacy et al., 2020).
  - Lack of knowledge and technologies, e.g., recycled materials may behave differently in the manufacturing process (Vermunt et al., 2019).

- Supply chain (supply):
  - Lack of knowledge about potential buyers of plastic waste.
  - Lack of access to recycling facilities (Mhatre et al., 2021).
  - Transportation (to recycling facilities) and storage issues of plastic waste.
  - Uncertainty about the quality of waste can be a challenge for recycling processes.
  - Lack of recycling technologies.
- Economics (supply):
  - High price of secondary materials (recycled) in comparison with primary materials.
  - Low prices of primary (virgin) materials in the market makes it more difficult for companies to create or maintain an economically viable business model.
  - Insufficient funds to pursue plastic recycling (Khan et al., 2020).
- Consumer (demand):
  - Plastic packaging waste from consumers goes to landfill.
  - Skills and knowledge (sorting).
  - Lack of responsibility.

Opportunities for a Circular Plastics Industry

The plastics and plastic packaging industry is characterized by a resource-intensive manufacturing process, requiring millions of tonnes of raw materials and generating large volumes of post-consumption waste. Therefore, elimination of unnecessary plastic products, design choices for secondary (recycled) materials, effective collection systems, and recycling technologies might open up opportunities for a transition towards a circular plastic industry (Table 7.1).

7.2 Circular Performance of the Lithuanian Plastic Industry

The analysis of the CE indicators of the plastics industry is done by comparing macro-economic indicators which could help to evaluate the circularity. Five areas are distinguished to present the results, which are presented in the methodology section (see Chapter 3).

The plastics industry has the Nomenclature of Economic Activities (NACE) classification code C22, “Manufacture of rubber and plastic products”. Due to the limited statistical information about some specific indicators, we take aggregated information for the C20–C22 sectors, where this code means “Manufacture of chemical, pharmaceutical, rubber and plastic products”.

Table 7.1 Opportunities for a circular plastic industry

Strategy	– Use of cutting-edge technologies (e.g., advances in mechanical and chemical recycling) – Use of digital technologies, such as big data technology and machine learning techniques (Lacy et al., 2020) – Circular sourcing
Product design and materials	– Use of recycled plastics (bottles, packaging)
Cleaner production	– Reduction of energy use by focusing more on renewables – Reduction of pollution
Usage & product life-cycle extension	– Responsible use of plastic packaging from the perspective of both manufacturers and consumers
Waste management	– Recycling technologies allowing low-cost recycling for high-value applications – Waste management companies should provide the necessary training programmes, guidelines, and facilities to organizations – Government or other relevant institutions should assist in establishing a networking platform to facilitate the sale or reuse of plastic waste (Khan et al., 2020)

Vision and strategy. The vision and strategy section presents the motivation of plastic and rubber manufacturing companies to implement environmental innovations. We select two indicators to analyse: environmental protection expenditure and environmental protection investment.

The results of the analysis show that the total amount of environmental protection expenditures was the highest in 2015 (€1.36 million) and the lowest in 2017 (€6.13 million). As presented in Fig. 7.1, protection expenditure for ambient air and climate decreased from 2015 through to 2018. The expenditure for waste-water management grew in the period 2016–2018, while expenditure for waste management decreased significantly in 2017 and grew again in 2018.

Expenditure on waste management was 89.5% of the total in 2018. The expenditure for other environmental protection activities was very volatile throughout the period. Companies tried to abandon internal environmental costs and tended to buy in external environmental services, as seen by the rise in this expenditure category from 24.9% in 2015, to 90.4% in 2018.

Environmental protection investment was quite low at between 0.2% and 1.9% of total investment. Investment grew in 2016–2018, but is still much lower than environmental expenditures. The highest amount of environmental protection investment is found in the year 2015 (€1.2 million), decreasing to €0.2 million in 2018. We note that, in 2018, 100% of environmental protection investment is targeted at environmental protection activities and there is clearly no interest in investing in production processes.

According to the Eurostat database, the leaders by investment amount are Czech Republic (€13.9 million), the Netherlands (€12.2 million), Belgium (€3.0 million),

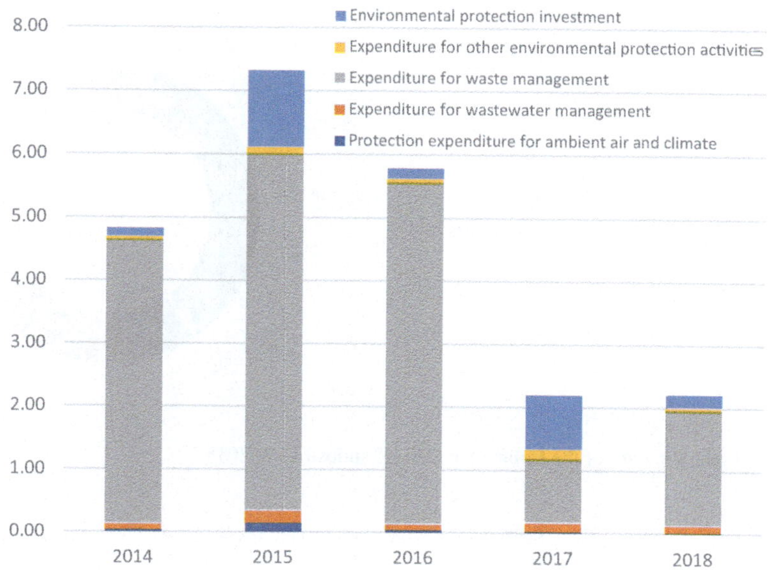

Fig. 7.1 Environmental expenditure and investment in plant and equipment for pollution control by the Lithuanian C20–22 industries in 2014–2018 (€ million)

and Slovenia (€0.2 million), all of which tend to invest more in plant and equipment linked to cleaner technology than for pollution control.

Raw materials, secondary raw materials, and eco-design. The use and complexity of raw materials are best described by the input structure of the Lithuanian C20–22 industries. However, there is a limited amount of data to analyse the use of secondary raw materials in particular industries, as well as eco-design changes. However, eco-design structure is partly reflected by input complexity. The inputs into the Lithuanian rubber and plastic products manufacturing industry are much simpler than those into furniture manufacturing.

As presented in Fig. 7.2, the value-added at basic prices accounts for about 40% of the input into the C20–22 sectors. Chemical and pharmaceutical products (such as paint, varnish, glue) account for 18% of the input of furniture manufacturing, and about 14% of the input is used to purchase products from other companies in the same sector. Expenses for wholesale and retail account for a relatively large share of the sector's input, at 10%.

The electricity, gas, water supply and environmental services, transportation and storage, and taxes on intermediate and final products each account for 2%, whereas only 1% of the input structure go to each of the following; products from paper products and printing, coke and refined petroleum, fabricated metal products, and other business sector services.

Cleaner production. While analysing the Lithuanian C20–22 industries, the indicators of energy and emissions related to cleaner production were selected for review.

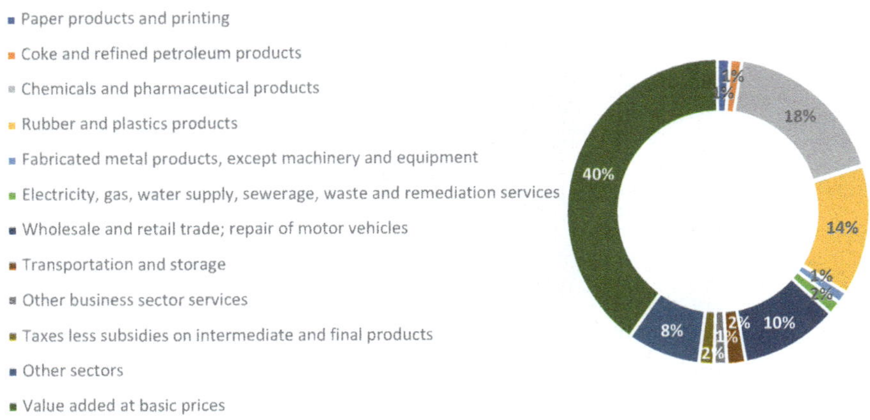

Fig. 7.2 Input structure of the Lithuanian C20–22 industries in 2015

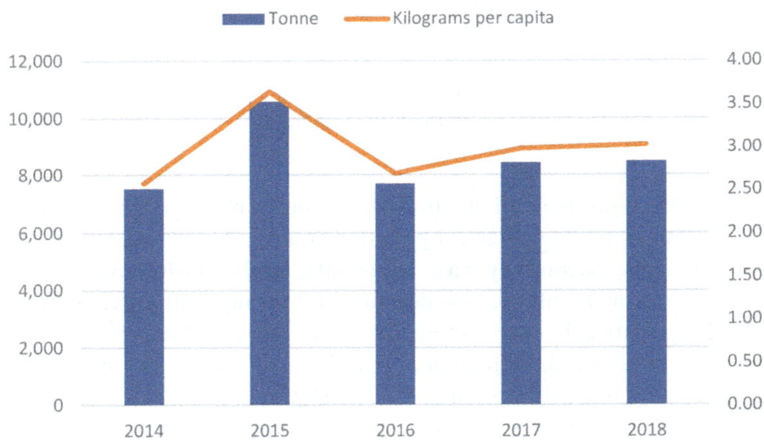

Fig. 7.3 CO2 emissions from the Lithuanian C20–22 industries

According to Fig. 7.3, CO2 emissions decreased to 7716 tonnes in 2016 and grew over the next two years to 8503 tonnes in 2018. During the period 2014–2018, the average value of CO2 emissions was 8567 tonnes, or 2.99 kg per capita; in 2018, it was 3 kg per capita, compared to Slovakia, with the highest value at 141.7 kg per capita, followed by Slovenia (45.1 kg), Luxembourg (29.4 kg), and Czech Republic (21.3 kg).

This indicator significantly decreased in Malta (by 19% in 2018), Cyprus (by 15% in 2018), and Luxembourg (by 13% in 2018), whereas strong growth was found in Latvia (16% in 2018) and Slovakia (10% in 2018).

The analysis of energy use shows an increasing demand for energy in the Lithuanian C20–22 sectors. The average growth in energy use was 11% across the period from 2014 to 2018. In 2018, energy was consumed mainly from electricity (77.9%), then natural gas (6.7%), and transport diesel (9.3%). The highest use of the SOEs was in Czech Republic in 2018, but the largest user of renewable energy was Estonia (6.6%). Denmark (2.4%) uses renewable energy in these sectors, while in other countries, the renewable energy input was zero.

The majority of SOEs use electrical energy as the main energy source for the manufacturing of rubber and plastic products. We identified five countries with completely different structures of energy products. In Ireland, transport diesel use is 95%. The second is Belgium, with 36% of the energy used coming from wood and wood waste, and 23% from electrical energy. In Finland, 32% of the energy is used from other petroleum products, and 27% from electrical energy. Liquid biofuels (40%) and transport diesel (24%) are the main energy products in Estonia, whereas in Slovenia, the main energy products are transport diesel (36%), natural gas (19%), and electrical energy (18%).

Consumption, reuse, repair. The consumption analysis is done by analysing output measures in 2015 from the OECD database. The results show that the main consumers of Lithuanian C20–22 products were households (20%) and companies inside the sector (13%) (see Fig. 7.4).

The construction sector uses about 10% of plastics, while 8% of the output is used by transportation and storage, and 7% by the food products, beverages, and tobacco industry. Both wholesale and retail trade and other manufacturing sectors use about 6% of produced products, 4% goes to chemical and pharmaceutical products, and 3% goes to agriculture, forestry and fishing, and electrical equipment. All the remaining sectors of the economy collectively consume about 17%.

According to OECD data, exports US$25.7 million in 2015, resulting in an import surplus of 2%.

Waste management. The production of rubber and plastic generated 2.2 million tonnes of waste in the Lithuania in 2018. This is measured every two years and has

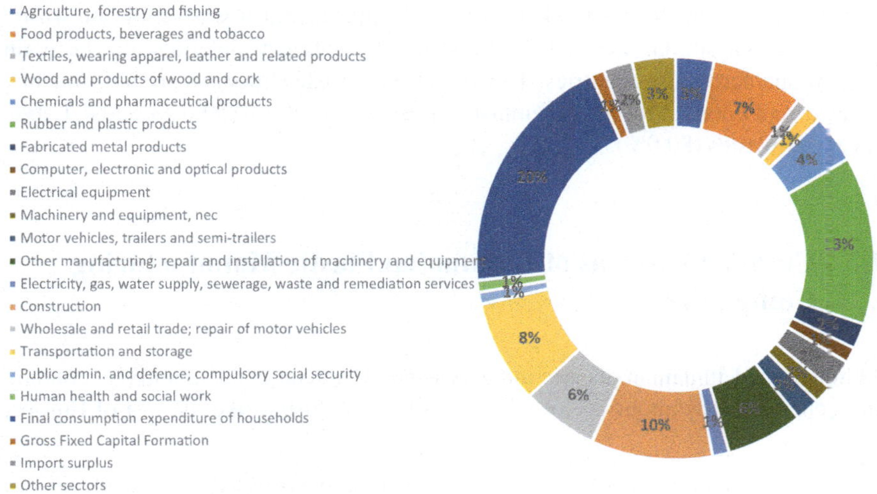

Fig. 7.4 Use structure of the output of the Lithuanian (C20–22) industries in 2015

Fig. 7.5 The structure of generated waste from the Lithuanian C20–C22 industries in 2018

decreased by 0.3% from 2016, whereas compared to the period of 2014–2016 it has increased by 3.5%.

The results of the analysis show that most of the waste consists of other mineral wastes (98.2%) (see Fig. 7.5), while plastic wastes account for 0.69%, mixed and undifferentiated materials 0.23%, and metal ferrous waste 0.15%.

A comparison of the waste generated in Lithuania with other SOEs shows that the Lithuanian C20–22 industries generate the highest amount of waste. A similar value of generated waste is found in Belgium (2.1 million tonnes). All other selected countries have a waste volume of less than 1 million tonnes. The waste structure is very different in other SOEs, where spent solvents, chemical wastes, plastic waste, household and similar waste, mixed and undifferentiated materials are the main types found across the countries. The exceptional waste structures are in Lithuania, Finland, and Latvia. Most of the Finnish waste consists of soil (59.6%), and in Latvia is vegetal wastes (80.0%).

7.3 Circular Patterns of Lithuanian Plastic Manufacturing Companies

Although the Lithuanian plastic[7] industry is not dominant in the country's economy and generates only about 1% of GDP, the plastic industry, like the rest of Europe,

[7] Officially (according to the NACE classification) the industry is called Rubber and Plastics, but in the book we refer to it collectively as the plastic industry.

is on the threshold of revolutionary transformations, caused by the EU directive on disposable plastic restrictions, and is an important and active participant in the search for technological solutions and innovations.

Details of our survey are given in Chapter 4. This chapter presents the results for the plastics companies surveyed. Almost all the plastics companies are operating in both national and international markets. Most participants are medium sized or large companies, both by number of employees and revenues (see Fig. 7.6). It is noticeable that only 15% of those that participated in the survey do not invest in green technologies or have no data on such investments. On the other hand, we see that at least 22% of them invest between 21 and 30% in green technologies of total investments.

The survey results of the CE in Lithuanian plastic manufacturing companies are visualized in Fig. 7.7.

At the vision and corporate strategy level, the largest focus is on digitalization. Digitalization, materials science, and additive manufacturing taken together are transforming the plastics industry. This transformation has implications not only for process and production efficiency, but also for international competition, as it can

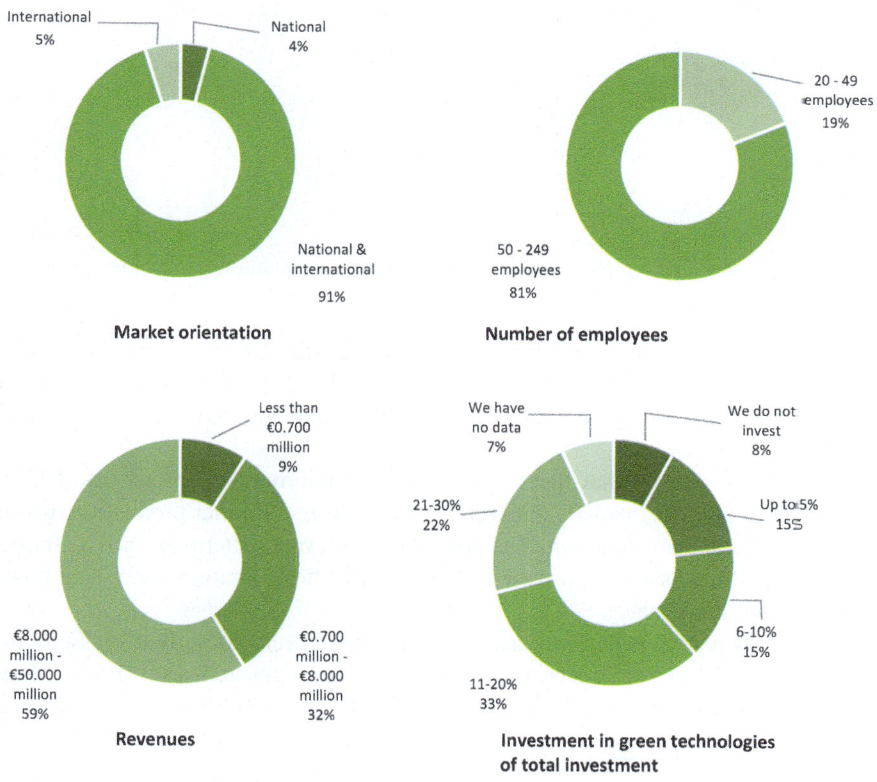

Fig. 7.6 Surveyed plastics companies' characteristics (2019)

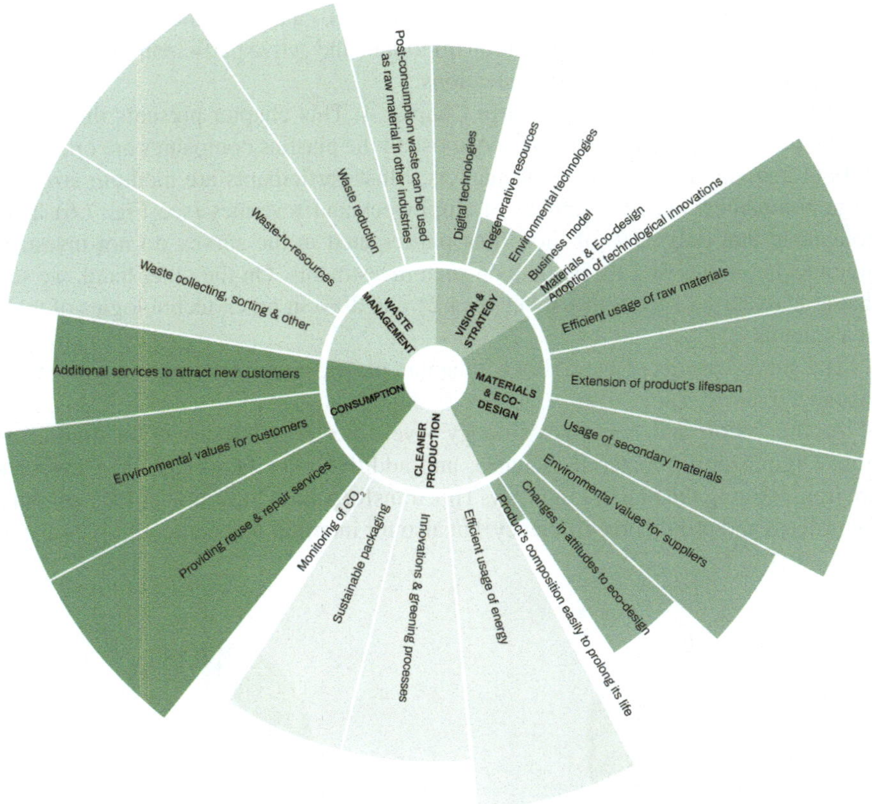

Fig. 7.7 The portfolio of relevant patterns of the CE in Lithuanian plastic manufacturing companies

allow smaller producers to enter the market and acquire technological capabilities that were previously only available to medium-sized and larger players.[8] Lithuanian plastics companies' strategies and focus on digitalization are thus in line with global trends.

The survey showed that there is an active transformation towards the CE in this sector in all areas, namely materials and eco-design, cleaner production, waste management, and consumption. The portfolio of relevant patterns of the CE shows the start of a transformation from a narrow resource flows strategy (dominant now) to a close-the-loop one.

As regards materials and eco-design, the priorities (very strongly expressed) are the efficient use of raw materials, product lifespan extension, use of secondary materials, and environmental values to suppliers, which indicates the prevalence

[8] Digital transformation of the plastic products factory. https://www.competition.org.za/ccred-blog-digital-industrial-policy/2020/4/21/digital-transformation-of-the-plastic-products-factory.

of eco-efficient strategies. The focus on secondary materials is aligned through all company activity areas. Furthermore, the surveyed companies are proactively creating environmental values for suppliers. Changes in attitudes to eco-design take place as well. However, experimenting with product composition patterns is not their focus.

The surveyed companies do not see serious challenges regarding cleaner production, because they have already focused on the efficient use of energy, innovation, and greening processes, as well as sustainable packaging. Their cleaner production process is based on renewable energy sources, mainly from solar energy. It is important to note that Lithuanian plastic manufacturers are orientated to export and their key consumers are foreign companies (B2B), which impose additional environmental requirements in terms of product quality and cleaner production processes. However, the companies do not measure negative environmental impact, such as CO2 emissions. This might be explained by the fact that the survey was dominated by medium-sized companies, and only the largest companies have legal obligations to monitor and report on emissions.

The plastics companies do not face huge challenges in terms of industrial waste management, because this area is more mature, especially waste collection, sorting systems, waste to resource, and waste reduction. The extreme interconnection with other industries via various types of packaging, their technological readiness for recycling, and a well-developed reverse logistics system in the whole ecosystem proves the possibility for companies to use post-consumption waste as material in other industries.

Plastic companies aim to create environmental values for customers. The problems caused by plastics are receiving a lot of political, regulatory and social attention, and plastic companies are paying attention to the problems caused by plastic consumption. Another important fact is that the plastic manufacturers are in the middle of the value chain and do not usually have a direct connection with the product after its market life, especially in export markets. The responsibility for collecting plastic lies with the final consumer goods industry. The results also indicate that, currently, manufacturers do see a significant role in closing the loops, as production and consumption systems are interconnected via developed reverse logistics systems.

The analysis of factors motivating the plastic manufactures to transition to the CE is presented in Fig. 7.8.

The key drivers are external financial support (this might be related to the adoption of expensive technologies), proper tax policy, and product certification. As the EU has introduced restrictions on the use of primary plastics, and the industry is looking for technological solutions to meet this requirement, the certification of secondary raw materials and of the product itself are critical to the quality of other products. Creating innovation requires a combination of financial and human resources and competencies, so it is not surprising that external financial support is an important incentive for companies to implement circular innovation based solutions, raised due to legal regulation.

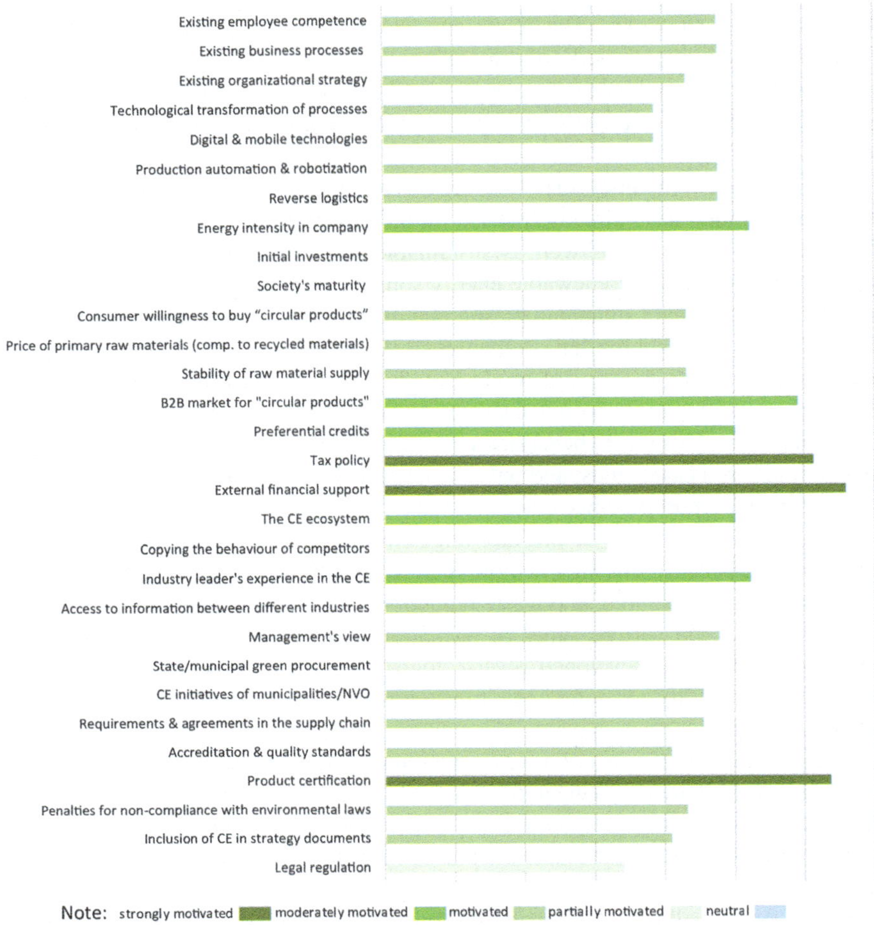

Fig. 7.8 Factors that influence plastics manufacturers to move towards the CE

7.4 Best Practices of Plastic Circular Business Models

The Lithuanian chemicals, plastics, and packaging sector has production capacity across all of the stages of the chemicals value chain, from production of primary and intermediate goods to the sale and distribution of the finished products or plastic packaging.[9] The primary production of plastics is limited to a few facilities, some owned by foreign companies.

The Lithuanian plastic packaging industry has implemented a successful bottle deposit system, that will be discussed later as a best practice case study. The country also plays an important part in the plastic bottle production industry. In addition,

[9] PPMI (2021). "Report on the Lithuanian Industrial Landscape and its Potential to Integrate into European Value Chains".

there are already innovative market players chemically recycling PET, such as the Neo Group (See Footnote 13 in Chapter 6). Eurostat reports that, in 2018, the level of plastic recycling reached 69%, which means that Lithuania ranks first in the EU. Lithuanian plastic manufacturers are also export-orientated companies at the EU level and are active participants in the search for technological solutions and innovations.

One of the main problems, which also exists globally, is the low quality of post-consumer plastic, due to disparate plastic waste collection policies and practices, which makes it difficult to create closed circular loops. The other threat in the plastics industry is related to the large differences in the quality of secondary materials in different EU countries. In addition, the highest quality secondary materials are sold to the highest bidder, who may not be in Lithuania (See Footnote 13 in Chapter 6).

A few exemplary Lithuanian companies that have formulated a sustainability strategy, as well as reverse logistics systems, are presented in Table 7.2.

Neo Group was founded in 2004 and is now one of the largest producers of polyethylene terephthalate (PET) granules and aromatic polyester polyols (APP). The plant produces over 450,000 tonnes per year, or 14% of European production of PET granules for food and beverage packaging, of which about 90% is shipped to Poland, Scandinavia, and other European regions, serving 300 packaging companies across more than 30 countries.

Materials and eco-design. In 2021, the Neo Group started supplying the first batches of PET pellets using 25% recycled material. The product, named "Neopet Cycle", is based on chemical recycling technology developed by the company's engineers and scientists, and currently patented by the Neo Group in the EU. This innovation allows beverage packaging manufacturers to meet the EU target for the use of secondary raw materials earlier than the 2025 deadline. All Neo Group product elements are fully recyclable.

Cleaner production. At the end of 2020, a 1000 kW solar power plant started operating on the roof of the warehouse where the finished product is stored. Through a series of energy efficiency projects, the company has managed to reduce its electricity consumption per tonne of product produced by more than a third. From 2019, all electricity consumed by the Neo Group is green. The company follows its integrated quality and environmental management system that meets ISO 9001 and ISO 14001 international standards and requirements. The company calculates and monitors its carbon footprint and provides public environmental reports through the relevant channels, as well as engaging and collaborating with its raw material suppliers to calculate their carbon footprint and adopt mitigation strategies.

Plasta is an advanced, modern, experimental plastics manufacturing company. Plasta is one of the largest secondary polyethylene raw materials processors and manufacturers in the world, manufacturing more than 500,000,000 plastic bags per year, as well as other plastic products. The company recycles over 34,000 tonnes of plastic waste per year, and almost 98% of production is made from secondary raw materials. More than 22,000 tonnes of Plasta products are made from its own produced secondary raw material, which is 100% recycled post-consumer waste. In the year 2000, Plasta was awarded an ISO 9001:2015 certificate.

Table 7.2 Lithuanian best practices of plastic companies cases

Company	Product features	Business model	CE aspects
Manufacturers			
Neo Group[10] A range of high-quality polyethylene terephthalate (PET) resins and polyols	Quality	Efficient use of resources (narrow resource flows) Eco-design	– Green energy – Innovation ("Neopet Cycle") to implement the EU 2025 requirements for the use of secondary raw materials
Plasta[11] Plastic garbage bags, films, sheets, and granules	Quality Durability	Efficient use of resources (narrow resource flows) Eco-design	– Principle of working without waste – Green energy – The Blue Angel labels – Innovation – Public education and information initiatives – Digital solutions – Sorting of waste inside the company and encouraging employees to sort at home – Financial support

(continued)

[10] Neo Group https://neogroup.eu/en/company/about-us/.

[11] Plasta https://www.plasta.lt/en/about-us/.

Table 7.2 (continued)

Company	Product features	Business model	CE aspects
Reverse logistics			
Užstato Sistemos Administratorius (USAD) (Deposit system)[12]	Close accessibility Convenience Clarity of rules Publicity Differentiation according to customer profile (individual, business, public organizations)	Resource recovery Public information and education	– Collection infrastructure development – Activity is based on the principle of producer responsibility – Public education and information programmes – Using an electric vehicle – Transparency – Mediation for financial support purposes

[12] Užstato Sistemos Administratorius https://grazintiverta.lt/en/about/74.

Materials and eco-design. When designing new products, the company considers their environmental impact, minimizes potential pollution, and pursues greening policies. Knotties patent is a unique patented bag technology with advantages such as reducing CO2 emissions and requiring a lower consumption of raw materials. Knotties bags are especially handy to use thanks to their exceptionally long handles and large opening, allowing the perfect utilization of the entire volume of the bag.

Cleaner production. The company seeks to implement the principle of zero waste and saving energy, tools, and equipment in the production process. Plasta buys electricity from renewable energy sources. In 2020, Plasta was awarded the German Blue Angel label, which confirms the compliance of the production processes and products with high standards related to the environment, health, and performance.

Waste management. Plasta promotes the use of recycled products and raw materials, choosing recycled paper, textiles, and other products wherever possible. They not only sort their own waste, such as plastic, glass, and paper, but they also encourage employees and suppliers to the same. The company supports green, environmental, and pollution-reducing associations, to the greatest extent possible, as well as individuals, projects, and educational institutions researching and developing measures to reduce pollution.

Consumption. The company is reducing their own consumption by replacing work tools with electronic solutions, and refurbishing and using old, second-hand items, providing that the quality does not suffer. They publish educational materials through paid and free channels, take an interest in the care of children and youth education, and initiate and participate in other educational projects.

The deposit system has been operating in Lithuania since 2016. The non-profit organization "Užstato Sistemos Administratorius" (USAD) was established by Lithuanian beverage producers, importers, and sellers, which manage the system on the principle of extended producer responsibility. At the end of 2022, the company had 17 employees and 2021 revenue amounting to €35.5 million (2020–€27.24 million). USAD receives revenues from three sources:

- Subsidies from beverage producers and importers (about 50% of total revenue).
- Secondary raw materials sold (about 30% of the total revenue).
- Not withdrawn deposits (about 20% of the total revenue).

The price of the deposit for one-way packaging under the system is approved by the Minister of Environment of the Republic of Lithuania for a period of at least one year. The value of the packaging deposit approved in October 2015 was €0.1 and has remained unchanged (with a perspective of 2023).

USAD collects 90% of the empty beverage cans and 92% of the one-way glass and plastic bottles, marked with the deposit system mark, that are sold each year. The deposit is applicable to the following types of one-way packaging:

- Glass (except fruit-wine, fruit-wine-based drinks, and fruit-wine cocktails in one-way glass packaging).
- PET.
- Metal.

The deposit system applies to one-way, single-use packaging of the following beverages: beer, cider, fruit-wine, other fermented drinks, alcoholic cocktails, and non-alcoholic drinks, such as soft drinks, table water, natural mineral water, spring water, bottled drinking water, juice, and nectar. There are around 3000 manual collection points and reverse vending machines around the country, mainly located near supermarkets in all 60 municipalities.

All packaging collected under the deposit system are recycled. To be more precise, in 2020, a total of 24,697,061 tonnes of packaging was collected for further processing.

USAD also implements public education and information activities such as communication and publicity on social networks, online media, national and regional press, radio broadcasting, radio games, integration into summer festivals and events, social initiatives, organization of excursions to the USAD Computing Centre, and others. According to public opinion, the system contributes to the clean-up of the environment and helps to reduce the amount of litter found in forests, lakes, and other natural sites.

USAD provides annual enforcement, financial, public education, and outreach reports (quarterly and annually), showing collection rates and operating costs. It also publicly provides information on collected packaging by municipalities. To ensure a transparent process and to avoid inaccuracies, USAD employs independent auditors who audit rates on an annual basis.

Companies that have a contract with a deposit system administrator can donate the funds recovered from the deposit to another organization, such as an animal shelter. Individuals can also donate deposits to support various USAD initiatives. For example, in 2020, at the suggestion of USAD, funds collected from the deposit of disposable packaging donated by many people were transferred to two directorates of Lithuanian regional parks. USAD also uses an electric car to collect disposable beverage packages from offices, restaurants, and hotels around the capital city, Vilnius.

Key Highlights

- The Lithuanian plastic industry is highly technologically developed, with an increasing focus on green and circularity-oriented innovations.
- Business models embedded in the plastic industry are starting a transformation from a strategy to narrow resource flows (dominant now) to a close-the-loop one.
- Eco-design is gaining importance, although there is much room for improvement in technological readiness.
- Plastic manufacturers are connected with other industries via developed reverse logistics systems to close the loop, despite the fact that they sell their products to other manufacturers and retailers.
- The Lithuanian deposit system serves as a successful proof of concept of a circular supplies business model and gathers around 92% of the one-way glass and plastic bottles, marked with the deposit system mark, that are sold each year. It is also educational.

- There is also a need for delivery/reverse logistics business models for other types of plastic packaging. Technology and knowledge are available, but regulations and guidelines need to be developed and agreed upon.
- European education and innovation policies, followed by R&D related instruments, remain important horizontal drivers to foster circularity in the Lithuanian plastics industry.

References

Bocken, N., Morales, L. S., & Lehner, M. (2020). Sufficiency business strategies in the food industry—The case of Oatly. *Sustainability (Switzerland), 12*(3). https://doi.org/10.3390/su12030824

Bocken, N. M. P., Pauw, I., Bakker, C. A., & van der Grinten, B. (2016). Product design and business model strategies for a circular economy. *Journal of Industrial and Production Engineering, 3*(5), 308–320. https://doi.org/10.1080/21681015.2016.1172124

Ellen MacArthur Foundation. (2016). *The new plastic economy: Rethinking the future of plastics.* https://ellenmacarthurfoundation.org/the-new-plastics-economy-rethinking-the-future-of-plastics

Ellen MacArthur Foundation. (2019). *Vision for a circular economy for plastics.* https://ellenmacarthurfoundation.org/plastics-vision

European Commission. (2018). *Plastic Waste: A European strategy to protect the planet, defend our citizens and empower our industries.* https://ec.europa.eu/commission/presscorner/detail/en/IP_18_5

Guldmann, E., & Huulgaard, R. D. (2020). Barriers to circular business model innovation: A multiple-case study. *Journal of Cleaner Production, 243*, 118160. https://doi.org/10.1016/j.jclepro.2019.118160

Khan, O., Daddi, T., Slabbinck, H., Kleinhans, K., Vazquez-Brust, D., & De Meester, S. (2020). Assessing the determinants of intentions and behaviors of organizations towards a circular economy for plastics. *Resources, Conservation and Recycling, 163*(105069). https://doi.org/10.1016/J.RESCONREC.2020.105069

Lacy, P., Long. J., & Spindler, W. (2020). *The circular economy handbook: Realizing the circular advantage* (p. 363). Springer, ISBN 978-1-349-95967-9. https://doi.org/10.1057/978-1-349-95968-6

Mah, A. (2021). Future-proofing capitalism: The paradox of the circular economy for plastics. *Global Environmental Politics, 21*(2), 121–142. https://doi.org/10.1162/glep_a_00594

Mhatre, P., Panchal, R., Singh, A., & Bibyan, S. (2021). A systematic literature review on the circular economy initiatives in the European Union. *Sustainable Production and Consumption, 26*, 187–202. https://doi.org/10.1016/j.spc2020.09.008

Paletta, A., Leal Filho, W., Balogun, A. L., Foschi, E., & Bonoli, A. (2019). Barriers and challenges to plastics valorisation in the context of a circular economy: Case studies from Italy. *Journal of Cleaner Production, 241*(118149). https://doi.org/10.1016/J.JCLEPRO.2019.118149

Plastics Europe. (2019). *Plastics—The facts 2019.* https://www.plasticseurope.org/en/resources/market-data

Rossi, E., Bertassini, A. C., Ferreira, C. dos S., Neves do Amaral, W. A., & Ometto, A. R. (2020). Circular economy indicators for organizations considering sustainability and business models: Plastic, textile and electro-electronic cases. *Journal of Cleaner Production, 247*. https://doi.org/10.1016/j.jclepro.2019.119137

Stumpf, L., Schöggl, J.-P., & Baumgartner, R. J. (2021). Climbing up the circularity ladder?—A mixed-methods analysis of circular economy in business practice. *Journal of Cleaner Production*, 316(128158). https://doi.org/10.1016/J.JCLEPRO.2021.128158

Urbinati, A., Chiaroni, D., & Chiesa, V. (2017). Towards a new taxonomy of circular economy business models. *Journal of Cleaner Production, 168*, 487–498. https://doi.org/10.1016/j.jclepro.2017.09.047

Vermunt, D. A., Negro, S. O., Verweij, P. A., Kuppens, D. V., & Hekkert, M. P. (2019). Exploring barriers to implementing different circular business models. *Journal of Cleaner Production, 222*, 891–902. https://doi.org/10.1016/j.jclepro.2019.03.052

Chapter 8
Concluding Remarks and Insights

Abstract The chapter briefly reflects the main findings from the research on circular business models in specific manufacturing industries in small open economies in the European Union. This chapter also presents insights into a future circular economy in small open economies by identifying main threats to circular success and providing scenarios for circular business model development in manufacturing industries.

Keywords Industry-specific · Circular business model · Scenarios for circular transition · Future circular economy

8.1 What Changes Need to Be Made to Business Models in a Transition to the CE?

The concept of the circular economy (CE), systems thinking, and collaboration is necessary to address problems of resource scarcity, overconsumption, waste, and environmentally unsustainable business practices. There is a growing desire for manufacturing companies to become both more aware of their environmental impact, and to accept greater responsibility for the ecological damage they cause. Circular innovations, based solely on economic motives (which are certainly important) reflect an anthropocentric approach, focusing on resource efficiency and waste minimization. On the one hand, this positive approach encourages a reduction in the use of rare and critical materials, and also takes into account what should be done with the waste, such as recycling or reuse. However, the CE is much more than a recycling economy. Anthropocentric assumptions do not fundamentally change how manufacturing companies design products, and nor do they shift consumer habits and attitudes.

The scientific literature provides a wide variety of circular business models, demonstrating that the CE topic is relevant and interesting, not only for researchers and policymakers, but also for managers and other practitioners who seek to implement circular business models practically. The existing gap between theoretical circular business models and their implementation shows that the CE is still a new

© The Author(s), under exclusive license to Springer Nature Switzerland AG 2023

L. Dagilienė et al., *Circular Business Models in the Manufacturing Industry*, Studies in Energy, Resource and Environmental Economics,
https://doi.org/10.1007/978-3-031-28809-8_8

phenomenon for many companies, and they require a lot of capabilities, knowledge, and resources to find the most effective solution for how to manage their businesses in alignment with the CE principles. Incremental business models show that some companies try to reduce their negative impact on the environment instead of eliminating it by integrating a certain circularity in order to achieve efficiency.

The factors that influence the transformation of business models may differ among different companies and industries. Manufacturing companies can face many factors that can encourage or hinder their transition to more circular business models. Drivers and barriers can arise from a multi-level perspective. Barriers to circular transformation can be uncertainty around regulations, a lack of consumer interest and awareness, changing consumer preferences and fast fashion, a lack of financial and technological resources or difficulties in accessing them, a lack of management support, expertise and knowledge, and a shortage of implementation tools. Key drivers for circular transformation are clear legislation and external financial support, consumer acceptance of circular products and services, the need for certification, resource scarcity, technological and social innovation, and collaboration.

The analysis of circular business models in a local context allows for a better understanding of how to achieve circularity at the national or regional level, which is critical for the assurance of circularity solutions throughout the entire supply chain and ecosystem. The development of product-service systems (PSSs), focused on circularity, might open up new opportunities for the transition to circular business models. Companies should orientate towards higher-quality circularity strategies, starting with circular product and service design.

8.2 How Can European SOEs Be Characterized in the Context of the CE?

More than half of the European Union (EU) countries are small open economies (SOEs), and the homogeneous transformation towards the CE across the EU significantly depends on these countries, and the fact that they are small, economically, appears to be no special handicap in the transformation towards CE. The specific role of SOEs in the EU transformation is related to their viability, flexibility, greater openness to change, agility, and decision-making efficiency.

We analyse 16 European SOEs that were selected on the basis of having a small population, an advanced economy (income per capita), and trade openness. From the statistical overview of the main macro-economic indicators, we find some with a higher-than-average GDP, such as the Netherlands, Belgium, Luxembourg, and Denmark, and some with a lower-than-average GDP, such as Slovenia, Slovakia, Latvia, Lithuania, and Cyprus. The results show that economically stronger SOEs create more green innovation and have higher resource productivity. Though moderate in size, they use their economic growth to improve the social conditions of employees by increasing wages.

A sectorial analysis of selected SOEs enabled us to identify the strongest countries in each industry. We observe that leading countries in an industry tend to implement more circular activities, specifically investing in cleaner production, waste, and energy use reduction.

8.3 What Are the Key Drivers, Barriers, Challenges, and Opportunities for the Lithuanian Manufacturing Industry in a Transition to the CE?

We surveyed 139 Lithuanian manufacturing companies to identify relevant CE patterns across the value chain, and the factors influencing their transition to the CE. The results show that their main focus in terms of the value chain is on waste management, though more and more attention is being paid to cleaner production processes, which could ensure the efficient use of raw materials and energy.

Our study shows that the factors driving the transition to the CE are ambivalent. Depending on the contextual circumstances, the same factor can be both a driver and a barrier, encouraging or hindering the transition of manufacturing firms towards CE. In general, the most motivating factors for manufacturing companies to CE are external financial support (e.g., governmental initiatives and financial mechanisms), followed by technological drivers such as production automation and robotization, and the technological transformation of production and business processes, while barriers include green procurement and reverse logistics.

Lithuanian manufacturing companies with biological cycles are more interested in technological solutions, which could lead to efficiencies, while those with technical cycles are highly motivated by requirements and agreements in the supply chain, corporate strategy, and access to external funding.

Another important contribution of this study is to provide industry-specific insights into circular business models, encompassing key patterns, barriers, challenges, and opportunities from previous research, combined with our original survey data.

8.4 Industry-Specific Insights

1. The **textile industry** has a relatively large economic, environmental, and social impact throughout the value chain, as well as on the whole ecosystem. The Lithuanian textile industry has started the transformation towards circularity; however, looking through the whole national ecosystem, linear supply chain elements are still dominant, meaning that, for example, most industrial and post-consumer waste is incinerated or sent to landfill. Lithuanian textile manufacturers, which are export-orientated subcontractors, focus mostly on eco-efficiency, through

energy (mostly solar) and material optimization, and cleaner production through technological adaptation (narrow the loop). From a CE point of view, Lithuanian textile manufacturers still lack eco-design solutions and novel business models orientated to product life-cycle extension. The principles of the CE are more intensively implemented in the use of natural and homogeneous fibres (linen, cotton, wool), while the principles of a linear economy are dominant in those using synthetic and composite fibres. Our research results are in alignment with those of Franco (2017), Koszewska (2018), Lacy et al. (2020), and Huang et al. (2021). The main challenge for the manufacturers is the uncertainty about the possibilities for further use of industrial waste, which arises from a lack of cooperation between them and companies in other sectors, as well as the lack of textile waste recycling technologies and/or technological unreadiness for recycling.

Factors that encourage Lithuanian textile manufacturers towards circularity depend on the business model chosen by the company. If a textile manufacturer works on a business-to-business basis and the products are exported, the brand name's requirements, agreements in the supply chain, and technological progress affect businesses the most. If the company operates a business-consumer model (especially in the Lithuanian market), customer segments and relationships, and the customer's willingness to buy sustainable products, affect business the most. Our results are in line with Koszewska (2018), Lacy et al. (2020), and Salvador et al. (2021).

The overview of circular business models in the Lithuanian textile industry demonstrates that manufacturers still treat the circular business models as experimental, and the potential of the CE has not yet been fully explored, discovered, and exploited.

Analysing the measures that stimulate the industry towards circularity the most, we recommend implementing measures focused on the national (macro), industrial (meso), and enterprise (micro) levels to ensure the systematic transformation of the whole ecosystem.

- Macro-level measures should focus on technological readiness for recycling, and the development of textile waste collection and sorting systems.
- Meso-level measures should encourage collaboration among textile manufacturers and companies from other industries.
- Micro-level measures should focus on solutions related to cleaner production, eco-design, and compliance with environmental requirements, as well as implementation of novel business models orientated to product life-cycle extension.

2. The **furniture industry** is witnessing increasing demand for cheaper and more accessible furniture products, which leads to the use of low-quality materials and unsustainable design standards that usually do not consider reuse and product life extension. Therefore, the furniture industry is considered to be problematic in the context of the CE.

Eco-efficiency through energy and material optimization is quite common in the EU furniture industry, including that in Lithuania, and this approach creates a competitive advantage. From the CE point of view, the furniture industry still lacks novel business models orientated towards sufficiency and overconsumption and giving a second life to furniture products. Product-service business models are not widespread, though they do offer a promising opportunity, specifically for the office furniture industry.

The Lithuanian furniture industry is highly technologically developed, with an increasing focus on digitalization. Furniture manufacturers are advanced in waste management and quite well interconnected with international value chains. Business models embedded in the economics of Lithuanian furniture are orientated towards eco-efficiency through input material optimization and cleaner production processes. Eco-design is gaining importance, although there is much room for improvement. Only the most sustainable furniture companies pay attention to human-centric design issues, product integrity, and sustainable materials. The weak spot is its vague contribution to closing the loop, because the manufacturers sell furniture products to large furniture retailers and do not contribute to reverse value chains.

Factors that encourage Lithuanian furniture manufacturers towards circularity support a techno-centric approach and include the importance of RPA, digital and mobile technologies, and the technological transformation of production and business processes. Intensive adoption of innovative technological solutions results in strong competitiveness and might also contribute to circularity. Collaboration-related factors, such as market requirements for quality management standards and product certification, and agreements in the supply chain, also foster manufacturers' motivation towards the CE.

3. Closing the loops in plastic production and the use of plastic products is highly important. The **plastic manufacturers** are in the middle of the value chain, so factors that encourage these companies towards circularity are related to technological specifications and quality requirements for plastic products, legal requirements from producers, agreements in the supply chain, and technological progress (like factors common to the business-to-business model). The Lithuanian plastic industry is highly technologically developed, with an increasing focus on innovations in alignment with the CE. Eco-design is gaining in importance, although again, there is much room for improvement in terms of technological readiness. However, eco-design choices also depend on the type of manufacturer and plastic product itself (e.g., whether it is a commodity, a component, or a plastic product for the end user). Plastic manufacturers are well connected with other industries via well-developed reverse logistics that seek to close the loop, despite the fact that they sell their product to other manufacturers or retailers.

The overview of circular business models in the Lithuanian plastics industry indicates that circularity is more mature and, although narrow-the-loop strategies still dominate, close-the-loop strategies are being adopted. This is due to the reverse logistics system embedded in the whole ecosystem, innovations, and active collaboration among different companies driven by extended producer responsibility. The catalyst for the progress of circularity is the technical capacity for recyclability and reusability.

8.5 The Future of the CE

The CE is an economic model which, in a relatively short period of time, has gained a significant traction in government, business, and with individual. Despite the critical debates among researchers (Bauwens et al., 2020; Gregson et al., 2015; Hobson & Lynch, 2016; Korhonen et al., 2018) of the transition to a circular and sustainable economy, most research focuses on how the CE is being implemented today, yet with a clear vision of a sustainable and circular future. However, existing guidance and research of the CE lacks the necessary understanding of how to go from the present to the future (Bauwens et al., 2020). The comprehensive and critical research about the challenges and threats to the CE may help us avoid a systemic failure within the CE.

CE policies, companies, and the engagement of civic society offer a promising way to speed up circular transitions, but external negative events and uncertainties might dramatically affect the speed and scale of this transformation. Therefore, there is a need for better understanding of the future in order to build the CE.

There are a number of external threats that may influence the further development of the CE.

The Russian–Ukrainian war, Brexit, the global economic slowdown due to government responses to the COVID-19 pandemic, and other national and regional shocks, are having a dramatic effect on business development and are destabilising the economic and political situations. Each shock and geopolitical conflicts can reshape or postpone future business strategies and innovations, and drastically affect the speed and scale of a transition to the CE. For example, before the start of the COVID-19 pandemic, environmental sustainability was one of the major concerns of industry due to the growing environmental legislation and public pressure to address climate issues. This was especially acute for industries such as plastics and the oil industry. However, a few weeks after the pandemic began, single-use plastics became very popular again (Mah, 2021), because the focus moved to health and product safety issues leading to increasing volumes of packaging and disposable surgical masks. According to the World Health Organization (2022), tens of thousands of tonnes of extra medical waste from the response to the COVID-19 pandemic have put tremendous strain on healthcare waste management systems around the world, threatening human and environmental health and exposing a dire need to improve waste management practices. The world's major economic powers are politically differentiated, and economies are partially closed and operating in a linear, protectionist manner (Marjamaa & Mäkelä, 2022).

According to our research, the common unexpected and uncontrolled challenge for Lithuanian manufacturing companies to implement a transition to the CE was the COVID-19 pandemic, which had a three-fold effect on the aspiration of textile and clothing companies to implement the principles of the CE: negative, neutral, and positive. The companies most sensitive to the coronavirus crisis postponed plans to implement the principles of the CE because all their efforts were directed to survive, i.e., ensuring income and stabilizing the situation, preserving jobs, and therefore, there was little room for additional investments in eco-innovation and circularity. For example, those companies whose main export market was the UK experienced two economic shocks, namely **Brexit** and the coronavirus crisis, so their priorities were maintain market share. Other companies, especially those that had already started implementing some CE principles, continued to do so and did not give up their strategic aspirations. The third group of companies were those that saw the CE as an opportunity to stay in the market. These were rather small, incumbent companies working as contract manufacturers, which sought to turn the principles of the CE to their competitive advantage. The response of Lithuanian manufactures to COVID-19 is correlated with the results of research conducted in other countries (Seetharaman, 2020; Bayram et al., 2020; Hermundsdottir et al., 2022). The researchers identify two types of strategic responses, namely protective/reactive, which typically implies postponing investments and laying off employees, and proactive, which typically implies accelerating strategic actions, such as adopting new technologies and innovative business procedures. However, the claims that any economic shock is identified as an opportunity for CE are becoming increasingly dominant in the scientific research. If we muddle through every new crisis based on the current economic model, using short-term solutions to mitigate the impact, future shocks will continue to surpass capacity. It is necessary, therefore, to devise long-term risk-mitigation strategies and sustainable fiscal thinking with the view of shifting away from the current focus on profits and disproportionate economic growth (Haigh & Bäunker, 2020). As the global economy recovers from COVID-19, it has become more apparent that there is a strong sense of interconnectedness between environmental, economic, and social sustainability (Bauwens et al., 2020). The pandemic has been described as an opportunity to further entrench digital transformation without the "digitalism", which is an extreme and adverse form of connectedness (Bayram et al., 2020). Green strategic responses positively mediated the impact of COVID-19 on environmental innovation change (Hermundsdottir et al., 2022) due to stakeholder relationships, reputation, and innovation capacity (Huang et al., 2020). The integration of sustainability at the corporate strategic and operational levels may make companies much more agile in responding to future unexpected events.

At the time of writing, it is too early to assess the impact of the **Russian-Ukrainian war**, but it will definitely have a huge effect on corporate circular strategies First of all, the invasion of Ukraine is causing a massive humanitarian crisis. Meeting the basic needs of people for food and shelter, and the psychological safety of Ukraine and the other neighbouring nations, is a gargantuan task for the global community (McKinsey & Company, 2022a). In addition, various humanitarian crises sharply increase the demand for social and medical services, which then generate even greater volumes of waste. Focusing only on the threats posed by war to the transformation of companies towards CE, we can identify two specific dangers.

- **Energy crisis.** Energy policy is rotating towards secure access and source diversification. McKinsey & Company (2022b) forecasts that global energy consumption will grow by 14% by 2030 and the role of electricity in the final consumption mix is projected to grow from around 20% today to 40% by 2050. Renewables are expected to become the new baseload, accounting for 50% of the power mix by 2030 and 85% by 2050. While acceleration of renewable energy can solve part of the puzzle, gas will remain an important source, and nuclear and coal may become larger components of the fuel mix to secure supply, particularly to mitigate potential gas shortages. The implications for achieving net zero emissions targets are not yet clear.

- **Resource crisis**. Tense political relationships and conflict intensify the competition for critical materials, equipment, and commodities. The real and perceived need for secure access to natural resources, materials, and advanced equipment (e.g., neon, nickel, palladium, and semiconductors) are likely to grow and further intensify the race between nations and companies to secure supplies. For example, due to the war in Ukraine and subsequent sanctions against Russia, imports of wood and biofuels from the East to Lithuania almost dried up, as it is now prohibited to directly or indirectly import, buy or transport wood products originating in Belarus. In the absence of imported biofuel, the country's producers face an increasing demand for local raw materials. As a resource-poor region, Europe is highly dependent on international trade, imported energy, and materials. Consequently, the price of essential raw materials and energy is rising. However, these geopolitical threats and uncertainties might manifest as an incentive for technological and social innovations aimed at using materials and minerals more effectively, taking into account the needs of future generations.

Climate change is increasingly disrupting the established economic balance. Scorching heat, heavy rains, and hurricanes affect the supply and demand for natural resources, fossil fuels, and can destroy economic infrastructure. In order to restore the balance, governments and companies first and foremost aim to satisfy the primary needs of consumers and employees, while the CE remains a secondary aspiration. On the other hand, these changes in climate are an indicator that circular activities must be developed urgently.

While the **population of the world is increasing,** together with rising consumerism, we have the same limited natural resources. It is still a question of how to motivate consumers to buy eco-design products and how to motivate companies to adopt eco-design principles.

In addition, the struggle between **democratic and less democratic countries** over values, and the resulting conflicts, can lead to changes in foreign policies. This leads to restrictions on mutual trade, the opportunity to purchase technology, restrictions on investment, and on people's movement. Affected businesses are forced to adjust their value chains and reassess the risks arising from business relations with non-democratic countries. From a CE perspective, the evaluation of value chains in the face of changing political interests can encourage companies to look for cooperation opportunities with neighbouring countries in developing new technologies, processing production resources, and trading intermediate products. In addition, a positive effect on pollution levels is expected due to the shortening of transport routes.

The research results justify the necessity for building future scenarios and increase awareness among businessmen, policymakers, and the whole of society in order to create a sustainable future.

8.6 Scenarios for Circular Business Model Development

The future cannot be predicted, but according to Svenfelt et al. (2019), alternative futures must become visible because they affect our cognitive perceptions of the realm of possibilities, and thus influence today's decision-making. Many companies need to decide how to act now, in anticipation of longer-term disruptions. Many business leaders are trying to move their organizations from reacting in an ad hoc manner to each disruption to a foundation of greater resilience, staying alert to what is over the horizon, and building capabilities to continually manage uncertainty.

Some of the scenarios for circular business model development are more probable than others, given the phenomenon of path dependency, existing production value chains, and consumption patterns, both locally and globally. Based on our research and identified drivers and barriers experienced by manufacture companies in the transformation towards CE, we identified four possible circular business model development scenarios in the SOEs:

- Twin transformation, leading to circular and digital upscale.
- Technological transformation, leading to eco-efficiency and weak circularity.
- Regional transformation, leading to local circular ecosystems.
- Partial transformation, leading to a mixture of linear and circular economies.

Twin transformation focuses on digitalization as the key catalyst in the CE transition. The upscale of circularity programmes are implemented at global level. The equal focus and change dynamics are on both circular production systems and consumption.

This twin transformation scenario is very much part of the EU political agenda, through prevalent strategies for 2030 or 2050. This scenario correlates very much with Marjamaa and Mäkelä (2022) who identify an optimistic future of the CE, a circular success story. The projected time is 2050, by which time the CE principles will have been fully adopted and the CE becomes the normal economy. The most significant global environmental problems have been brought under control with the help of technology. The everyday life and earning logic of companies are in line with the CE, and all materials circulate several times, creating turnover and business. Businesses based on services, digital platforms and solutions, proactive service and maintenance, modular design, reuse, life-cycle extension, leasing, lending, and repairing demonstrate successful circular business models. Even chemicals and wood fibres can be leased. New companies, innovations, and jobs are constantly being created, and the CE arises within industrial ecosystems.

Technological transformation leads to eco-efficiency and weak circularity. The focus is on production systems and digital technologies, while patterns of growing consumption do not change. This scenario depends primarily on technological innovation and the centralization of political and economic decision-making in the hands of governments and a few large industrial leaders. Such trends occur in the plastics or furniture industries, where many manufacturers sell goods to one or more focal companies that control global value chains. The government's main role is to set targets and standards for eco-efficiency and recycling, as well as to support certain priority industries. While creating the industrial circular roadmap, Lithuania identifies key demonstrating sectors that are extremely important because of their high-value-added and negative environmental impacts. The idea of sector prioritization leads to innovation-led policy instruments to drive R&D investment and circular innovation. Focal companies and leaders in the manufacturing value chains respond to these incentives and create circular innovations. The main rationale is that humans can protect nature by using technology to "decouple" negative impacts from nature (Bauwens et al., 2020). In this scenario, the transition to circular business models is mainly supply—or production-oriented (i.e., product design, and cleaner production and supply chain activities), driven by large industrial companies, and consumers either accept or reject circular product innovations, without drastically changing their consumption patterns. Sustainable business is not trending and consumer behaviour is based on the rapid satisfaction of short-term desires. This scenario is very close to that of circular modernism, as elaborated by Bauwens et al. (2020). From the perspective of Lithuanian manufacturing, there is a very strong focus on the role of digital technologies.

Regional transformation leads to local circular ecosystems. The focus is on consumption systems and servitization business models, while patterns of consumer behaviour change locally. Peer-to-peer circularity (Bauwens et al., 2020) and local circles (Marjamaa & Mäkelä, 2022) are similar to scenarios that emphasize greater consumer responsibility and circular business models orientated on product life-cycle extension. In the local circles scenarios (Marjamaa & Mäkelä, 2022), there is sufficient demand for CE products and solutions, but CE businesses are still in the early stages of development. Hyperglobalization has shifted to a smaller, environmentally conscious version of everyday life. The circularity and recycling obligations of companies at the legislative level are minimal. Large companies, with the help of technology, move towards the responsible management of resources and closing-the-loop business models. Recycling works extremely well and, as before, the reduced volume of waste is taken to landfill. The support of the government, as well as the EU, plays a key role through financial support and R&D investment policy. Slowing-the-loop models, such as prolonging product life cycles and product-service systems, are mainly implemented by small, incumbent companies.

The megatrends of increasing political tensions and a drive to sustainability push more towards the shortening of global value chains and favouring regionalization (Mariotti, 2022). Transitioning to regional value chains promotes shorter supply chains that are more resilient to material and energy disruptions caused by pandemics, war, and other uncertainties. Emphasis is placed on the control of value chain activities through digital technologies, collaboration efforts, and localization. Digitalization delivers both resilience (through remote control) and geographic flexibility (through the replacement of labour-intensive activities with technology-intensive ones) (Mariotti, 2022).

Partial transformation is mixture of linear and circular economies This scenario is close to the structural, regulated circularity outlined by Marjamaa and Mäkelä (2022) and the planned circularity of Bauwens et al. (2020). State policy and a top-down approach play an important role in this scenario. An innovation system is encouraged, developing technologies more focused on even stricter waste management. Pandemics occur quite frequently and require state-led control. Strong control at the EU level, strong national control, taxation, and regulation creates the basis for CE and sometimes strict regulations that stifle consumer behaviour. CE is considered labour-intensive and bureaucratic because it involves different methods, technologies, and measurements, and it is not positively perceived (Marjamaa & Mäkelä, 2022). Large companies have dedicated low-carbon and CE strategies. Some business models are successful, but not enough to change the linear economic paradigm. The CE principles, such as refuse, reduce, reuse, recycle, and recover, are mainly approached through low-tech innovations (Bauwens et al., 2020) and regulations such as setting hard caps on resource consumption or banning certain materials. However, overall resource and energy efficiency have reduced the use of natural resources to more sustainable levels. However, much remains to be done to reach a level that is truly ecologically sustainable.

Obviously, hybrid forms of different development scenarios can exist. Currently, it seems that the focus is stronger and faster on reshaping production systems through effective waste management systems, cleaner production technologies, sustainable product design, and closed value chains, and less on changing consumer patterns so they broadly accept circular business models, rather than seeing them as a niche phenomenon.

There is still a lot of uncertainty around how each of these challenges, and new ones that we have not yet considered, will play out. However, we can state that the future circular of the economy depends on us, namely on our vision, willingness, initiatives, and competencies. Through our research, we aim to increase knowledge now about the possibilities that are open to companies to become more circular, and thus contribute to the creation of a circular success story.

References

Bauwens, T., Hekkert, M., & Kirchherr, J. (2020). Circular futures: What will they look like? *Ecological Economics, 175*(November 2019), 106703. https://doi.org/10.1016/j.ecolecon.2020.106703

Bayram, M., Springer, S., Garvey, C. K., & Özdemir V. (2020). COVID-19 digital health innovation policy: A portal to alternative futures in the making OMICS J. Integrat. Biol. https://doi.org/10.1089/omi.2020.0089

Gregson, N., Crang, M., Fuller, S., & Holmes, H. (2015). Interrogating the circular economy: The moral economy of resource recovery in the EU. *Economy and Society, 44*(2), 218–243. https://doi.org/10.1080/03085147.2015.1013353

Haigh, L., & Bäunker, L. (2020). Covid-19 and the circular economy: opportunities and reflections.

Hermundsdottir, F., Håkon, H. D., & Aspelund, A. (2022). Analyzing the impact of COVID-19 on environmental innovations in manufacturing firms. *Technology in Society, 68*,. https://doi.org/10.1016/j.techsoc.2022.101918

Hobson, K., & Lynch, N. (2016). Diversifying and de-growing the circular economy: Radical social transformation in a resource-scarce world. *Futures, 82*, 15–25. https://doi.org/10.1016/j.futures.2016.05.012

Huang, W. S., & Chen, L. T. (2020). Nguyen Corporate social responsibility and organizational resilience to COVID-19 crisis: an empirical study of Chinese firms *Sustainability, 12*(21). https://doi.org/10.3390/su12218970

Korhonen, J., Nuur, C., Feldmann, A., & Birkie, S. E. (2018). Circular economy as an essentially contested concept. *Journal of Cleaner Production, 175*, 544–552. https://doi.org/10.1016/j.jclepro.2017.12.111

Koszewska, M. (2018). Circular economy—Challenges for the textile and clothing industry. *Autex Research Journal, 18*(4), 337–347. https://doi.org/10.1515/aut-2018-0023

Lacy, P., Long. J., & Spindler, W. (2020). *The circular economy handbook: Realizing the circular advantage* (p. 363). Springer, ISBN 978-1-349-95967-9. https://doi.org/10.1057/978-1-349-95968-6

Mah, A. (2021). Future-proofing capitalism: The paradox of the circular economy for plastics. *Global Environmental Politics, 21*(2), 121–142. https://doi.org/10.1162/glep_a_00594

Mariotti, S. (2022). A warning from the Russian-Ukrainian war: Avoiding a future that rhymes with the past. *Journal of Industrial and Business Economics*. https://doi.org/10.1007/s40812-022-00219-z

Marjamaa, M., & Mäkelä, M. (2022). Images of the future for a circular economy: The case of Finland. *Futures, 141*, 102985. https://doi.org/10.1016/j.futures.2022.102985

McKinsey & Company. (2022a). *War in Ukraine: Lives and livelihoods, lost and disrupted*. https://www.mckinsey.com/business-functions/strategy-and-corporate-finance/our-insights/war-in-ukraine-lives-and-livelihoods-lost-and-disrupted

McKinsey & Company. (2022b). *Global Energy Perspective 2022b*. https://www.mckinsey.com/~/media/McKinsey/Industries/Oil%20and%20Gas/Our%20Insights/Global%20Energy%20Perspective%202022b/Global-Energy-Perspective-2022-Executive-Summary.pdf

Seetharaman, P. (2020). Business models shifts: impact of covid-19 Int. J. Inf. *Manag*, 54, 102173. https://doi.org/10.1016/j.ijinfomgt.2020.102173

Svenfelt, A., Alfredsson, E. C., Bradley, K., Fauré, E., Finnveden, G., Fuehrer, P., & Öhlund, E. (2019). Scenarios for sustainable futures beyond GDP growth 2050. *Futures, 111*, 1–14. https://doi.org/10.1016/j.futures.2019.05.001

World Health Organization. (2022) https://www.who.int/news/item/01-02-2022-tonnes-of-covid-19-health-care-waste-expose-urgent-need-to-improve-waste-management-systems

The manufacturer's authorised representative in the EU is Springer Nature Customer Service Centre GmbH, Europaplatz 3, 69115 Heidelberg, Germany. If you have any concerns regarding our products, please contact ProductSafety@springernature.com

Printed and bound by CPI Group (UK) Ltd, Croydon, CR0 4YY
30/09/2026
02225262-0010